CHARLEMAGNE'S COURTIER

D1016517

READINGS IN MEDIEVAL CIVILIZATIONS AND CULTURES: III
series editor: Paul Edward Dutton

CHARLEMAGNE'S COURTIER

THE COMPLETE EINHARD

edited and translated by

PAUL EDWARD DUTTON

broadview press

Canadian Cataloguing in Publication Data

Einhard, ca 770-840
Charlemagne's courtier: the complete Einhard

(Readings in medieval civilizations and cultures)
Includes bibliographical references and index.
ISBN 1-55111-134-9

1. France — History — To 987 — Sources. 2. Carolingians — Sources. I. Dutton, Paul Edward, 1952-   . II. Title. III. Series.

DC73.2 1998   944'.014   C97-932743-1

Broadview Press • Post Office Box 1243, Peterborough, Ontario, Canada K9J 7H5

in the United States of America: 3576 California Road, Orchard Park, NY 14127

in the United Kingdom: B.R.A.D. Book Representation & Distribution Ltd., 244A, London Road, Hadleigh, Essex SS7 2DE

Broadview Press gratefully acknowledges the support of the Ontario Arts Council and the Ministry of Canadian Heritage.

COVER ILLUSTRATION: Saint Michael. An ivory carving (34 cm x 10 cm.) dating from around 800 A.D. Museum für Kunsthandwerk, Grassimuseum, Leipzig.

Book design by George Kirkpatrick.
PRINTED IN CANADA

CONTENTS

LIST OF ILLUSTRATIONS AND MAPS

Figures

Maps

PREFACE

The first graduate essay I can remember writing was one on Einhard and Carolingian pessimism. I recall being frustrated, as graduate students often are, by my inability to lay my hands all at once on everything about the topic and to swallow it whole. Twenty years later, this little collection of sources is the result, the very book I wish I could have laid my hands on for an afternoon when I was a green and hungry graduate student.

The reader of this book is, however, forewarned that its title is misleading, since Einhard was not only Charlemagne's courtier, but also Louis the Pious's. Nor is Einhard complete here, for how could one ever hope to squeeze into one small book all the scattered pieces produced and materials touched by someone as busy as Einhard once was. Still it would not be unfair to characterize Einhard's contact with Charles the Great as the defining experience of his life, and I have tried to include here all the works that have been assigned to him with confidence by scholars; and that has over the last century been a shrinking repository, since scholars no longer assign annals or passion poems to his authorship.

This book was prepared with students in mind and should not be thought of as a critical contribution to the study of Einhard's writings, one that would surely demand and deserve critical Latin texts with facing translations, variants, notes, and extended commentaries. Someday Einhard's collected writings will be so treated, but the readers of this book will find instead a rather rough and ready translation of his collected works that seeks to be nothing more than helpful. Einhard is not always the easiest Latin writer to translate. His voice is often overly rhetorical, saying in twenty words what might have been said in ten. It is puzzling that Lupus of Ferrières should have praised Einhard for writing simple sentences of moderate length, since in translating I constantly wanted to simplify and break down complex and overlong sentences. And how should a translator treat Einhard's formal voice? In an effort to restore Einhard's personal agency, I have on occasion translated "we" as "I", but the reader will need to remember that Einhard often spoke as the head of various households and communities of monks. His collective voice probably carried great authority in the ninth century, but it was also a conventional mode of expression that can sound distant and fussy to the modern ear. His abstract characterizations of himself, particularly in his letters, as "Smallness" and "Tininess" also sound particularly strange and unnatural today, but may, for that very reason, for their air of medieval role playing, be particularly worth preserving, and so I have. In fact, the changing sound of Einhard's voice as one moves from the *Life of Charlemagne* to the *Translation and Miracles of the Blessed Martyrs, Marcellinus and Peter* and from his business to personal letters is a great challenge for the translator to capture and for the reader to try to hear.

I am much in debt to those many scholars who have previously edited and translated various works of Einhard. In an earlier book in this series, *Carolingian Civilization: A Reader*, I had revised translations by S.E. Turner, B. Wendell, and H. Preble. Each of those translations was serviceable, but the act of revising them for a modern audience convinced me that a systematic set of new translations based on the best available editions would be useful. I have also collected together the thoughts of Einhard's contemporaries on his life and work, translated those charters or portions of charters in which he was a central participant, and inserted a translation of Einhard's 'On the Adoration of the Cross' in the personal correspondence with Lupus of Ferrières where it seems to belong.

Square brackets in the translations contain information added for the sake of explanation and clarification. They also enclose words such as antecedents and transitional phrases not specifically found in Einhard's writings, but which English prose seems to want. Internal references such as [5.3.2] direct the reader to see part 5, book 3, section 2 of the primary sources in the reader.

Many people have helped me at one stage or another as I worked on this book. I would especially like to thank David Ganz, who is at present preparing a new study of Einhard, for his generous and invaluable advice and correction. Others kindly endured and entertained my many questions: John Contreni, Herert Kessler, Gustav Komarek, Hilmar Pabel, John Shinners and Mary-Ann Stouck. Fred Kyba of the Instructional Media Centre at Simon Fraser University prepared some of the illustrations that accompany this book and Jaclynne Campbell, a graphic designer of the same Centre, readied the computerized reconstructions of Einhard's triumphal arch. The Bibliothèque Nationale of Paris, the Österreichische Nationalbibliothek of Vienna, the Bibliothèque Publique et Universitaire of Geneva, the Burgerbibliothek of Berne, and the Grassimuseum, Museum für Kunsthandwerk, of Leipzig kindly gave me permission to print illustrations from their libraries. The plans of Einhard's basilicas come from Otto Müller's work. Stuart Daniel made the maps herein. Caroline Suma of the library of the Pontifical Institute of Mediaeval Studies and Jane Schuele and Florine Muhlenbruck of the Benedictine College Library supplied materials otherwise inaccessible to me. As always the Inter-Library Loans Office of the W.A.C. Bennett Library at Simon Fraser

University was constantly helpful. I cannot conclude without expressing my gratitude to Don LePan, who first suggested the idea for this reader, and to Barbara Conolly and George Kirkpatrick of Broadview Press, who helped me to produce the book in its final form. To all of these my thanks and deepest gratitude.

Fortunately the essay I wrote on Einhard in 1976 has long since disappeared from sight, but whatever I thought then, I am now convinced that Einhard was not a pessimist by any reasonable definition of the word. Indeed, whatever confidence I myself once had in the knowability of Einhard and the full range of his work in Charlemagne's world has steadily waned as I worked on this little reader, and that too is as it should be.

AN INTRODUCTION TO EINHARD

Einhard and Charlemagne have traveled through history together, at least as we have always imagined them, the little biographer and his towering subject. Their relationship has always struck observers, including Einhard himself, as that of a nurturing father and his adopted son. But it would do no harm for us to scratch a little at the varnish that lies thick and yellowing over this familiar portrait. Beneath it the searcher may come upon another image, the one that too often lies hidden behind the figure of Charlemagne himself, even in the title of this collection of readings. The adventurous reader may wish, in fact, to reverse the process, to consider whether s/he ever sees Charlemagne at all or only Einhard's particular act of remembering him.

But, just as it is imperative for students to assess Charlemagne independently of Einhard's account, it is also important to try to take the measure of Einhard apart from Charlemagne. That is not to say that one can ever be fully understood without the other, but the whole of Einhard's life was not encompassed by Charlemagne. Virtually all his writing was done after Charlemagne died in early 814. His surviving compositions neatly cover the last twenty-five years of his life and his career as a lay abbot and man of property dates from Louis the Pious's time as well.

His noble lineage came from his parents, Einhard and Engilfrit, who held property near the Main River in eastern Francia [see 1.14 and 3.6 below]. Einhard may have been their eldest or only child and was probably born around 770 not long after Charlemagne became king. His parents sent him to be educated at the monastery of Fulda [see Map 3], perhaps, as has been suggested, because his small size made it unlikely that he could take up a military career. At Fulda he learned Latin and immersed himself in the Bible and the classics. He wrote out six charters while resident at Fulda, three of them dated to the period between 788 and 791 [3.1-6]. Einhard was already in his early 20s when the abbot of Fulda, Baugulf, to whom Charlemagne sent his famous letter on educational reform [see *Carolingian Civilization* 13.7], apparently recommended him to Charlemagne's attention as a learned young man who would be useful at court [see 1.14 below]. Given the king's drive to improve official literacy within the kingdom, Charlemagne and his court must have been on the lookout for excellent and energetic officials in order to extend and improve the workings of the palace and the administration of the kingdom. There was also a standing need to replace those court officials and schoolmasters who had already departed.

When Einhard appeared at court around 791-92, Charlemagne's first great collection of scholars was already dissolving. Alcuin had been at court for a decade, but he was to depart for Tours in 796. Paulinus of Aquileia was gone by 787, and had been preceded home by another Italian, Paul the Deacon. Even Peter of Pisa was likely gone for good by the time Einhard arrived. The new court circle of Charlemagne was dominated by Angilbert, Theodulf of Orléans, and Alcuin's own students, men like Fridugis and the poet Modoin.

Charlemagne's court must have been very near the pinnacle of its vigor and accomplishment in the 790s when Einhard arrived. It was an exciting time to be a courtier. The Avars had finally been conquered in 795-96 and the treasure from their Great Ring fueled the new-found prosperity of the Carolingians. Einhard may never have been a warrior, but he slipped easily into the life of a courtier. He was assigned a variety of roles that made him an exceedingly useful and prompt presence at court.

The portrait of Einhard drawn by his contemporaries in these early years is consistent and fond. Both Alcuin and Theodulf characterized him as small and energetic, though the one seems to have done so with more love than the other [1.3 and 1.6]. Theodulf's relationship with Einhard, as with so many others, may have been strained by his sharp wit and aggressive nature [1.7]. He complained that Einhard, on occasion, avoided him, but he effectively sketched Einhard as a man in constant motion, scurrying here and there, books in hand, little legs awhirl.

The early reports of those at court also portray Einhard as a poet and learned man. Alcuin told Charlemagne in 799 that Einhard, their intimate assistant, could easily explain difficult problems of grammar and arithmetic to him in Alcuin's absence, and he wondered why Einhard, fine poet that he was, had not replaced him as the master of the court school [1.1-2]. Modoin, in his list of successful court poets, counted Einhard as one of that charmed circle of poets – Angilbert, Alcuin, and Theodulf – who had achieved great names and fortunes at Charlemagne's court because of their expert command of song [1.5]. This was exalted company, indeed, but where is the poetry on which Einhard's reputation rested? Alcuin spoke of his command of Trojan epic, that is, of Virgilian verse [1.2]. Now it has been suggested that the most famous epic of the ninth century, the incomplete but brilliant *Charlemagne and Pope Leo*, may have been composed by Einhard, but the matter is far from sure. The attribution of the poetic *Passion of the Martyrs of Christ, Marcellinus and Peter* to Einhard is easier to dismiss. For one thing, as Marguerite Bondois long ago pointed out, Einhard seems to have known next to nothing about the specific history of his saints, which is the subject treated in detail in the *Passion*. Moreover, that hagiographic piece cannot have been written before

828 and, therefore, could not have been the basis for Einhard's early reputation as an epic poet. It is that early, epic poetry that one would want to see, if
one could. Moreover, if Einhard was one of the chief poets celebrated at
Charlemagne's later court, why did he not receive, as the others did, a classical
poet's name?

Instead Einhard had two nicknames. Early on he was called the Nard or
Nardulus, Little Nard, perhaps because of simple homophony. The nard was a
rare and fragrant oil, but unless Einhard smelled especially good, it is difficult
not to imagine that his first nickname was a product of its trivial similarity to
the '-hard' ending of his name. Even today one hears children in schoolyards
making play with the sounds of their classmates' names, sometimes coining
less than kind endearments.

The other nickname given to Einhard early on by Alcuin was taken from
the Bible, for Bezaleel was the exquisite craftsman assigned to Moses by God
[Exodus 31:1-5]; he was expert not only in making things of brass, silver, and
gold, but in cutting stones and working in wood. When Alcuin and Theodulf
employed this nickname [1.2 and 1.7], they did so without explaining what it
meant, but surely theirs was a nominal metaphor to type Einhard as an expert
in many of the minor arts. In the 820s, Walahfrid Strabo compromised the
metaphor by explaining it, but he leaves us in no doubt as to Einhard's considerable understanding of the visual arts [1.9]. Hrabanus concurred [1.17].
The material case for Einhard as an aesthete and patron of art is suggestive, if
not particularly tangible. Paris, Bibliothèque Nationale, fr. 10440 [see Figs.6-7]
preserves a lifesize drawing from the seventeenth century of a small, silver triumphal arch that Einhard donated to one of his dependent churches. The
donor's inscription [Fig. 5], however, is somewhat ambiguous, since it states
that Einhard "set up" (ponere) and dedicated the arch. Ponere could be taken to
mean "made" or "fashioned", but curavit would seem to suggest that he
arranged for others to carry out the work. For this reason it seems better to
assume Einhard commissioned the piece, perhaps even specifying its dimensions, actual design, and iconography, but asked others to make it. Even in the
Translation and Miracles of the Blessed Martyrs, Marcellinus and Peter, we see him
ordering a new reliquary, not making it himself [5.1.10]. And he asked mem-
bers of his household to prepare gifts for Lothar and his wife Ermengard, in
this case apparently not even specifying what the objects were to be [6.54].
But Einhard moved in a world of painters [6.45], reliquary-makers [6.30], tile-
makers [6.38], royal scribes [7.6], organ builders [5.4.11], and palace workmen
[5.4.12], and he knew how to employ them to advantage.

His tastes in art, as in so much else, were classical or, rather, late antique,
but these may have been the wider tastes of Charlemagne's court. The lost

silver arch had figures that are reminiscent of the forms found on late ancient ivory carvings. Indeed, the ivory that graces the cover of this book, with its gently curved figure of the archangel Michael wrapped in swirling cloth and standing with angelic abstraction upon a tormented little dragon, belonged to the same world. This piece too was probably produced at Aachen during Einhard's time. From his own writings [6.30] we know that Einhard was a reader of Vitruvius, the ancient expert on architecture. In the letter he wrote to his student Vussin, he recalled a reliquary fashioned with classical columns that had been carved in ivory. Fragments of these miniature columns may survive today in the Landschaftsmuseum in Seligenstadt. Lupus of Ferrières also thought that Einhard could lay his hands upon the alphabet of ancient capital letters that the royal scribe Bertcaud had inscribed and, in fact, at the very end of a copy of Victorius of Aquitaine's calculus, a book that Bernhard Bischoff associated with Lupus, one finds just such a scheme of capital letters [7.6 and Fig.14]. Is this then Lupus's copy of Einhard's book and Bertcaud's letters? Indeed, one has to wonder if Einhard himself composed the inscription and designed the arch that once rose above Charlemagne's tomb [2.31], since some of its vocabulary was favored by him and he remained in 814 the ultimate overseer of royal works.

But whether he was himself the direct fabricator of anything, or at least of anything that survives, may never be known. Part of our problem, of course, is that our view of what an artist was is too modern, too shaped by Italian Renaissance ideas of individual and inspired creativity. Perhaps Einhard's contemporaries thought of artists the way we think of architects today: the credit belongs to the person who conceives and organizes the artifact, not to its mere executor. If so, Einhard was the Bezaleel of his day, for if Charlemagne was the first and material cause of Aachen's splendor, it was Einhard's creative spirit that brought much of it about. When Hrabanus in Einhard's epitaph [1.17] said that it was through Einhard that Charlemagne accomplished so many fine things, he was probably thinking of Einhard as the beautifier of the palace.

The standing assumption that Einhard was centrally involved in the construction of the court chapel of St-Mary at Aachen [see Fig. 3] may be true, but it is unfortunately supported by little direct evidence. Since Odo of Metz was the architect of the palace chapel, Einhard was probably something more akin to its project manager, one of the facilitators of the building campaign in Aachen. He cannot have been the first such, since the project was probably under way before he had even arrived at court as a young recruit. And he was not the last. Late in his reign, Charlemagne put Ansegisus in charge of the royal works at Aachen, but his direct superior and overseer was Einhard

[1.12]. Still, by the mid-790s, Einhard may have been the chief enabler of the rising building. No wonder, then, that the other courtiers who saw him at the time thought of him as constantly busy, always rushing here and there. The wide range and variety of building trades necessary for such an immense building project must have made Einhard's participation essential and may explain why some contemporaries marveled at his knowledge of such a wide range of crafts [1.9 and 1.17]. It is also worth noting that in the *Life of Charlemagne* [2.26] he himself drew particular attention to the metalwork of the great chapel, but had nothing to say about its impressive architecture. He may have been a Bezaleel, but we need to remember how important the minor arts were to the Carolingians, for theirs was not a world dominated by a taste for the monumental and gigantic, but for things small, precious, and portable; or so it must seem to modern scholars who are forced to sift through the surviving particles of their lost world.

One of Einhard's own churches partially survives today. The hall church at Steinbach, just outside Michelstadt, was consecrated in 827 and was originally intended to be the site of Einhard's burial. The nave of the small church, which rises over a solid Carolingian crypt, has six square piers supporting arches that once opened into side aisles, which have long since been suppressed. The nave ends in a shallow apse. Each side aisle originally possessed its own narthex entranceway and a small chapel in the east end [see Fig. 10]. The west end of the church may once have possessed as many as five doors. With its varied roof line and complexly articulated outer wall, the church at Steinbach must have seemed a visual wonder to its rural visitors. Einhard was proud of his new building, which he had built at his own expense between 815 and 827 [5.1.1]. It was for this newly completed and consecrated church that Einhard first sought to obtain saints' relics. But the martyrs refused to remain in Michelstadt or, at least, the interpreters of their wishes thought they should travel north to Mulinheim, which later on was renamed Seligenstadt, the site of the blessed martyrs [1.16]. There Einhard had a new and still larger church constructed in the 830s [see Fig. 11], into which the martyrs' ashes were eventually translated and Einhard himself was finally entombed. This church was almost twice as large as the one at Michelstadt, but had a more familiar design with two side aisles, a long nave, and a coherent complex of connected chapels in the east end.

Not long after he arrived at Charlemagne's court, Einhard had already assumed an important and respected place there. The poet Theodulf saw him saddled not only with an armful of books, but with the heavy burdens of court business [1.6]. At least twice during Charlemagne's reign, we know of Einhard's involvement in high affairs of state. For it was he who, as a special emissary in 806, carried Charlemagne's partition of the kingdom between his three living sons, the so-called 'Division of the Kingdom', to Pope Leo III in Rome [see 1.4 and *Carolingian Civilization* 22]. In 813 Charlemagne convoked the Diet of Aachen to consider the matter of his succession now that only one of his sons still lived; it was apparently Einhard who, speaking on behalf of certain noble interests, publicly acclaimed Louis the Pious's elevation to co-imperial status [1.11].

Einhard's career is surprisingly obscure in the first decade after Charlemagne's death, though it can be assumed that, for the benefit of Louis the Pious, he carried on many of the functions he had performed for his father. He would, therefore, have been found at certain times of the year at the imperial court assembled in such places as Aachen and Ingelheim to wait on Louis's needs, to write letters and laws. Louis himself spoke of the need to reward Einhard for his service [see 3.7]. Some of the letters Einhard composed for the emperor survive in Einhard's collected letters [see 6.19-21, 39], and he gave Louis and his wives advice on matters of state. As well, Hubert Mordek noted that in a memorandum about the matters to be discussed at an upcoming meeting to be convened under Louis one of the items reads:

> 17. Concerning the long-term possession of churches that cannot be defended through the years, as, for instance, is the case we have in [the village of] Colonia, which was handed over to [the monastery of] St-Bavo during the time of King Pepin.

It would not surprise us to learn that Einhard, the abbot of St-Bavo and a key member of Louis's court, had a hand in preparing memoranda of this sort. But whatever his involvement was in this case, there can be little doubt that he played an active role in the operations of Louis the Pious's government. One of Einhard's letters [6.34] may even be taken to mean that Louis had at one point appointed him the tutor, or should that be counselor, of his son Lothar. For all his busy work on Louis's behalf and, perhaps, even as a reward for his essential role in Louis's elevation, Einhard received properties from the new emperor.

Had he ever received lands or revenues from Charlemagne? If not, how had he supported himself for twenty years in Aachen, where he may have been resident all year round? Modoin characterized Einhard as one who had become rich along with Charlemagne's other poets [1.5]. Did he merely mean that he had received high offices and royal favor or something more substantial? When Ansegisus took charge of the royal works under Charlemagne, Einhard was already called an abbot [1.12], though that may have been to give him a later office and not one that he actually held under Charlemagne. But what are we to make of Einhard's own comment in the preface to the *Life of Charlemagne* that he owed Charlemagne "both in life and death" [2.preface]? Is it possible that the old king in his last days had recommended to his son and successor that his faithful courtier Einhard should be rewarded with lands? Again we do not know, but the problem of how Einhard supported himself and his household for twenty years in Aachen still remains to be solved.

Early in 815 the new emperor granted Einhard and his wife Emma the substantial properties of both Michelstadt and Mulinheim or Seligenstadt [3.7]. A few months later he reconfirmed the immunities of the monastery of Blandin in Ghent, which Einhard was to hold as lay abbot [3.8]. Four years later, as the lay abbot of St-Bavo, also in Ghent, Einhard received the reconfirmation of its immunities [3.9]. In the same year, Einhard and Emma stipulated that their holdings in Michelstadt should pass to the monastery of Lorsch on their deaths [3.10]. The reader should notice that the donors did not also give the Seligenstadt properties to Lorsch. One of the most interesting of Einhard's charters is the survey of the Michelstadt properties that Einhard had his notary Luther draw up [3.11]. In reading this document, one bounces from oak tree to stream, along rivers and brooks, to villages and hills, past now long forgotten places, one of which bears Einhard's name. One also sees in these charters a few of Einhard's legal actions as lay abbot, leasing land and facilitating the exchange of peoples. Einhard's principal holdings were located in three areas: in Michelstadt and Seligenstadt [Map 3], at his two monasteries at Ghent [Map 1], and at St-Servais in Maastricht [Map 2]. But he also had property interests near Paris [6.2 and 3.13] and at Fritzlar [6.37]. In the *Translation and Miracles* we also learn that he held the churches of St-Salvius in Valenciennes [5.4.10] and St-John the Baptist (Domnanae) in Pavia [5.1.6] as benefices. The former was a benefice of Louis, the latter "of kings", presumably meaning Louis the Pious and Lothar I, and was held in 827 as his notary Ratleig passed through Italy [see Map 4]. Between 816 and 823, Einhard also held the monastery of Fontanelle (St-Wandrille) in Normandy [1.12 and Map 4].

We should be thankful for Einhard's relative prosperity, for it may have been the landed wealth of the 820s that allowed him, at least partially, to begin extricating himself from court. For it was probably time away from court that fostered his burgeoning writing career. It was a simple fact of Carolingian court life that people at the palace had less need to write to each other, but when away from court needed to write a great deal in order to communicate with the powerful people who could give them lands and shape their destinies. The thousand preoccupations and demands of duty at court must have given even energetic Einhard little free time. But in the late 820s and 830s Einhard's center of intellectual gravity was shifting to his local estates and to his new religious enthusiasms.

Einhard's most famous book was written after Charlemagne's death, but just when has always been unclear. Dates from as early as 817 to as late as 836 have been proposed. The first two contemporary references to the famous book come from Gerward, Louis the Pious's librarian, and the young monk Lupus of Ferrières. Gerward attached a set of dedicatory verses to the copy of the biography he presented to Emperor Louis [see 1.8]. The date of Lupus's first letter to Einhard [7.1], in which he praises the *Life of Charlemagne*, has been the subject of considerable debate. The letter cannot have been written before 830 and Lupus's first stay at Fulda, but some have argued that it was written as late as 836 during the monk's second visit to Fulda. Given its introductory and rather callow quality, it would seem to belong to Lupus's youthful first visit rather than his more mature second. But whatever the date of Lupus's first letter, Gerward's short dedicatory poem still seems to be the earliest public acknowledgment of the existence of the biography and of Einhard's authorship. The description of Gerward that Einhard himself supplies in the *Translation and Miracles* [5.4.7] is interesting in this regard. He says of 828 that Gerward was "already at that time" the palace librarian. This might lead one to suspect that Gerward had not long held the office, but had been appointed relatively recently. As Louis's librarian, therefore, he may not have been in a position to present the emperor with a copy of the biography much before 826 or 827. It is also not impossible that both Walahfrid [1.9] and Ermold [1.11] already knew of the existence of the *Life of Charlemagne* by 829. Walahfrid's titular reference to *Einhartus Magnus* reminds one of Gerward's *Einhardus magnificus* [1.8], but the librarian's clever epithet may have been designed for Louis's benefit, since it could be taken to mean 'one who makes much of a thing'. Walahfrid's *magnus* may also contain an allusion to Einhard's fame as the biographer of the Great One. Ermold's portrait of Einhard worshipping the very ground on which Charlemagne walked may be an allusion as well. Gerward, Walahfrid, and Ermold all knew, of course, that it was Louis who buttered their bread and they may have been reacting to Einhard's high praise of Charlemagne, who was in little favor at the early court of his son. Gerward seems to have wanted, with his poetic preface to Louis's personal copy of the biography, to balance things, to provide an almost lapidary antidote for the considerable flattery of Charles that was to come by beginning with Louis's own greatness, lifting his name to the stars. This interpretation of the early allusions to Einhard as the great one's biographer would fit with Heinz Löwe's suggestion that the *Life of Charlemagne* was probably written around 825-826.

Matthew Innes and Rosamond McKitterick recently returned to the older argument that a library catalogue from Reichenau written in the early 820s must push the date of the composition of the biography back to the early years of Louis's reign. They would associate the work with Louis's restructuring of the kingdom in 817. Unfortunately the catalogue entry in question does not specifically cite Einhard or the biography by name, and the date of the catalogue itself remains controversial. Moreover, it is difficult to reconcile a date of composition for the biography as early as 817-18 with the content of the biography itself: in particular, the noble and generous treatment of Bernard of Italy and his five sisters would have been a very daring position to take in 818 [2.19], and for that matter at any point prior to Louis's public penance in 822 for Bernard's death. Moreover, the biography likely was not written before the Abodrites revolted in 817 or the wooden arcade at Aachen collapsed on Louis and his company on Maundy Thursday (9 April) 817, for both events seem to be alluded to by Einhard [2.12 and 2.32], though neither of those references is beyond variant interpretation. Was Einhard's memory confused because much time had passed before he wrote about the latter incident, or was he willfully confusing chronology?

Another indication that the biography may have been written closer to the mid-820s is its description of Charlemagne as a family man, since this emphasis may have been Einhard's rebuttal of the famous dream of Wetti from November 824 in which the emperor was envisaged standing on an illumined plain while an animal gnawed at his genitals. Wetti's angel proclaimed that Charles deserved to suffer such torment because of his lecherous life. The vision quickly began to circulate in written form, saying publicly what many churchmen knew to be true: that Charles could not escape in death the punishment he deserved for the sins he had committed in life. In 827 Walahfrid Strabo himself set the vision to verse. Einhard's portrait of Charlemagne as a family man may appear almost apologetic in this light, part of an attempt to answer Charlemagne's critics with a pointed defense of his domestic life. In the second decade of the ninth century, Charlemagne's reputation stood at virtually its lowest point in all of western history. His son and even the royal Frankish annalist were quick to recognize Charlemagne's injustices, the filth of his palace, his own lust, and the failure of his last military campaign. Ermold and Louis's advisers seem, moreover, to have thought that Charlemagne had been too concerned with war; he was the great *belliger*, the bringer of war. Einhard's rather dry account of Charlemagne's wars is almost an anti-epic [see 2.6], perhaps in order to de-emphasize a side of

Charlemagne that was no longer fashionable. And so the reader passes straight from war to peace, from the Charlemagne Einhard hardly knew to the one he knew very well, all of which may reflect Einhard's sensitivity to the images of Charlemagne that were circulating in the 820s.

Why all the fuss about dating the *Life of Charlemagne*? It is an important issue, because if we knew when Einhard composed the biography we might be able to understand somewhat better the author's intentions and the relative emphases buried in his work. If it was written as early as 818, it might well have had a tone imparted by Louis the Pious's reform of the palace and kingdom early in his reign; if written as late as 829–830, it might refer to the troubles of the rebellion of Louis's sons that were then looming. But the author may not have wanted the biography, with its classical tenor and scrambling and confusion of Carolingian references, to be pinned down too closely. Within the last few years distinguished scholars have with great conviction read the biography as either pro-Louis or anti-Louis. That very indeterminacy may actually help us to place the *Life of Charlemagne* down in the mid-820s when Louis the Pious's reign seemed to begin to drift and others were writing symbolically allusive compositions of their own. Walahfrid Strabo's poem on the statue of Theoderic, in which Einhard was called The Great [1.9], is equally suggestive and indeterminate. Both works are tantalizingly allusive and may have been designed to supply Louis and his world with mirrors in which to search for veiled truths. There is evidence, after all, that the biographer was politically astute or, at least, aware of where the troubled waters lay. There is, for instance, no mention made of Charlemagne's 'Division of the Kingdom' of 806, which Einhard himself had carried to Rome. Was it excluded from the biography because he considered it a document that had no force after 813 or because it was one that, despite its importance to understanding Charlemagne's view of succession, ran counter to Louis's view (prior to 830) of an indivisible empire, the one enshrined in the *Ordinatio imperii* of 817 [see *Carolingian Civilization* 27], to which he had been the sole heir and which Lothar would in turn inherit? Whatever his reason, Einhard made a deliberate choice not to mention the arrangement, and its omission should alert readers to the careful nature of Einhard's selection of materials, both what he includes and what he excludes. His high and historically vague praise, for instance, of Charlemagne's farsighted preparations for dealing with raids by the Northmen and Moors [2.17] has always seemed to reflect the hindsight of someone situated in Louis the Pious's Francia [see 6.22] rather than Charlemagne's.

The *Life of Charlemagne* is without doubt the jewel of early medieval biographies, and in a recent paper David Ganz noted that it has survived in over 100 manuscripts, thus also making it one of the Middle Ages' most popular secular works. But it has also been dismissed by some as a derivative work, since Einhard drew upon Suetonius's *Lives of the Caesars*, a work that he had probably first seen as a student at Fulda, for the structure and some of the language of his portrait. The biography of Augustus, in particular, influenced Einhard's design. But it would not do to exaggerate Einhard's dependence on Suetonius or to cast Charlemagne as a thirteenth Caesar, for the purposes and conclusions of the two authors were strikingly different. Suetonius may have striven to balance his portraits of imperial vices and accomplishments, but in the end he exposed and effectively condemned the many vices of even Augustus. Einhard, on the other hand, has hardly a negative word to say about his king, and when he does his comments are enclosed in careful qualifications. In this way he explained and accounted for Charlemagne's harsh and arbitrary actions as unusual lapses. In fact, both Einhard [2.20] and the reviser of the *Royal Frankish Annals* (for 792) blamed Fastrada for Charlemagne's troubles with noble conspirators. But Einhard was also selective in his critical comments. He did not mention, for instance, the execution of thousands of Saxons at Verden at all, but was prepared to issue his own quiet complaint over the shallowness of Charlemagne's legal reforms [2.29].

But as Siegmund Hellmann in an old and important study and Matthew Kempsall in a new and insightful one have both argued, the *Life of Charlemagne* is a work informed by sophisticated literary strategies and influences. Einhard's models may be less Suetonian than Ciceronian and classical, for the Carolingian biographer may actually have set out to treat his famous subject according to non-Suetonian categories. Some of these were supplied by Ciceronian ideals of eloquence and classical notions about how one was to measure and present the *magnanimitas* or greatness of a ruler. Although Walahfrid supplied formal chapter titles and breaks for the short biography, Einhard himself imagined his work as a continuous sketch. Why, after all, would one further categorize what was already so manifestly categorical in treatment?

Part of the enduring appeal of the *Life of Charlemagne* is that it has resisted being precisely pinned down. It has stubbornly refused for over a thousand years the most persistent efforts to assign it and its author to a particular cause or event. Can one doubt that this was a deliberate authorial strategy adopted by "prudent Einhard" in order to protect and hide himself by removing his personal voice from the biography, as best he could? It has surely, if only accidentally, added to the allure of a piece that cannot be too easily known or personalized. In its structural simplicity the biography charms its readers, leading them ever closer to Charlemagne himself, to the great man as he was at home.

Why, in fact, does the *Life of Charlemagne* bend so many of the facts we know about events? Was this a product of poor memory, distant memory, a lack of handy archival materials, an overdependence on a model — as for example in his contrived and false construction of portents – or a purposive and deliberate strategy for shaping material to convey indirect messages to king and court?

Einhard certainly thought of himself as a member of that court, as a courtier of both Charlemagne and then his son. The audience for his two books was the circle of people he knew at court. His letters bounce the reader back and forth between the concerns of his various households or *familiae* and those of the court. The rhythms of his annual life also swung between these two poles, since when he was at Michelstadt in the 820s or Seligenstadt in the 830s, he was always aware that the court was out there waiting to engage and threaten him. There was no escaping it. And when at court, he needed via letters and messengers to handle the distant affairs of his properties and to collect the provisions he needed for his residence in Aachen [6.23].

Einhard was, by all accounts, an extremely careful courtier. Some of his contemporaries did not hesitate to call him the most prudent of all the men at court [1.13]. This carefulness extended to his writing. One of the distinct peculiarities of the *Life of Charlemagne*, after all, is that Einhard did not attach his name to the work. This was not, I suspect, an accident of manuscript transmission, for both Gerward [1.8] and Walahfrid [1.14] went to some trouble to identify Einhard as the biographer. Apparently the book circulated as early as the late 820s and as late as the 840s in copies without the author's name attached. Why did Einhard wish to hide even his name? Was it an example of his modesty or an attempt to preserve some small measure of anonymity? With anonymity went humility, of course, and the diminutives of the preface – his little training and small reputation – were meant to conjure up images of humble, little Einhard. But those in the know certainly knew who had written the biography, and Gerward simply assumed that Louis either knew or could figure out who had written the biography of his father.

But Walahfrid felt a particular need [1.14] to explain who Einhard was. Did he do this without a deeper purpose? When he edited Thegan's *Life of Louis*, Walahfrid added a brief introduction in which he briefly commented on the author's noble anger at Louis's lowborn enemies, but in Einhard's case he went much further and supplied readers with a detailed sketch of Einhard and the times through which he had lived. His was a contextual interpretation of the *Life of Charlemagne*, for he was keen to see Einhard as a survivor of the enveloping turbulence of Louis the Pious's reign. But this praise may have been backhanded, for Walahfrid seems to have wondered after Einhard's death how Charlemagne's courtier, The Great Einhard, had survived all the troubles that had so swiftly brought Louis and his loyal courtiers down. Walahfrid himself had been one of those overthrown by the politics of rebellion in the

830s. His short sketch, so simple in its measured praise of Einhard, may contain a certain criticism of Einhard's guarded and careful nature – too prudent a courtier, after all, Walahfrid may have thought. Still, his piece was the first in a long series of attempts to restore a historical context to Einhard's naked composition, to dress it in some of the contextual clothes it seems to want.

There is another matter about the biography that has received even less attention than its date and authorship: the question of the biography's specific audience. It is not impossible that Einhard wrote the biography or, at least, its preface for a specific individual, as David Ganz has suggested, since in that preface Einhard submitted the book to some unnamed person (*tibi*). But, even if Einhard sent the biography and preface to an acquaintance or fellow courtier, he may still have had several readers in mind, the greatest congregation of which was certainly the collection of his fellow courtiers at the palace. Gerward's little verses prove that the book was there [1.8]. But if the *Life of Charlemagne* was written originally for a specific person, its message might be read in a different light, as the memoirs of one courtier for the education and training of another. Seen in that light, the biography of Charlemagne would stand like Hincmar of Rheims's *On the Governance of the Palace* [see *Carolingian Civilization* 72] as a briefing manual, as one courtier's reflections on what the court had once been like and should be like again. Neither Lupus nor Walahfrid read it in that vein, but rather, as one would have expected learned courtiers and would-be courtiers to read it, as a reflection of the flowering of civilization in an earlier and more enlightened age. Whatever its date of composition, audience, or meaning, the *Life of Charlemagne* quickly became a classic in such circles. Lupus of Ferrières could not restrain his admiration for its elegant style and high purpose [7.1]. But in the early 830s Lupus was a young monk on the make, not yet a courtier, and he was seeking Einhard's favor. What he wanted, in part, was to lay his hands on Einhard's library, for Lupus seems to have loved rare books almost more than the people who owned them.

The *Life of Charlemagne* is a great work of medieval historiography for many reasons, not the least of which is its powerful simplicity. It seems, on the surface, a straightforward book, but its brevity conceals and intrigues, leading us deeper into material that hides as much as it reveals. Almost as important as what Einhard tells us, after all, is what he does not. He has relatively little to say about the meaning of empire to Charles's court and next to nothing about the doctrinal controversies that raged inside and outside the court and kingdom: nothing on adoptionism, the procession question, or the iconodule issue. Alcuin and Peter of Pisa receive their due in the book, but Paul the Deacon and Paulinus of Aquileia, who had departed from Aachen before Einhard arrived, are not mentioned. Theodulf surfaces only impersonally as a witness to the last testament. Louis the Pious himself is not a prominent figure in the biography. Nor does Einhard address the problem of partible inheritance which had so concerned Charlemagne and continued to worry his son Louis.

But if the *Life of Charlemagne* seems simple, straightforward, and short, the *Translation and Miracles* has struck some modern readers as fantastic and bizarre. Indeed, nothing could have prepared the readers of Einhard's imperial biography for the *Translation and Miracles*, some portion of which may have surfaced as early as late 830 or early 831. The translation of the relics themselves had occurred in October 827 and was reported by the royal Frankish annalist as if it were a matter of importance to all Francia. Once again Einhard was at the leading edge of the intellectual currents of his day, now not the world of sublime poetry in the intimate circle of a great king and his playful bards, but the world of popular religion being tested by Carolingians in the countryside of northern Europe. Though curmudgeons like Claudius of Turin and even Agobard of Lyons may have been unsympathetic toward expressions of popular religion, Einhard embraced the cult of the saints with exhilarating enthusiasm in the late 820s. In 826 the archchaplain Hilduin had enshrined the relics of Saint Sebastian in St-Médard of Soissons. They were said to have immediately brought about a great number of miraculous cures – evidence, thought Hilduin, of Christ's powerful presence and local immediacy in Soissons. Einhard, who was just then founding his own church at Michel-stadt, sought relics for its dedication. It is the history of the translation, of the aquisition and *adventus* of the saints, of the intrigues and deceptions that he and the saints suffered, and of their many marvelous and manifest works, that fill his book. The translation of the relics also marked a new phase in Einhard's life, as he slowly disengaged himself from court and active royal service, or rather sought to transfer his service to the care of his saintly patrons.

The reasons why Einhard wrote this book were far from simple, and not completely unconnected to the *Life of Charlemagne*, which may have been composed not very many years before. The opening lines of the *Translation and Miracles* may even contain an apologia not just for Einhard the hagiographer, but also for the biographer. Why else would one write about just and holy men, he asks, except to provide examples whereby the living might emend their lives? But if he began by nodding in the direction of Charlemagne and his earlier work, he quickly turned toward those Carolingian skeptics who doubted the power and efficacy of the saints. He needed to answer the rumors then circulating that his relics had been divided and their integrity compromised by the theft committed by Hilduin's agent. This theft should give pause to those readers tempted to think that Hilduin and Einhard were insincere hucksters anxious to dupe a superstitious age, for both were prepared to go to extraordinary lengths to acquire and keep relics, even if it meant risking high political animosities. Nor were they religiously naive, for they understood that there was trickery about in the relics trade. Einhard asked Deusdona to supply him with "genuine relics" [5.1.1], which seems to suppose the existence of false relics. And, indeed, Einhard knew Deusdona to be a dealer in false goods and half-truths. His man, Ratleig, would finally find the true relics on his own.

Einhard was ill, apparently with a disease like dysentery, in the spring and early summer of 830 [6.41], and, perhaps, all the more aware of his need for saintly help. But it may have been that illness, which conveniently coincided with the rebellion of 830, that provided him with the opportunity to hole up at Seligenstadt and begin or continue writing the *Translation and Miracles*. His book thus had both personal and political agendas; at points it even recommends political and social reforms [5.3.13-14].

Einhard was, in both his formal compositions, engaged in hoarding reputation for personal advantage. In the first, he styled himself the keeper of Charlemagne's memory; and in the second, he secured and promoted his personal connection to the saints. He presented himself, in fact, as the driving force behind the translation of the martyrs. His desire to acquire relics was the motivating factor, he cut the deal with Deusdona, sent Ratleig, received the relics, recovered the relics from Hilduin, sent portions of them to other churches, and kept careful reportorial watch on the miracles performed.

But in the *Translation and Miracles* Einhard also remained a royal courtier. One needs to examine closely just when Einhard finally circulated his account of the translation. The last dated miracle occurred on 28 August 830 [5.4.18]. That year had been a difficult one for Einhard and his king. Louis's sons had revolted in the spring and had captured the emperor and his wife. By October in an assembly held at Nijmegen, however, Louis had reasserted his authority. He made a special point, according to his biographer, the man popularly known as the Astronomer, of accusing Abbot Hilduin of hostility and resistance to the imperial will. Another biographer, Thegan, lumped Hilduin in with the other rebels of the spring. Hilduin fell far and fast, ending up spending the winter of 830-31 in a tent outside Paderborn. Given Einhard's careful nature it is unlikely that he would have circulated or, perhaps, even written the second book of the *Translation and Miracles*, with its damning portrait of Hilduin, while the abbot was still a great power at court. In many ways Hilduin is the chief villain of the whole work. He is not just one of those figures such as Deusdona and the scurrilous Hunus, who represent forces that would frustrate the rightful progress of the martyrs to Einhard; he is the last and greatest obstructionist. Although one particle of the relics was generally thought to possess the power of the whole, Hilduin had colluded in the unnatural and unkind separation of two saintly companions. Einhard presents the abbot's final hesitation in handing over the separated relics in strikingly unfavorable terms. Indeed, Hilduin had earlier let it be known that he would accept the judgment of no one – which must have included the emperor himself – who said that he should part with the relics [5.2.1]. Einhard was quick to pass on this hearsay as evidence of Hilduin's overweening pride. Contemporary readers at court would have nodded in assent and recognized Hilduin's pride as the underlying cause of his contumacy. Moreover, Hilduin kept Louis himself away from Einhard's relics for a time [5.2.6], an act that must have seemed to Einhard to have denied the salvific grace of the saints to an emperor much in need of it at the time. In Einhard's view, Hilduin had done everything he possibly could to delay the transfer of the saints and to put Einhard, their rightful servant, in a humiliating and subordinate place.

In fact, St-Médard would still claim in the early 840s to possess the remains of Marcellinus and Peter [see *Carolingian Civilization* 44.3.2]. One should note that the *Royal Frankish Annals* entry for 827 in which the translation of Marcellinus and Peter was reported made no mention of Einhard at all. Was that because Hilduin prior to Easter 828 still claimed a portion of the relics for St-Médard and was not yet willing to place them completely in Einhard's hands? Did Hilduin, in fact, cheat Einhard one last time? He made him wait for the relics and charged him the enormous sum of 100 gold pieces for their return, but did he in the end still pass along bogus bones? It is a classic con-artist's technique, after all, to make the victim of deception stew in anticipation, making him all the readier to accept fraudulent goods as genuine. Einhard may never have detected that final deception, if it occurred, but he took timely revenge for his earlier frustration. In the late summer and early fall of 830, with Hilduin in public disgrace, Einhard wrote some portions of the *Translation and Miracles* and publicly unmasked Hilduin's dishonesty, pride, and greed. Moreover, late in the *Translation and Miracles* [5.4.14] Einhard's relics bested those of Hilduin, carrying out a miracle that Hilduin's Saint Sebastian had been unable to bring about. Einhard also cast doubt on the relics of Saint Tiburtius, suggesting that not even Hunus had believed in their authenticity [5.1.5]. Thus the rivalries of the Carolingian court spilled over into the invisible realm of the saints where powerful courtiers were still looking for their own holy patrons and protectors, for the means to gain saintly advantage over their enemies.

At one level, then, Einhard's translation history is a self-serving whodunit intended to restore the reputation of Einhard's relics before a public that had heard stories questioning their legitimacy and integrity. The first book of the *Translation and Miracles* is also a gripping specimen of Carolingian travel writing, but the reader should notice that it works as a pilgrimage in reverse. In most pilgrimage accounts, all the hindrances and adversities of the road are encountered on the way to the goal, be it Rome, St-James of Compostella, or Jerusalem. The trip back was generally a mere afternote, often adorned with few details. Einhard's account of the *Translation and Miracles* works in the opposite direction, for little information about the journey to Rome is supplied, but a great deal about the trip to Michelstadt with its incidents of intrigue, treachery, and triumphal advent [see Map 4]. What the reader needs to appreciate is that the true pilgrimage or home-coming was that of the martyrs themselves and that their voyage was not a return trip, but one that only began in Rome with the discovery of the holy bones. It was the saints' journey north to Einhard that was religiously remarkable.

One also needs to appreciate that the prevailing theory was that the saints were fully present and powerful in their bones and that they would not, indeed could not be made to go where they did not wish to go. They refused, for instance, to stay in Michelstadt, where Einhard had all along thought they belonged, but rather wanted to travel to a place which at the time must have had a less than fully suitable church to hold them and their petitioners. Throughout his book, it is clear that Einhard thought of the martyrs as active and living presences and that he was merely and sincerely collecting the evidence of their agency and intervention in the world. Now the fact that the saints were believed to inhabit their bones, to be truly and powerfully present in them, meant that it was technically impossible to steal them, since they would go only where and when it suited them. Einhard may have reasoned along these lines as he indirectly solicited and then unashamedly broadcast Ratleig's violation of Roman tombs and his theft of relics. In 826 Hilduin had been anxious to have the *Royal Frankish Annals* report that the pope himself had granted his request for the relics of Saint Sebastian, and the Astronomer would wrongly grant Einhard the same privilege posthumously [1.13]. But, at some level, Einhard was aware that he was planning a major theft. He and Deusdona might try to excuse their larceny on the pretext that the tombs of the martyrs in Rome were neglected and the saints uncared for [5.1.1], but the excuse-making suggests they knew that their trade in bones was not absolutely licit.

Einhard, however, needed to see Hunus's theft of relics from Ratleig in a different light, as the unnatural and unholy separation of martyrs who belonged together, bound by their boonship [5.1.5]. Still, the logic was weak and Einhard did not wish to dwell for too long on the problem. For despite the good reasons for stealing a saint's bones, the thieves still knew it was robbery. Ratleig and his companions may have surrounded their theft with holy acts by fasting for three days and praying at the doors of the churches they robbed, but they knew they were engaged in grand larceny. Ratleig hid out in Rome, stole into the crypts at night, listened for signs of detection, had his gang of grave-robbers split up as they left town, and was wary of a papal party he feared might be on their trail. Nor were they the best of crooks; they couldn't even figure out how Deusdona had learned that they were operating without him, though they must have stood out like sore thumbs in Rome. Only when they finally crossed the Alps and no longer feared being caught did Ratleig openly display the saints. Now, in a striking elevation of their public role, the martyrs were escorted north as though they were the highest church dignitaries. Theirs was now a triumphal procession ending at each village in an elaborate *adventus* or arrival celebration. Einhard's literary genius is evident once again as he filled his pages with dramatic tension expressing his own profound sense of wonder.

Einhard's theology of the relics was relatively simple, though encumbered by a somewhat opaque vocabulary. He knew and stressed at several points that the saints, as powerfully present in their bones, merely interceded with Christ on behalf of their petitioners [5.3.preface, 5.3.2, 7.4]. Thus, the sick prayed to the saints, who in turn prayed to Christ. But it was Christ's divine power that produced miraculous cures, in part because the saints were in favor with him and stood close to his side. For the most part, Einhard spoke of these cures and miracles as being achieved *per merita sanctorum*. Though I have for the sake of convenience and consistency translated this phrase as "through the merits of the saints", *merita* is a particularly slippery word that Einhard never clearly explained. At some points, it seems that one could susbstitute *per intercessionem martyrum* for his formula, as he himself does, but that would be to confuse the process with the cause. In fact, at 5.3.15, he speaks of *per merita et intercessionem sanctorum* and thus separates out two aspects of the saints' role. What Einhard seems to have meant by *merita*, therefore, is something closer to the "virtuous credits" that Marcellinus and Peter had accrued in heaven because of their holy lives and precious martyrdoms. Christ was prepared to listen to their petitions on behalf of Christians who were specially deserving because the saints, by their very lives and deaths, had earned his special attention. Not being a theologian, for whom consistency is everything, Einhard occasionally lost tight control of his formula. On several occasions he spoke of miracles occurring *per virtutem sanctorum* [5.3.5 and 5.3.12] and *per potestatem sanctorum* [5.3.15], which could lead an uncareful reader to assign direct agency to the saints. The sick people who prostrated themselves before the relics must have rarely made the careful distinctions that Einhard knew needed making. They imagined instead that the two saints took a hands-on approach to curing even the deformed, as with one at each end they pulled twisted limbs straight [5.3.9].

But to return to stylistic matters, how does one account for the change of prose styles between the *Life of Charlemagne* and the *Translation and Miracles*? Was it simply the case that in the former Einhard had relied on his ancient models to achieve a classical, imperial biography with longer sentences and classical vocabulary? Or were the effective audiences different, since the translation story sought to spread popular word of the efficacy of the relics? Einhard's different voices in the two works were deliberately chosen. He began the biography by denying that he could ever achieve a true Ciceronian style, but that was his goal, the one Lupus so warmed to. He ended the *Translation and Miracles* by consciously defending the vulgarity of the prose style he had employed, prepared to stare down his detractors. He only hoped that his critics wouldn't curse as they impugned him and his popular book.

The fourth book of the *Translation and Miracles* does contain some fairly crude accounts of the saints' various cures as they moved through the countryside like some traveling medicine show, but these were accounts produced at other churches and inserted into the work by Einhard [5.4.9-14]. The three little registers or calendars of miracles included in the fourth book are more interesting than students sometimes suppose. They remind one, in their almost totemic structure, of the ancient stelae found at the temples of Asclepius, which recount the incubation cures of those who had visited and slept with the pagan god. Einhard himself was anxious to demonstrate the potency of the martyrs' relics, but to do so he needed to isolate them from other forces and other saints. The three external registers proved, he may have thought, that everywhere the saints went, miracles, like Mary's little lambs, were sure to go. It should be noticed that Einhard had not allowed his relics to wander too far afield, for St-Bavo in Ghent, St-Salvius in Valenciennes, and St-Servais in Maastricht were all churches under his direct control. Indeed, the dates of the three calendars are worth noting, for it is almost as if one could follow the relics from place to place over four months in 828. But the dates overlap at points and George, the Venetian organ builder, had arranged for the relics to be picked up in Aachen and Einhard himself may have carried the relics to Maastricht [5.4.14]. One could conclude that in 828 Einhard divided up and permanently alienated portions of the relics from Seligenstadt, since he said in the 830s that the relics continued to bring about cures in those other places [5.4.8].

Each of the little books is also different in language and emphasis. George, for instance, fairly consistently associated miracles at St-Salvius with the celebration of the Mass [5.4.10], a connection not specifically drawn by the others. Moreover, did Einhard himself write the last of those accounts, the one from St-Servais? At several points in 5.4.14 (on 4 and 10 June) he relates, in the first person, events in which he directly participated. If Einhard did compose that work, or a portion of it, why did he feel the need to present it as the work of the monks of St-Servais?

Einhard and his various churches certainly benefited from the publicity stirred up by the relics. He used his particular devotion to the martyrs as a means of persuading the emperor and empress to give him special relief from his public commitments, and he received financial advantages for his churches. But the cult of the saints as promoted by Hilduin and Einhard should not be reduced to crass commercialism, since everything suggests their deep belief and sincerity. One only needs to study the depths of Einhard's despair and utter disappointment when the saints failed to save his wife Emma from her final illness in order to gauge the sincerity of the hope he had placed in the power of his saints [7.3].

It might almost be argued that the *Translation and Miracles* was as influential, at least in terms of spawning a genre, as the *Life of Charlemagne*. For while the latter had few direct imitators, so inimitable was its subject and style, the translation story would effectively shape and guide the creation of a subgenre of hagiography, the translation histories, that would achieve great prominence and importance in the central Middle Ages.

It would probably be inaccurate to think that Einhard's own religious beliefs changed radically in the 820s, though with his rise to lay abbacy and with the onset of old age and illness, the features of his personal life may have begun to sharpen his particular religious needs. Once again, however, in his dealings with Deusdona, the relics salesman, one sees Einhard as energetic as ever and prepared to invest a great deal in an unusual and somewhat risky enterprise. The results in the short run, at least, were extremely rewarding, for his possession of the saints allowed Einhard to achieve new preeminence and prominence. Even archbishops now asked him to supply them with relics [6.10], for Einhard's saints had returned him once again to the very center of things, where he had not been since the dissolution of Charlemagne's court and the various disruptions of the late 820s. In this light, the *Translation and Miracles* is the natural successor to the remembered world of the *Life of Charlemagne*, but it was now a world inhabited by a different circle of powerful people, by new and invisible friends and by true believers, a spiritual court of Einhard's own making.

Einhard's correspondence is one of the fullest collections of Carolingian letters, but it is also one filled with intriguing problems. The collection has survived in only one damaged manuscript, which was once in Laon (Paris, B.N. lat. 11379). Gaps in the letters are indicated by ellipses [...] in the translations below. Virtually all the letters come from the last fifteen years of his life, many from the last decade. It has long been thought that the collection was copied out at St-Bavo, which may be true, but that need not mean that the letters are particularly concerned with that monastery. In fact, though St-Bavo, Blandin, Maastricht, St-Cloud, and Fritzlar are all mentioned in the letters, the great majority concern Seligenstadt. Was the collection then one that began as Einhard's own letter book or register of letters that happened to pass through and be preserved by scribes at St-Bavo? The collection is representative of a certain portion of Einhard's correspondence, but it is far from complete. The spottiness and disorganization of the collection is all too apparent. In his letter to Gerward [6.14], Einhard talks about an important earlier letter that seems at first to be missing. But a later letter in the collection [6.41] could well be that missing letter. The letter to Lupus [7.3], however, is not preserved in the collected letters, but only in Lupus's own collection. Was this an accident of transmission or the result of the letter writer's own notion of what was worth preserving or, rather, what he chose not to preserve? Letters he received from elsewhere rarely survived. The letter he and others received from the cathedral of Sens is printed as an appendix to part 6 below.

Although Hampe and others carefully reordered the letters into a reasonable chronological sequence, in the translation below I have restored the letters to their original order in the unique manuscript and have provided Hampe's letter numbers in parentheses. It can be argued that, as in some archaeological dig, the original context and placement of a piece in the strata of this collection have informative and meaningful values of their own. Despite some chronological anomalies such as the Bernharius letters [6.31-32], the manuscript does preserve some revealing chronological and thematic patterns of its own. Thus, the letters to Lothar fall fairly early in the collection, the letters to Louis the German fairly late. The letters during the first rebellion hang together [6.40-44] as do those of the second [6.46-48, 53-54], while the letter on the appearance of Halley's Comet in 837 is late in the collection [6.61]. There also seems to be some rough thematic groupings of material in the collection. Those letters, for instance, that concern people seeking refuge at Seligenstadt, a subject not taken up in the *Translation and Miracles* for some reason, occur early in the collection.

Two of the most political of Einhard's letters actually survive in their best copies outside the original collection, or, rather, they were added to the manuscript of the collection on a separate folio written by another scribe. Folio 20 of Paris, B.N. lat. 11379 contains a partial copy of letter 34, which is perhaps the most forthright and so extraordinary of Einhard's letters, his rebuke of the recently rebellious Lothar; it also contains a complete copy of an important letter to Louis the Pious in which Einhard pleaded early in the 830s for the emperor's special patronage and protection of the saints and their new church [6.appendix.A]. Where did these letters come from and do they suggest that there once existed another collection of Einhard's important letters?

The collection of letters contains a particular body of Einhard's letters that may have had some utility at a place such as St-Bavo, not just as the great Einhard's letters, but as an example book for writing business correspondence. In fact, letters written by others follow Einhard's. In the manuscript the collection was given the title, "A Little Book of Letters". In that light, it might be viewed less as Einhard's book of letters than as a book of specimen letters with all the historical confusions and anomalies that arise from that other ahistorical purpose. This may help us to account for why so many names have been dropped from the manuscript, generally being replaced with a single initial or N. The latter stood in some cases, if not in all, for *Nomen* or Name, that is to say, a blank. Letter 31, for instance, lists the recipient as N. in the salutation, even though we know from the body of the letter that it was addressed to Bernharius. Perhaps these names and their historical significance held little importance for the scribe of the manuscript or for monastic readers.

The letters show us Einhard acting as an agent of the emperor, as a local patron, as a lay abbot, as the holder of properties, as an influential referee, as a marriage broker, and as an intellectual and friend. Along with the *Translation and Miracles*, they take us into the daily life of the Carolingian world, where the price of roof tiles, the eruption of blood feuds, and the arrangement of marriages daily preoccupied lords like Einhard. Once again, Einhard's witness to the Carolingian world is rich and precious.

But the collection of Einhard's letters is more complex than students might at first assume. There are few letters from others to Einhard in the collection, so that we almost exclusively encounter a one-sided correspondence and cannot easily judge Einhard's role in the thrust and parry of correspondence. A particular problem for both the translator and the reader are the formal salutations and valedictions in the collection, in which Einhard frequently demeans and humbles himself. We should, perhaps, give these no more thought than we do when we write "Dear Mr. Jones" to someone we may neither know nor like. But they do belong to a particular and characteristic voice that Einhard assumes in many of his letters, as does the epistolary exaggeration and panegyrical tone taken in the letters to his superiors. We should not allow the shifting tones of Einhard's voice in these letters to people placed at different levels of society to escape our attention entirely, for they reveal something of the intricate hierarchical character of Carolingian society and Einhard's reinforcement of it.

Nor can we afford to assume that Einhard was always completely honest or forthright in his letters. He was, for instance, careful to guard his secrets and not to put things in letters that might compromise him should the letter fall into the wrong hands [6.56]. The letters written during the two rebellions of 830 and 833 are among the most guarded in all his correspondence. Indeed, it is difficult to know where he fixed his loyalties during these years. But readers of the letters are, at least, allowed to suspect that this was a function of his guarded epistolary voice, and even then, to qualify further, of the voice we meet in the surviving letters. Einhard himself was probably responsible for removing his more direct and politically sensitive correspondence from the record. The several letters he wrote in early 830 as revolt broke out and he was unable to comply with changing imperial commands provide a study in the difficulties of a courtier's life in times of crisis and how Einhard used letters to try to protect himself and his reputation. There are few letters in the collection, in fact, that might be called personal; one needs to turn to the Lupus correspondence to appreciate that there were other epistolary worlds Einhard once occupied that are now entirely lost to us. Perhaps the compiler of the collection or Einhard himself simply thought that his monks did not require access to private correspondence of the sort he shared with Lupus.

Those who read the fascinating exchange with Lupus of Ferrières quickly realize that letters are missing from their exchange and that even the specific dating of the letters is somewhat uncertain. Still it does seem possible to see an approximate order and meaningful patterns in the letters that survive. Lupus's first letter to Einhard [7.1] was written around 830 during his first visit to Fulda. In it he expressed the hope that he might borrow Einhard's copy of Aulus Gellius's *Attic Nights*. Six years later in 836, in the last surviving letter [7.6], he informed Einhard that he hoped that he would soon be able to return that very book. Theirs was, to some degree, a tightly circumscribed and formal epistolary exchange; they didn't talk of politics or people, but of books and personal problems, philology and travel plans. But the correspondence is also one-sided, since Lupus in shaping his own letter collection kept or copied out only one of Einhard's letters [7.3], and this one was doubtless preserved because it set up Lupus's own long letter of consolation on Emma's death [7.5]. By placing the Einhard materials at the start of his collection, Lupus may also have wanted his readers to appreciate how intimately he had known the great old man, formerly of Charlemagne's court. But the real treasure in their correspondence is Einhard's letter, the one on Emma's death in 836, for it is one of the most touching and human of all the Einhard documents. Lupus's long letter of reply can strike the modern reader as strangely ineffective and cold, since it fails to meet Einhard in the depths of his emotional heart, but seeks to guide him intellectually out of his state of profound despair. But it belonged to a much older and richer genre of consolation, one to which Einhard himself had had recourse in his letter to the dying Bernharius [6.32]. But the formulaic and commonplace nature of Lupus's letter makes it seem at points a rhetorical exercise rather than a response on some deeper emotional level. The poignancy of Einhard's letter comes precisely from the fact that his grief was grounded in a personal and particular loss, and no universal consolation of Lupus's sort could ever salve a wound as individual as Einhard's was.

Einhard's last work, his 'On the Adoration of the Cross', is either a long letter or a short theological treatise. It has been placed in the correspondence with Lupus, because it properly belongs to their exchange of letters. At the start of the work, Einhard informs Lupus that he had worked on his question about the adoration of the cross when he was troubled by recent events, meaning, we must suppose, the sickness and death of Emma. Among his question-filled letters to Einhard, Lupus had apparently asked about the adoration of the cross. Did this lost letter precede or follow Einhard's letter [7.3]? In his letter of consolation on the death of Emma [7.5], Lupus thanked Einhard for dedicating the little book to him, which he may have received while working on his own lengthy letter. Letter 7.5 is so obviously an answer to 7.3 that it is difficult to know where exactly the 'On the Adoration of the Cross' fitted into this exchange. Lupus had clearly already received 7.3 and was hard at work on 7.5 when the treatise hit his writing desk.

But if its place in their exchange of letters is not entirely clear, its context and circumstances are. Though Lupus may have asked a brief question about the adoration of the cross, Einhard subordinated that issue, as well he should, and took up a problem that concerned him more profoundly: the nature of prayer and why it sometimes fails. In 7.3 he had confessed to Lupus that his deepest disappointment during Emma's illness had been that his prayers to the saints had accomplished nothing. After all that he had done in his devotion to them, Einhard may have felt almost cheated in early 836 when the saints ignored his prayers and Emma died. Thus, he turned his reply toward a consideration of proper prayer. His short treatise may propound rather unremark-able theology, but it is in its own way a remarkably human document, since it was a theology fashioned out of the crucible of his own suffering. His reflec-tions may even have had a certain therapeutic value, as he tried to work out his relationship with the saints and with God in the light of his own recent crisis of faith.

There had, of course, been a good deal of Carolingian reflection on the cross. Hrabanus Maurus had already produced his famous, illustrated *On the Praises of the Holy Cross* [see Figs. 2 and 12], but there were doubters. Claudius of Turin thought that the adoration of the cross was a dangerous practice, because there was almost nothing that could not then be adored, since every-thing connected with Christ's earthly presence – wood, mules, boats, mangers, old rags – would have to be adored [see *Carolingian Civilization* 35]. Einhard's own interest in the meaning of the cross apparently was of long-standing. He had probably thought of the cross in his role as the lay abbot of monasteries and their churches, all of which needed crosses. The silver arch he had had made served as the base for one such cross [see Figs. 5-9] he appar-ently gave to St-Servais in Maastricht. What one needs to imagine, in order to complete the effect, is the cross that surmounted that sumptuous silver pedi-ment.

But in 836 Einhard's preoccupation was more with prayer than with the cross. The last word on the matter was, however, granted to Lupus and he chose not to comment on or even engage Einhard's treatise or the reasons he wrote it. Instead, he asked the old man still more questions about rare books and rare words. One has to wonder how much Lupus lost in this exchange of letters through his own various inattentions and preoccupations. Louis the Pious's own visit to Seligenstadt in 836, as reported by the *Annals of Fulda*, seems to have been a more touching gesture of respect toward a valued ser-vant on the death of his wife, if we are allowed to surmise that that was why Louis visited his old courtier.

Einhard's relationship with Emma is a fascinating one to ponder, but there is too little material upon which to examine it in any depth. Had she gone from being his wife and companion to his spiritual sister and help-mate in his work as lay abbot? She surfaces only in the Michelstadt charters [3.7 and 3.10], three letters [6.15, 6.32, and 6.57], and in the Lupus correspondence. When had they married and where? Einhard along with Nithard and Dhuo-da was one of only a handful of prominent lay people who were important writers in the ninth century, and Emma herself may be another example of a Carolingian woman writer. Einhard and Emma seem not to have had chil-dren, or at least none that survived the first two decades of the ninth century, since in the charter from 819 [3.10] they held out the chance, which may have been just a standard legal clause, that they might still have offspring. Their marriage seems to have been a long one, lasting from at least 815, and probably much earlier, until Emma's death early in 836. Ironically the couple later had their names mistakenly substituted at Lorsch for those of a pair of legendary lovers, the courtier Angilbert and Charlemagne's daughter Bertha, who were caught in a compromising tryst at the winter palace by the emperor himself. But it would be wrong to read too much into Einhard's relationship with Emma, since we see too little of their life together in any of Einhard's writing. What cannot be mistaken is Einhard's profound distress at her death, though the reasons he gives for his despair may irk some modern readers. But we must be careful not to project modern values onto past emotions, for they were as filled with and defined by convention as are our own.

As dangerous as it is to try to assess the character of an individual who lived over a thousand years ago, one can at least identify some of the basic characteristics of Einhard's personality. He was not, it would seem, a particularly candid, audacious, or fearless fellow, but then his role at court and in the wider Carolingian world may not have allowed him the luxuries of willfullness and daring. Let invective belong to Theodulf, moral disapproval to Alcuin, outspokenness to Agobard, and authority to Charlemagne; Einhard would take usefulness as his chief asset. What seems to have particularly shaped Einhard's career was a gift for making himself useful and accommodating to his superiors and patrons. At virtually every stage of his long career he found ways of pleasing his many superiors: Baugulf, Alcuin, Charlemagne, Louis the Pious, Judith, Lothar, and the counts who sought out his letter-writing skills late in his life [6.63]. He seems to have impressed each of these people in turn with his utility and they soon found themselves depending upon him for his loyalty, prudence, and learning, all good courtly virtues. Each of them, to varying degrees, came to rely on him for his special skills in the art of accommodation and the prompt performance of duty.

The subtle patience revealed in his dealings with scoundrels like Deusdona and Hilduin was an indication of his defining virtue, that of extraordinary prudence. He could on occasion show his irritation with the likes of Hilduin, but even then he was careful not to offend directly until it was safe to do so. Indeed, his political letters are generally studies in restraint. The corrective letter to Lothar [6.34] may reveal real courage, but it was the censorious courage expected of a pedagogue for a fallen student and strikes a tone not unlike the one he took in the letter to another of his charges [6.30]. And the transmission of the archangel Gabriel's message of reform to the emperor [5.3.13] was a bold gesture, but it was also one he was careful to keep private. Nor was Einhard ever embroiled centrally in any controversy or scandal, as even the aged Alcuin had once been.

Perhaps, as Walahfrid seemed to imply, his small size had done a great deal to form his character, forcing him away from the battlefield and toward a career as a consummately wise and careful courtier. Though Walahfrid thought that Einhard had suffered a great deal from his tininess, we can see that the little man himself played upon the theme and used his size to epistolary advantage. Thus, when writing to the mighty of the world, he played off his Smallness against his correspondents' Greatness in a complex game of flattery and self-abasement. He may have been one of many individuals in Carolingian society who profited from being non-threatening. The abstract characterizations with which he spoke of himself as PARVITAS, PVSILITAS, IMBECILLITAS, PVSILLANIMITAS, and TENVIS PERSONA certainly belong to the medieval topos of humility, and Lupus employed a limited version of the same. But in Einhard's case these epithets had a real referent in his small size and his correspondents were doubtless aware of that dimension to their word play. Walahfrid went one step further, for in his Theoderic poem, written while Einhard was still an important figure at court, he turned Einhard's size into a theological lesson, for God could choose anyone to succeed, he wrote, no matter how weak or impaired he might seem [1.9].

Einhard's own preferred epithet was PECCATOR or sinner. He applied this word to himself in at least sixteen letters, the dedicatory inscription on his silver arch, two charters, and the preface to the Translation and Miracles. This characterization served, as it were, as his individualized sign, but it may not have had its roots in some deep sense of guilt. The charter in which Einhard and Emma donated Michelstadt to Lorsch [3.10] begins with some general reflections on the fallen state of humankind, but these should not be personalized. In fact, Einhard seems to have thought of the Carolingian people in general, and not just its rulers, as sinful [5.3.14 and 6.61]. The conception of himself as a sinner certainly belonged to the image of smallness and humility Einhard was drawing for himself. But was it an epithet he took in mid-career at Louis the Pious's court with its changing religious tastes, which were now more monastic and less Pelagian? Was even the taking of this epithet then another indication of Einhard's adaptibilty and conformity, or did it belong to the same inner drive that led him to embrace the saints so passionately in the 820s? One of his first uses of the epithet, after all, may have been on the charter from September 819 when he and Emma granted Michelstadt to Lorsch [3.10, and see 3.8.3].

In a world full of bitter rivalries and embattled palatines, Einhard succeeded in winning the favor of even his rivals. One of his great gifts, as his letters suggest, may have been that he threatened few other courtiers and no counts or kings. Theodulf, Walahfrid, and Ermold all seem to have had a grudging respect for him, though none could be called a friend. Einhard did have friends, but friendship at the heights of Carolingian society was always difficult, complicated as it was by the competitive nature of court life and the jockeying for royal favor by suitors. Gerward may have been, as Josef Fleckenstein suggested, one of Einhard's better friends, but in Einhard's one letter to him [6.14] the tension between the two of them is thick. For Gerward was, by this point, fully the emperor's man and he and, perhaps, his boss had grown weary of Einhard's excuses and his trading on the saints. The disaster of 830, when Louis and his men were overthrown, hit Einhard hard. He had been away from court when the rebellion broke out, but was reluctant to return and expose himself to a turbulent, remade court with its new power structures and shifting allegiances. His health, he claimed, had taken a turn for the worse. Whether his illness was real, feigned, or merely exaggerated, it was convenient and bought him the time he needed to retreat by boat to St-Bavo and ultimately, he thought, to his saints at Seligenstadt. He sent out three letters – to the emperor, empress, and some high member of court such as Gerward – to explain his absence, and to protect his reputation for loyalty and obedience [6.40-42]. Arthur Kleinclausz went to considerable trouble to try to prove that Einhard was truly ill in 830, and he may have been, but it is striking that he fell sick again in 833-834 when political crisis again struck and the sons of Louis the Pious again overthrew their father [6.53]. Had Einhard hit upon a useful strategy late in life for avoiding committing himself too early in these dynastic disputes? If so, he was certainly not the first to plead illness as a way of avoiding life-threatening conflict. Nine hundred years earlier Cicero had booked off sick on the day of the battle of Pharsalus.

Was Einhard a good and fair adminstrator of the properties he held? He was certainly a pluralist, but that was not particularly frowned upon in the ninth century. Moreover, it can't have been easy in the ninth century to manage far-flung properties, but Einhard seems to have worked hard at running the three main groupings of his properties and visited them when he could. Emma, if we may judge by his letter of lament [7.3], was an invaluable supervisor of some of his households. Her own two letters [6.15 and 6.57] suggest that she too received *missi*, petitions for help, and inquiries, and acted upon them. At Blandin in particular one can see the extent to which Einhard's organizational skills came to bear on what may have been a previously disorganized monastic operation [see 3.8], but once again Einhard was careful to insure that the record of his activity was preserved as he would have wished it preserved. Was he a demanding overlord? It is noteworthy that his greatest frustration as a property holder was with distant properties such as Fritzlar over which he can have had but minimal control [see 6.37 and Map 3]. A great deal depended upon the quality of the ecclesiastical officials he appointed. The only one of these we are in a real position to judge is Ratleig, who had been a priest and his notary at Michelstadt [5.1.8]. His intelligence, determination, and loyalty to Einhard emerge clearly from the pages of the *Translation and Miracles*. Ratleig would, in fact, succeed Einhard as abbot of Seligenstadt [1.15], doubtless as Einhard's own choice. He continued Einhard's active promotion of the cult of the martyrs and commissioned Hrabanus Maurus to write a poem in their honor [1.15]. Did he also commission the composition of the *Passion of the Martyrs of Christ, Marcellinus and Peter*, after he became the abbot of Seligenstadt?

Monastic deputies or *vicedomini* were also crucial to the administration of Einhard's properties; we know the names of at least four and can see unnamed deputies at work at still other places. Einhard managed to build – and it was a considerable achievement in and of itself – at least two churches. The first of these, at Michelstadt, was paid for out of his own resources [5.1.1], while he seems to have built the church at Seligenstadt with the help of Louis the Pious and his sons [6.38, 46, 51, appendix.A]. His foundation of that church would be remembered with great reverence nine hundred years later in an engraving that shows him steering the ship of Seligenstadt, filled with the abbots who succeeded him [Fig. 1].

Was Einhard a good lay abbot? He was certainly conscientious, and it cannot have been easy for a layman to run several monasteries. He was excluded from full monastic life and must have suffered, if his experience was like that of other lay abbots, from the doubts and disapprovals of the monks placed under him. One has to wonder if his promotion and cultivation of the saints served as a bridging mechanism, as a way for Einhard to orchestrate the activities of his monks around his goals, rather than theirs. We shall never know, nor shall we ever know what deliberative role some monks may have played in shifting the relics from Michelstadt to Seligenstadt. Almost the last letter in Einhard's collection [6.64] is an impassioned command for the monks of Seligenstadt to attend to the saints, to pray for him, and to regulate their lives. The cult of the saints also allowed Einhard to give his several properties, the monasteries at Seligenstadt, St-Bavo, St-Servais, and, even, his benefice at St-Salvius, a common and uniting hagiographic purpose.

1. An engraving from 1707 of Einhard as helmsman of the church of Seligenstadt. He is the figure seated in the stern of the ship below a plaque identifying him as the abbot and founder of Seligenstadt. From the frontispiece to Johannes Weinckens, *Vir fama super aethera notus Eginhartus...* (1714).

It is extremely difficult to know a man who was as adept as Einhard was at hiding himself in busy work and in service to others. We come closest to him, I suspect, in the religious enthusiasm of the *Translation and Miracles*, which must be counted, aside from the letter about Emma's death, as the most heartfelt of Einhard's writings. No one who reads only the *Life of Charlemagne* should pretend to know Einhard. But dare we pit the pronounced classicism of his tastes in literature and art against the religous fervor of his later life? Certainly not, for both belonged to the same life; and we can imagine in the shallow line drawing of the lost triumphal arch and in something as precious as the ivory of the archangel Michael how these seemingly divergent tastes could fuse in the Carolingian mind.

Einhard was also fascinated by fantastic things, by the portents that had prefigured, he thought, the death of the emperor [2.32], by the startling appearance of Halley's Comet in 837 [6.61], and by the red liquid that dripped steadily from the saints' reliquary for seven days in 827 [5.1.10]. Classicism and a deep sense of wonder were but two of Einhard's varied responses to the world around him. My suspicion is that if more of Einhard's writings survived, these tendencies would become even more apparent, for they seem to have stood along with his guardedness, prudence, and usefulness as consistent features of his personality and personal interests. But it is also my sneaking suspicion that if more of Einhard's writings survived we might actually like him less, for just as Petrarch came to disapprove of the fuller Cicero he finally met in the *Letters to Atticus*, we too might find little Einhard a less tantalizing figure the more we learned of him. Life on the inside is, after all, filled with compromises, petty foibles, and incapacitating doubts that we on the outside scarcely have the right to judge.

Still, Einhard led a most interesting life, one filled with remarkable accomplishments, for he had not just stood in the presence of Charlemagne, but had actually assisted him in making the new administrative world of Aachen; and had not just watched, but had participated in the adornment of the great palace chapel, had seen its arches rise, and had heard the sound of hammers and the din of its workmen barking orders. He sealed his vision of that fleeting world in the crystalline amber of the *Life of Charlemagne*, which in its classical simplicity and careful symmetry is a work of enduring and unforgettable genius, as much Einhard's as Charlemagne's. But I would almost trade it, if I were forced, for the *Translation and Miracles*, which is a book whose psychology we have hardly begun to plumb. Even here in his various literary accomplishments, Einhard revealed once more his ability to meet, match, and shape the tastes of the times through which he passed. From epic poet to classical biographer, and from courtier to cultivator of the saints, Einhard was an adaptable creature of his times. The suppleness of his mind, his quickness as a courtier, and his intuitive grasp of his own talent and its limits allowed him not just to survive in the kingdoms and courts created by Charlemagne and his son, but to thrive.

SELECTED BIBLIOGRAPHY FOR STUDENTS

Some Primary Carolingian Sources in Translation

Allott, Stephen. *Alcuin of York, c. A.D. 732 to 804: His Life and Letters*. York: William Sessions, 1974.

The Annals of Fulda: Ninth-Century Histories, vol. II. Trans. and annotated by Timothy Reuter. Manchester: Manchester University Press, 1992.

The Annals of St-Bertin: Ninth-Century Histories, vol. I. Trans. and annotated by Janet L. Nelson. Manchester: Manchester University Press, 1991.

Carolingian Chronicles: 'Royal Frankish Annals' and Nithard's 'Histories'. Trans. Bernhard Walter Scholz with Barbara Rogers. Ann Arbor: University of Michigan Press, 1970.

Carolingian Civilization: A Reader. Ed. Paul Edward Dutton. Peterborough: Broadview Press, 1993.

Charlemagne's Cousins: Contemporary Lives of Adalard and Wala. Trans. Allen Cabaniss. Syracuse: Syracuse University Press, 1967.

Godman, Peter. *Poetry of the Carolingian Renaissance*. Norman: University of Oklahoma Press, 1985.

Herren, Michael W. "The 'De imagine Tetrici' of Walahfrid Strabo: Edition and Translation." *The Journal of Medieval Latin*, vol. 1 (1991), pp.118-39.

King, P.D. *Charlemagne: Translated Sources*. Lambrigg, Cumbria: P.D. King, 1987.

Loyn, H.R., and J. Percival. *The Reign of Charlemagne: Documents on Carolingian Government and Administration*. London: Edward Arnold, 1975.

Son of Charlemagne: A Contemporary Life of Louis the Pious. Trans. Allen Cabaniss. Syracuse: Syracuse University Press, 1961.

Carolingian History

Bullough, Donald. *The Age of Charlemagne*. London: Ferndale Editions, 1980.

Charlemagne's Heir: New Perspectives on the Reign of Louis the Pious (814-840). Ed. Peter Godman and Roger Collins. Oxford: Clarendon Press, 1990.

Duckett, Eleanor Shipley. *Carolingian Portraits: A Study in the Ninth Century*. Ann Arbor: University of Michigan Press, 1962; repr.1969.

Dutton, Paul Edward. *The Politics of Dreaming in the Carolingian Empire*. Lincoln: University of Nebraska Press, 1994.

Fichtenau, Heinrich. *The Carolingian Empire: The Age of Charlemagne*. Trans. Peter Munz. Oxford: Basil Blackwell, 1957.

Folz, Robert. *The Coronation of Charlemagne, 25 December 800*. Trans. J.E. Anderson. London: Routledge & Kegan Paul, 1974.

Ganshof, F.L. *The Carolingians and the Frankish Monarchy: Studies in Carolingian History.* Trans. Janet Sondheimer. Ithaca: Cornell University Press, 1971.

Halphen, Louis. *Charlemagne and the Carolingian Empire.* Trans. Giselle de Nie. Amsterdam: North Holland, 1977.

Heer, Friederich. *Charlemagne and His World.* New York: Weidenfeld and Nicolson, 1975.

McKitterick, Rosamond. *The Frankish Kingdoms under the Carolingians.* London: Longman, 1983.

Nelson, Janet L. *The Frankish World, 750-900.* London: Hambledon Press, 1996.

———. *Politics and Ritual in Early Medieval Europe.* London: Hambledon Press, 1986.

The New Cambridge Medieval History, vol.2: *c.700-900.* Ed. Rosamond McKitterick. Cambridge: University of Cambridge Press, 1995.

Noble, Thomas F.X. *The Republic of St. Peter: The Birth of the Papal State, 680-825.* Philadelphia: University of Pennsylvania Press, 1984.

Riché, Pierre. *The Carolingians: A Family who Forged Europe.* Trans. Michael Idomir Allen. Philadelphia: University of Pennsylvania Press, 1993.

Sullivan, Richard E. "The Carolingian Age: Reflections on its Place in the History of the Middle Ages." *Speculum,* vol. 64 (1989), pp. 267-306.

Intellectual and Art History

Backes, Magnus, and Regine Dölling. *Art of the Dark Ages.* Trans. Francisca Garvie. New York: Harry N. Abrams, 1970.

Bischoff, Bernhard. *Manuscripts and Libraries in the Age of Charlemagne.* Trans. and ed. Michael Gorman. Cambridge Studies in Palaeography and Codicology, vol. 1. Cambridge: Cambridge University Press, 1994.

Bullough, Donald. *Carolingian Renewal: Sources and Heritage.* Manchester: Manchester University Press, 1991.

Carolingian Culture: Emulation and Innovation. Ed. Rosamond McKitterick. Cambridge: Cambridge University Press, 1994.

Conant, Kenneth John. *Carolingian and Romanesque Architecture, 800 to 1200.* 2nd ed. rev. Harmondsworth: Penquin, 1978.

Contreni, John J. "The Carolingian Renaissance." In *Renaissances before the Renaissance: Cultural Revivals of Late Antiquity and the Middle Ages.* Ed. Warren Treadgold. Stanford: Stanford University Press, 1984, pp.59-74.

Deshman, Robert. "The Exalted Servant: the Ruler Theology of the Prayerbook of Charles the Bald." *Viator,* vol. 11 (1980). pp. 384-417.

Dutton, Paul Edward, and Herbert L Kessler. *The Poetry and Paintings of the First Bible of Charles the Bald.* In Recentiores: Later Latin Texts and Contexts. Ed. James O'Donnell. Ann Arbor: University of Michigan Press, 1997.

"The Gentle Voices of Teachers": Aspects of Learning in the Carolingian Age. Ed. Richard E. Sullivan. Columbus: Ohio State University Press, 1995.

Godman, Peter. *Poets and Emperors: Frankish Politics and Carolingian Poetry.* Oxford: Oxford University Press, 1987.

Hildebrandt, M.M. *The External School in Carolingian Society.* Education and Society in the Middle Ages and Renaissance, vol.1. Leiden: Brill, 1992.

Hinks, Roger. *Carolingian Art: a Study of Early Medieval Painting and Sculpture in Western Europe* (1935). Ann Arbor: University of Michigan Press, 1962.

Holländer, Hans. *Early Medieval Art.* Trans. Caroline Hillier. New York: Universe Books, 1974.

Hubert, J., J. Porcher and W.F. Volbach. *The Carolingian Renaissance.* Trans. James Emmons, Stuart Gilbert, Robert Allen. New York: George Braziller, 1970.

Kessler, Herbert L. *The Illustrated Bibles from Tours.* Studies in Manuscript Illumination, vol. 7. Princeton: Princeton University Press, 1977.

Kornbluth, Genevra. *Engraved Gems of the Carolingian Empire.* University Park: Pennsylvania State University Press, 1995.

Laistner, M.L.W. *Thought and Letters in Western Europe, A.D. 500 to 900.* 2nd ed. Ithaca: Cornell University Press, 1957.

Lasko, Peter. *Ars sacra, 800-1200.* Harmondsworth: Penquin, 1972.

Marenbon, John. *Early Medieval Philosophy (480-1150).* London: Routledge & Kegan Paul, 1983.

McCormick, Michael. *Eternal Victory: Triumphal Rulership in Late Antiquity, Byzantium, and the Early Medieval West.* Cambridge: Cambridge University Press, 1986.

McKitterick, Rosamond. *The Carolingians and the Written Word.* Cambridge: Cambridge University Press, 1989.

Morrison, Karl F. *The Two Kingdoms: Ecclesiology in Carolingian Political Thought.* Princeton: Princeton University Press, 1964.

Mütherich, Florentine, and Joachim E. Gaehde. *Carolingian Painting.* New York: George Braziller, 1976.

Nees, Lawrence. *A Tainted Mantle: Hercules and the Classical Tradition at the Carolingian Court.* Philadelphia: University of Pennsylvania Press, 1991.

Science in Western and Eastern Civilization in Carolingian Times. Ed. Paul Leo Butzer and Dietrich Lohrmann. Basel: Birkhäuser, 1993.

Religious and Social History

Brown, Peter. *The Cult of the Saints: Its Rise and Function in Latin Christianity.* Chicago: University of Chicago Press, 1981.

Dutton, Paul Edward. "Thunder and Hail over the Carolingian Countryside." In *Agriculture in the Middle Ages: Technology, Practice, and Representation.* Ed. Del Sweeney. Philadelphia: University of Pennsylvania Press, 1995, pp. 111-37.

Geary, Patrick J. *Furta Sacra: Thefts of Relics in the Central Middle Ages.* Princeton: Princeton University Press, 1978.

———. *Living with the Dead in the Middle Ages.* Ithaca: Cornell University Press, 1994.

McKitterick, Rosamond. *The Frankish Church and the Carolingian Reforms, 789-895.* London: Royal Historical Society, 1977.

Munz, Peter. *Life in the Age of Charlemagne.* London: Batsford, 1969.

Riché, Pierre. *Daily Life in the World of Charlemagne.* Trans. with an introduction by Jo Ann McNamara. Philadelphia: University of Pennsylvania Press, 1978.

Wallace-Hadrill, J.M. *The Frankish Church.* Oxford: Oxford University Press, 1983.

Wemple, Suzanne F. *Women in Frankish Society: Marriage and the Cloister, 500 to 900.* Philadelphia: University of Pennsylvania Press, 1981.

Einhard: Various Translations and Editions of his Works

Oeuvres complètes d'Éginhard. 2 vols. Trans. A. Teulet. Paris: Renouard, 1840-1843. Repr. Paris: Firmin Didot, 1856.

Charters

Chronicon Laureshamense. Ed. K.A.F. Pertz. In Monumenta Germaniae Historica: Scriptores. Vol. 21. Hanover: Hahn, 1869. Repr. Leipzig: Hiersemann, 1925, pp. 357-61.

Codex diplomaticus Fuldensis. Ed. Ernst F. J. Dronke. 1850. Repr. Aalen: Otto Zeller, 1962.

Codex Laureshamensis. Vol. 1: *Einleitung Regesten Chronik.* Ed. Karl Glöckner. Darmstadt: Verlag des historischen Vereins für Hessen, 1929, pp. 229-304.

Diplomata Belgica ante annum millesimum centesimum scripta. Vol. 1: *Teksten*; vol. 2: *Reproducties.* Ed. M. Gysseling and A.C.F. Koch. Brussels: Belgisch Inter-Universitair Centrum, 1950.

Eginhardi chartae. Ed. J.P. Migne. In Patrologiae Latinae, vol. 104. Paris: J.P. Migne, 1864, cols. 601–608A.

"Formulae Imperiales", no. 35. Ed. Wilhelm Schmitz. In Monumenta Germaniae Historica: Formulae Merowingici et Karolini Aevi. Ed. Karl Zeumer. Hanover: Hahn, 1886, p. 313.

Lokeren, A. van. *Chartes et documents de l'Abbaye de Saint Pierre au Mont Blandin à Gand depuis sa fondation jusqu'à sa suppression.* 3 vols. Ghent: H. Hoste, 1868, vol. 1, pp. 9–18.

Urkundenbuch des Klosters Fulda. Vol. 1.2: *Die Zeit des Abtes Baugulf.* Ed. Edmund E. Stengel. Marburg: N.G. Elwert, 1956.

The Life of Charlemagne

Early Lives of Charlemagne by Eginhard and the Monk of St Gall. Trans. and ed. A.J. Grant. New York: Cooper Square, 1966.

Éginhard, Vie de Charlemagne (1938). 5th ed. Ed. and trans. Louis Halphen. Paris: Belles Lettres, 1981.

Eginardo, Vita dell'imperatore Carlo Magno. Trans. Carmelo A. Rapisarda. Catania: Università di Catania, 1963.

Eginardo, Vita di Carlo Magno. Omikron, vol. II. Ed. Giovanni Bianchi. Rome: Salerno Editrice, 1988.

Einhard, The Life of Charlemagne. Trans. S.E. Turner. New York: Harper & Brothers, 1880. The same translation was printed with a foreword by Sidney Painter. Ann Arbor: University of Michigan Press, 1960.

Einhard and Notker the Stammerer, Two Lives of Charlemagne. Trans. Lewis Thorpe. Harmondsworth: Penguin, 1969.

Einhard, Vita Karoli Magni. Ed. and commented on by John F. Collins. Bryn Mawr Latin Commentaries. Bryn Mawr, Pennsylvania: Bryn Mawr College, 1984.

Einhard, Vita Karoli Magni. Vol. 1: *Text*; Vol 2: *Kommentar.* Ed. Franz Herrmann. Münster: Aschendorff, 1926. 4th ed. 1993.

Einhard, Vita Karoli Magni: The Latin Text. The Life of Charlemagne with a New English Translation. Ed. and trans. Evelyn Scherabon Firchow and Edwin H. Zeydel. Coral Gables: University of Miami Press, 1972.

Einhardi Vita Karoli Magni. 6th ed. Ed. O. Holder-Egger. In Monumenta Germaniae Historica: Scriptores rerum Germanicarum in usum scholarum. Hanover: Hahn, 1911; repr. 1965.

Einhard's Life of Charlemagne: The Latin Text. Ed. with introduction and notes, H.W. Garrod and R.B. Mowat. Oxford: Clarendon Press, 1915.

Einhards Vita Karoli Magni. Trans. Hans Fluck. Paderborn: Ferdinand

Schöningh, 1925.

"Einharti Vita Karoli Magni." Ed. Philipp Jaffé. In Jaffé. *Bibliotheca rerum Germanicarum*, vol.4: *Monumenta Carolina*. Berlin: 1867; repr. Aalen: Scientia, 1964, pp. 509-41.

Milde, Wolfgang and Wurzel, Thomas. *Einhard, Vita Karoli magni. Faksimileausgabe im Originalformat der Vita Karoli Magni aus Codex Vindobonensis 529 (Folios 1-13) der Österreichischen Nationalbibliothek*. Graz: Thomas Wurzel, 1991.

The Translation and Miracles of the Blessed Martyrs, Marcellinus and Peter

Einhard, Übertragung und Wunder der Heiligen Marzellinus und Petrus (1925). Trans. Karl Esselborn. Darmstadt: Historischer Verein für Hessen, 1977.

The History of the Translation of the Blessed Martyrs of Christ, Marcellinus and Peter: The English Version. Trans. Barrett Wendell. Cambridge, Mass.: Harvard University Press, 1926. Rev. in Paul Edward Dutton. *Carolingian Civilization: A Reader*, pp.198-246.

Translatio et miracula sanctorum Marcellini et Petri auctore Einhardo. Ed. G. Waitz. In Monumenta Germaniae Historica: Scriptores, vol. 15.1. Hanover: Hahn, 1888, pp. 239-64.

The Letters of Einhard

"Einharti epistolae." Ed. K. Hampe. In Monumenta Germaniae Historica: Epistolae, vol. 5. Hanover: Weidmann, 1898-99; repr. 1974, pp. 105-45.

"Einharti epistolae." Ed. Philipp Jaffé. In Jaffé. *Bibliotheca rerum Germanicarum*, vol.4: *Monumenta Carolina*. Berlin: 1867; repr. Aalen: Scientia, 1964, pp. 440-86.

"The Letters of Einhard." Trans. by Henry Preble, Annotated by Joseph Cullen Ayer, Jr. *Papers of the American Society of Church History*, vol. 1 (1913), pp.107-58; rev. in Paul Edward Dutton. *Carolingian Civilization: A Reader*, pp. 283-310.

The Correspondence with Lupus of Ferrières

The Letters of Lupus of Ferrières. Trans. Graydon W. Regenos. The Hague: Martinus Nijhoff, 1966, pp.1-17.

Loup de Ferrières, Correspondance. 2 vols. Ed. and trans. Léon Levillain. In Les Classiques de l'histoire de France au Moyen Age. Paris: Société d'Édition 'Les Belles Lettres', 1964, vol. 1, pp.3-51.

Servati Lupi epistulae. Ed. Peter K. Marshall. In Bibliotheca scriptorum Graecorum et Romanorum Teuberiana. Leipzig: Teubner, 1984, pp. 1-15.

Lupi abbatis Ferrariensis epistolae. Ed. Ernst Dümmler. In Monumenta Germaniae Historica: Epistolae, vol. 6. Hanover: Weidmann, 1902-25; repr. 1974, pp. 1-17.

'On the Adoration of the Cross'

"Einharti quaestio de adoranda cruce." Ed. K. Hampe, in Monumenta Germaniae Historica: Epistolae, vol. 5. Hanover: Weidmann, 1898-99; repr. 1974, pp. 146-49.

"La question de l'adoration de la Croix." Trans. Arthur Kleinclausz. In Kleinclausz, *Eginhard.* Annales de l'Université de Lyon, vol. 12. Paris: Société d'Édition 'Les Belles Lettres', 1942, pp. 249-55.

"Einhard beantwortet 836 Lupus von Ferrières dessen Quaestio de adoranda cruce." Ed. and trans. Karl Hauck. In *Das Einhardkreuz: Vorträge und Studien der Münsteraner Diskussion zum arcus Einhardi.* Ed. Karl Hauck. Göttingen: Vandenhoeck & Ruprecht, 1974, pp. 211-16.

Studies on Einhard

Anton, Hans Hubert. "Beobachtungen zum fränkisch-byzantinischen Verhältnis in karolingischer Zeit." In *Beiträge zur Geschichte des Regnum Francorum. Referate beim Wissenschaftlichen Colloquium zum 75. Geburtstag von Eugen Ewig am 28. mai 1988.* Beihefte der Francia, vol. 22. Sigmaringen: 1990, pp. 97-119.

Belting, Hans. "Der Einhardsbogen." *Zeitschrift für Kunstgeschichte*, vol. 36 (1973), pp. 93-121.

Beumann, Helmut. *Ideengeschichtliche Studien zu Einhard und anderen Geschichtsschreibern des früheren Mittelatlers.* Darmstadt: Wissenschaftliche Buchgesellschaft, 1969.

Bondois, Marguerite. *La Translation des saints Marcellin et Pierre: Étude sur Einhard et sa vie politique de 827 à 834.* Paris: Honoré Champion, 1907.

Brunhölzl, Franz. *Histoire de la littérature latine du Moyen Age.* Vol. 2: *L'époque carolingienne.* Trans. Henri Rochais and bibliographical additions by Jean-Paul Bouhot. Turnhout: Brepols, 1991, pp. 77-82, 280-81.

Brunner, Karl. *Oppositionelle Gruppen im Karolingerreich.* Veröffentlichungen des Instituts für österreichische Geschichtsforschung, vol. 25. Vienna: Herman Böhlaus, 1979, pp. 83-95.

Buchner, Max. *Einhards Künstler- und Gelehrtenleben: Ein Kulturbild aus der Zeit*

Karls des Großen und Ludwigs des Frommen. In Bücherei der Kultur und Geschichte, vol. 22. Bonn: Kurt Schroeder, 1922.

Bullough, Donald. "*Europae Pater*: Charlemagne and his Achievements in the Light of Recent Scholarship." *English Historical Review*, vol. 85 (1970), pp. 59-105.

Cahour, Joseph. *Petit lexique pour l'Étude de la 'Vita Karoli' d'Eginhard.* Paris: Editions de la Pensée Latine, 1928.

Declercq, Georges. "De *capitula adhuc conferenda* van Lodewijk de Vrome en der domeinen van de Gentse Sint-Baafsabdij in Noord-Frankrijk." In *Peasants and Townsmen in Medieval Europe: Studia in honorem Adriaan Verhulst.* Ed. Jean-Marie Duvosquel and Erik Thoen. Ghent: Snoeck-Ducaju & Zoon, 1995, pp. 325-45.

Dekker, Cornelis. "Saint-Bavon en Zélande." In *Peasants and Townsmen in Medieval Europe: Studia in honorem Adriaan Verhulst.* Ed. Jean-Marie Duvosquel and Erik Thoen. Ghent: Snoeck-Ducaju & Zoon, 1995, pp. 379-96.

Depreux, Philippe. *Prosopographie de l'entourage de Louis le Pieux (781-840).* In Instrumenta, vol. 1. Sigmaringen: Jan Thorbecke, 1997.

Dümmler, Ernst. "Ein Nachtrag zu Einhards Werken." *Neues Archiv*, vol. 11 (1886), pp.233-38.

Das Einhardkreuz: Vorträge und Studien der Münsteraner Diskussion zum arcus Einhardi. Ed. Karl Hauck. Göttingen:Vandenhoeck & Ruprecht, 1974.

Felten, Franz. *Äbte und Laienäbte im Frankenreich. Studien zum Verhältnis von Staat und Kirche im früheren Mittelalter.* In Monographien zur Geschichte des Mittelalters, vol. 20. Stuttgart: 1980.

Firchow, Evelyn Scherabon. "Einhard." In *Dictionary of the Middle Ages*, vol. 4. Ed. Joseph Strayer. New York: Charles Scribner's Sons, 1989, pp. 412-13.

Fleckenstein, Josef. "Einhard, seine Gründung und sein Vermächtnis in Seligenstadt." In Fleckenstein. *Ordnungen und formende Kräfte des Mittelalters.* Göttingen:Vandenhoeck & Ruprecht, 1989, pp.84-111.

———. *Die Hofkapelle der deutschen Könige.* In Schriften der Monumenta Germaniae historica: Deutsches Institut für Erforschung des Mittelalters, vol.16.1. Stuttgart: Anton Hiersemann, 1959.

Ganshof, F.L. "Eginhard à Gand." *Bulletijn der Maatschappij van Geschied-en Ouheidkunde te Gent: Bulletin de la Société d'histoire et d'archéologie de Gand.* (1926), pp. 13-33.

———. "Einhard, biographer of Charlemagne." In Ganshof. *The Carolingians and the Frankish Monarchy: Studies in Carolingian History.* Trans. Janet Sondheimer. Ithaca: Cornell University Press, 1971, pp.1-16.

Ganz, David. "Einhard's *Vita Karoli Magni*: Reception and Intention." A paper presented at King's College, London, 1996.

Grabar, André. "Observations sur l'Arc de Triomphe de la croix dit Arc d'Éginhard et sur d'autres bases de la croix." *Cahiers archéologiques*, vol. 27 (1978), pp.61-83.

Grierson, P. "The Early Abbots of St.Peter's of Ghent." *Revue Bénédictine*, vol. 48 (1936), pp.129-46.

Halphen, Louis. "Einhard, historien de Charlemagne." *Revue historique*, vol. 126 (1917), pp. 271-314. Repr. in Halphen. *Études critiques sur l'histoire de Charlemagne*. Paris: 1921, pp. 60-103.

Heinzelmann, Martin. "Einhards 'Translatio Marcellini et Petri': eine hagiographische Reformschrift von 830." Forthcoming.

Hellmann, Siegmund. "Einhards literarische Stellung." *Historische Viertel-jahrschrift*, vol. 27 (1932), pp.40-110. Repr. in Hellmann. *Ausgewählte Abhandlungen zur Historiographie und Geistesgeschichte des Mittelalters*. Ed. Helmut Beumann. Weimar: Hermann Böhlaus Nachfolger, 1961, pp.159-229.

Hessen im Frühmittelalter: Archäologie und Kunst. Ed. Helmut Roth and Egon Wamers. Sigmaringen: Jan Thorbecke, 1984.

Innes, Matthew. "Charlemagne's Will: Piety, Politics and the Imperial Succession." *The English Historical Review*, vol. 112 (1997), pp. 833-55

Innes, Matthew, and Rosamond McKitterick. "The Writing of History." In *Carolingian Culture: Emulation and Innovation*. Ed. Rosamond McKitterick. Cambridge: Cambridge University Press, 1994, pp.193-220.

Kempsall, Matthew S. "Some Ciceronian Models for Einhard's Life of Charlemagne." *Viator*, vol. 26 (1995), pp.11-37.

Kleinclausz, Arthur. *Eginhard*. In Annales de l'Université de Lyon, vol.12. Paris: Société d'Édition Les 'Belles Lettres', 1942.

Die Klostergemeinschaft von Fulda im früheren Mittelalter. 3 vols. Ed. Karl Schmid. In Münstersche Mittelalter-Schriften, vol. 8. Munich: Wilhelm Fink, 1978.

Lintzel, Martin. "Die Zeit der Entstehung von Einhards Vita Karoli." *Kritische Beiträge zur Geschichte des Mittelalters. Festschrift für R. Holtzmann zur sechzig-sten Geburtstag*. Ed. W. Möllenberg and M. Lintzel. Berlin: Emil Ebering, 1933, pp.22-42. Repr. in Lintzel. *Ausgewählte Schriften*. 2 vols. Berlin: Akademie, 1961, vol.2, pp. 27-41.

Löwe, Heinz. "Die Enstehungszeit der Vita Karoli Einhards." *Deutsches Archiv für Erforschung des Mittelalters*, vol. 39.1 (1983), pp.85-103.

Ludwig, Thomas. "Die Durchdringung von Mittelschiff und Querschiff in der Einhardsbasilika in Seligenstadt und in der St. Galler Plankirche." *Architectura*, vol. 24 (1994), pp.129-40.

Ludwig, Thomas, Otto Müller, and Irmgard Widdra-Spiess. *Die Einhards-Basi-*

lika in Steinbach bei Michelstadt im Odenwald. 2 vols. Mainz: Philipp von Zabern, 1996.

Montesquiou-Fezensac, Blaise de. "L'arc d'Éginhard." *Cahiers archéologiques*, vol. 8 (1956), pp.147-74.

Mordek, Hubert. "Livius und Einhard: Gedanken über das Verhältnis der Karolinger zur antiken Literatur." In *Livius, Werk und Rezeption. Festschrift für Erich Burck zum 80. Geburtstag.* Ed. Eckard Lefèvre and Eckart Olshausen. Munich: C.H. Beck, 1983, pp.337-46.

———. "Recently Discovered Capitulary Texts belonging to the Legislation of Louis the Pious." In *Charlemagne's Heir: New Perspectives on the Reign of Louis the Pious (814-840).* Ed. Peter Godman and Roger Collins. Oxford: Clarendon Press, 1990, pp. 436-53.

Pyritz, H. "Das Karlsbild Einharts." *Deutsche Vierteljahrschrift*, vol. 15 (1937), pp. 167-88.

Schefers, Hermann. "Einhard—ein Lebensbild auz karolingischer Zeit." *Geschichtsblätter Kreis Bergstraße*, vol. 26 (1993), pp.25-92.

———. "Einhards römische Reliquien. Zur Bedeutung der Reliquientranslation Einhards von 827/828." *Archiv für hessische Geschichte und Altertumskunde.* New Series, vol. 48 (1990), pp. 279-92.

Seeliger, Hans Reinhard. "Einhards römische Reliquien. Zur Übertragung der Heiligen Marzellinus und Petrus im Frankenreich." *Römische Quartalschrift für christliche Altertumskunde und Kirechengeschichte*, vol. 83 (1988), pp. 58-75.

Weinckens, Johannes. *Vir fama super aethera notus Eginhartus, quondam Caroli Magni cancellarius, dein antiquissimae et regalis nostrae ecclesiae Seligenstadiensis fundator, sub patrocinio sanctorum martyrum Marcellini et Petri; nunc autem illustratus, et contra quosdam authores vindicatus.* Frankfurt: Philipp Andrea, 1717.

Wolter, H. "Intention und Herrscherbild in Einhards Vita Karoli Magni." *Archiv für Kulturgeschichte*, vol. 68 (1986), pp.295-317.

REFLECTIONS ON EINHARD

1. SOME REFLECTIONS ON EINHARD BY HIS CONTEMPORARIES

1. Alcuin, A Letter to Charlemagne from April or May 799

Alcuin and Einhard would have been together at Charlemagne's court, chiefly at Aachen, for almost five years between 792 and 796 before Alcuin took up the abbacy of the monastery of St-Martin of Tours.

Source: translated from Alcuini Epistolae, ed. Ernst Dümmler, in Monumenta Germaniae Historica: Epistolae, vol.4 (Berlin: Weidmann, 1895; repr. Berlin: Weidmann, 1974), p.285.12-15.

I have sent to your excellency certain forms of expressions made clear by illustrations and verses drawn from [the writings of] that venerable father [Peter of Pisa]. [I have also enclosed] on the blank [piece of] charter you sent me some drawings of arithmetical problems for your amusement. May you now find dressed what came to me bare and think it appropriate that the [charter] that came to me dignified by your mark is [now] covered by my writing. And if those forms [of expressions] should have too few illustrations, Bezaleel [Einhard], your, no, rather, our close assistant, will be able to supply you with more [illustrations] of that father's verses. He is also able to understand the meaning of the figures in that little book of arithmetical learning.

2. Alcuin, Poem 26: "On the Court"

This undated poem may have been written not long after Alcuin left the court. Alcuin complained that the school he had done so much to develop was slipping away.

Source: translated from Alcuini Carmina, ed. Ernst Dümmler, in Monumenta Germaniae Historica: Poetae Latini Aevi Carolini, vol. 1 (Berlin: Weidmann, 1881; repr. Berlin: Hildebrand, 1964), p.245.18-22.

Why did the poet Virgil make mistakes all on his own at court?
Was that famous father still not worthy of having a master [under him],
Who might recite sublime poetry for the boys under the palace roof?
What shall Bezaleel, who is skilled in Trojan epic, do [now]?
Why, I ask, did he not take on the school as its father?

3. Alcuin, Poem 30.2, On Einhard's Small Size

This poem, also probably written after Alcuin's departure from court, likens Einhard to the fragrant nard or spikenard, a small but powerfully aromatic plant like jasmine. The poet's point may be that little Einhard now ran the domus, that is, the palace of Aachen itself. In this light, it should be remembered that after 800 Charlemagne was without a wife, who would normally have been in charge of the domestic operation of the palace. The absence of a queen may have enhanced the role of palace officials such as Einhard.

Source: translated from Alcuini Carmina, ed. Ernst Dümmler, in Monumenta Germaniae Historica: Poetae Latini Aevi Carolini, vol. 1 (Berlin: Weidmann, 1881; repr. Berlin: Hildebrand, 1964), p.248.1-8.

There is a small door and a small inhabitant in this temple.
Do not spurn, O reader, the nard, [though] small in size,
For the nard with its spiked shoot gives off a tremendous smell:
The bee [also] bears outstanding honey to you in its small body.
Notice that though the pupil is but a small part of the eye,
It rules with firm authority the actions of a vigorous body.
So that little Nard himself rules that whole house on his own.
Steadfast reader, say [with me]: "O little Nard, you small man, be well."

4. The *Royal Frankish Annals* (806) on the 'Division of the Kingdom'

In 806 Charlemagne, with three surviving, legitimate sons, decided to set out a partition of his kingdom that would minimize the possible sources of territorial friction between his sons in the days after his death. This partition was agreed to on 6 February 806 and Einhard carried a copy of the agreement to the pope in Rome not long afterwards. Charlemagne knew from personal experience with his brother Carloman that a struggle for power between his sons was inevitable and, indeed, upon Louis the Pious's death in 840, a civil war almost immediately broke out between his three sons. The 'Division of the Kingdom' of Charlemagne survives: see Carolingian Civilization 22.

Source: translated from Annales Regni Francorum, ed. G.H. Pertz and F. Kurze in Monumenta Germaniae Historica: Scriptores rerum Germanicarum in usum scholarum, vol.6 (Hanover: Hahn, 1895), p.121.

After those [Ventian and Dalmatian legates] had been dismissed, the emperor convoked an assembly of the chief men and magnates of the Franks concerning the establishment and maintenance of peace among his sons and about making a division of the kingdom into three parts, so that each of them might know what part he ought to protect and rule if he should happen to outlive [his father]. A record of this partition was made and confirmed by oaths sworn by the Frankish magnates. And rules for maintaining the peace were made. All these things were set down in writing and were conveyed by Einhard to Pope Leo [III], so that he might assent to them with his own signature. Once he had read these things, the pope gave his approval and signed [the document] with his own hand.

5. Modoin, *Eclogues*: On the Poets of His Age

The first of the Eclogues, *which were probably written in the first decade of the ninth century, contains a debate between an old and young man about the state of their time. Here the young man envies the material success of the older poets.*

Source: translated from Nasonis Ecloga I.82-92, ed. Ernst Dümmler, in Monumenta Germaniae Historica: Poetae Latini Aevi Carolini, vol. 1 (Berlin: Weidmann, 1881; repr. Berlin: Hildebrand, 1964), p.387.

We would also see that many other [poets] have been enriched
With similar rewards, but it would take a long time to deal with them all.
Instead look at how things work now in our own time:
For my smooth-talking [friend] Homer [Angilbert] is used
To pleasing Charles frequently with his learned verses.
If Flaccus [Alcuin] had not known how to make songs with a reed,
He would not have obtained so many of the benefits of this present life.
For a long time now Theodulf has played a sheperd's plain pipe;
And, by singing, he has earned many worldly goods.
Notice how the triumphant Nard, who is used to reciting Aonian verses,
Is aflush today with the highest of honors.

6. Theodulf, A Poem for Charlemagne on the Court

Theodulf and Einhard were fellow courtiers at the later court of Charlemagne. There are indications in this snippet taken from a much longer poem that Theodulf was aware of Alcuin's characterization of the little Nard, but he also hoped to secure Einhard's service as an ally in his poetic wars against the Irishman Cadac and others.

Source: translated from Theodulfi Carmina 25.155-160, 175-180, ed. Ernst Dümmler, in Monumenta Germaniae Historica: Poetae Latini Aevi Carolini, vol. 1 (Berlin: Weidmann, 1881; repr. Berlin: Hildebrand, 1964), pp.487-88.

May the little Nard always run back and forth with steps
    Like your feet, O ant, which come and go, again and again.
A great host lives in the small house of this man;
    Something great resides deep inside his small chest.

Now let him carry about his books, and now his other burdens,
  And now let him prepare darts able to slay the Irishman.
To him, while he is my companion here, I send these kisses,
  Which a savage wolf gives to you, my little, long-eared ass...

Let the decent deacon Fridugis stand alongside Oswulf,
  Both of them experts in the art, both of them very learned.
If the Nard and Ercambald should join up with Oswulf,
  They could comprise the three feet of one table.
This one is fatter, this one thinner than the other,
  But a still higher sort of measurement makes them equals.

7. Theodulf, A Chance Encounter with Einhard

Here Theodulf not only gives us an indication of Einhard's cautious and guarded character, but also of his own happily aggressive nature.

Source: translated from Theodulfi Carmina 27.45-48, ed. Ernst Dümmler, in Monumenta Germaniae Historica: Poetae Latini Aevi Carolini, vol. 1 (Berlin: Weidmann, 1881; repr. Berlin: Hildebrand, 1964), p.492.

Bezaleel suddenly spied the lazy wolf [Theodulf],
  And, fearing his alluring words, he fell silent.
After the wolf withdraws, feeling will return to his chest,
  [And] he will fill rivers, fields, and homes with his song.

8. Gerward, A Poetic Preface to the *Life of Charlemagne*

Gerward was Louis the Pious's palace librarian by at least 828 and it was in that capacity that he prepared a copy of the Life of Charlemagne *for the emperor.*

Source: translated from Gerwardi Versus, ed. Ernst Dümmler, in Monumenta Germaniae Historica: Poetae Latini Aevi Carolini, vol.2 (Berlin: Weidmann, 1884; repr. Berlin: Hildebrand, 1964), p.126.

For you, O greatest prince, Gerward, your obedient servant,
  Produced these little verses for your
Eternal praise and memory. For good reason
  He raises your distinguished name to the stars.
You, O reader, being wise will know that magnificent Einhard
  Wrote this account of the deeds of Charles the Great.

9. Walahfrid Strabo, "On the Statue of Theoderic"

In a complex and allusive poem written in 829, Walahfrid, newly arrived at the court of Louis the Pious, reflected on the monumental equestrian statue of the great Ostrogothic king, Theoderic, that stood in the palace courtyard at Aachen. He also proceeded to review various court personalities; the one preceding Einhard in the poem is Hilduin of St-Denis, the archchaplain.

Source: translated from Walahfridi Strabi Carmina 23.221-226, ed. Ernst Dümmler, in Monumenta Germaniae Historica: Poetae Latini Aevi Carolini, vol. 2 (Berlin: Weidmann, 1884; repr. Berlin: Hildebrand, 1964), p.377. See also Michael W. Herren, "The 'De imagine Tetrici' of Walahfrid Strabo: Edition and Translation," The Journal of Medieval Latin 1 (1991), pp.128-29.

About Einhard the Great
Our respect for this great father should be no less [than it was for Hilduin].
To begin with Bezaleel ingeniously and prudently understands
All the [various] works done by artisans: thus, finally,
God, himself the highest, selects the weak and scorns the strong.
For what great man ever received greater [gifts]
Than those we are amazed to see shine forth from this tiny, little man?

10. A Cleric Sends Louis the Pious his Opinion on the Trinity

An unidentified cleric wrote to the emperor while Einhard was still at court, thus prior to 830. Although he addresses his argument on the Holy Trinity's reflection of the triple nature of the human soul to Louis, he fully expected that Einhard as a high advisor of the emperor would see the letter.

Source: translated from Ad Epistolas Variorum Supplementum, 1, ed. Ernst Dümmler, in Monumenta Germaniae Historica: Epistolae, vol.5 (Berlin: Weidmann, 1899; repr. Berlin: Weidmann 1974), p.616.15-21.

May these things, O my pious emperor, about which many opinions exist, suffice. I, being a pesky fly, wrote these things for you as though to someone who didn't [already] know them, because it pleased me to write something to you [Louis], the very adornment of our age. What came to my mind I have composed, revised, and sent... O Einhard, should you chance to read this letter, don't be surprised to find me in error, but rather I hope that you will be surprised to see that I have said anything correctly.

11. Ermold the Black, "A Poem in Honor of Louis the Pious"

At the imperial diet of Aachen in 813, Einhard spoke in favor of Louis the Pious's elevation as co-emperor. Ermold the Black was in exile around 829-830 when he included this account of the diet in his long poem in honor of Louis.

Source: translated from Ermoldi Nigelli Carmina, In honorem Hludowici 2.31-48, ed. Ernst Dümmler, in Monumenta Germaniae Historica: Poetae Latini Aevi Carolini, vol. 2 (Berlin: Weidmann, 1884; repr. Berlin: Hildebrand, 1964), p.25.

> Then Einhard, who was much loved by Charles
> And who had a quick mind and was full of goodness,
> Falls before [Charles's] feet and kisses the ground where he walks.
> This learned man first begins with the following advice:
> "O emperor, celebrated on high and on earth and sea,
> You who are bestowing your imperial name upon your son,
> There is nothing we can add to your plan,
> Nor has Christ given any human a better plan than this.
> I urge you to carry out, as soon as possible, everything
> That merciful God directed you in your heart to do.
> O kind one, you have a son with an extremely fine character,
> Who, because of his merits, is able to hold your kingdoms.
> All of us, both the high and the low, want this man,
> The church wants him, and Christ himself supports him.
> After the bitter passing of your power he will be able
> To maintain the law with force, intelligence and faith."
> With happiness Caesar nodded in approval and prayed to Christ,
> And he sent for his son to come quickly to him.

12. *The Acts of the Abbots of Fontanelle*

In 823 Ansegisus succeeded Einhard as abbot of the monastery of Fontanelle or St-Wandrille in Normandy. The celebrated account of the deeds of the monastery's abbots was probably written between 830 and 840 under Ansegisus's charge.

Source: translated from Gesta sanctorum patrum Fontanellensis coenobii (Gesta abbatum Fontanellensium) XIII.1-2, ed. F. Lohier and P.L. Laporte (Rouen: Lestringant, 1936), pp.94, 96. See also Gesta abbatum Fontanellensium, 17, ed. Samuel Löwenfeld, in Monumenta Germaniae Historica: Scriptores rerum Germanicarum in usum scholarum (Hanover: Hahn, 1886; repr. 1980), p.50.

Moreover, while [Ansegisus] was holding the aforementioned [monastery of] Fly by the rules of a praecarial grant and benefice, the lord king [Charlemagne] appointed him the superintendant of royal works at the royal palace of Aachen under Abbot Einhard, the most learned of all men. [Ansegisus] administered that office most nobly and conducted himself prudently in all his duties. He carried out with great energy the many legations ordered by that same king....

Thus in the third year of the empire of Emperor Louis [that is, 816], Trasarus, the abbot of this monastery [of Fontanelle], retired with the permission of the emperor to the place of his birth. He returned to Benevento in Campania and was honorably received by Duke Sigo, whom he had baptized. After him, Einhard held this monastery for almost seven years. Only then, when the monastery had been voluntarily given up, did the Lord Ansegisus take over the governance [of Fontanelle], following, it is right to believe, a divine command and a grant of the most glorious Emperor Louis. This occurred in that year already calculated above [that is, 823].

13. The Astronomer, *The Life of the Emperor Louis*

The biography of Louis written by an unidentified courtier popularly known as the Astronomer was probably written in the 840s.

Source: translated from Astronomus, Vita Hludowici Imperatoris, 41, ed. Ernst Tremp, in Monumenta Germaniae Historica: Scriptores rerum Germanicarum in usum scholarum, Separatim editi, vol. 64 (Hanover: Hahn, 1995), p.442.

In that very year [that is, 827], Einhard, the most prudent man of his time, having been inspired by a passion for holy devotion sent [men] to Rome and, with the pope's approval, arranged for the bodies of the saints Marcellinus and Peter to be carried to Francia. And, at his own expense, he housed them with due propriety in his own territory. There, even now, because of the merits of those saints, the Lord works many powerful miracles.

14. Walahfrid Strabo, His "Prologue" to the *Life of Charlemagne*

Sometime after the deaths of both Louis the Pious and Einhard in 840, Walahfrid supplied the Life of Charlemagne *with a prologue, chapters, and titles.*

Source: translated from Walahfridi Prologus, ed. O. Holder-Egger, Einhardi Vita Karoli Magni, 6th edition, Monumenta Germaniae Historica: Scriptores rerum Germanicarum in usum scholarum (Hanover: Hahn, 1911; repr. 1965), pp.xxviii–xxix.

Einhard is known to have sketched the account of the life and deeds of the most glorious Emperor Charles that is found below. Among all the courtiers of the palace at that time, this man received surpassing praise not only for his knowledge, but also for the complete integrity of his character. It is also known, since he was present at most of these events, that he made his account even stronger by [his personal] attestation to the simple truth [of things].

He was born in eastern Francia in a district called Maingau. He received the first rudiments of his boyhood education at the monastery of Fulda in the school of St-Boniface, the martyr. From there Baugulf, the abbot of that monastery, sent him to the palace of Charles, not, however, because of the nobility which was so obvious in him, but rather because of the specialness of his capacity [for learning] and his intelligence. For even then in that monastery he [had] shown great signs of the wisdom that later on shone forth so clearly [from him].

[Charles] was, of course, the keenest of all kings in zealously searching out and supporting wise men so that they might pursue knowledge without material worry. Almost the whole of the kingdom granted to him by God had been, as I might put it, wrapped in fog and blindness. But, with a new ray of universal knowledge almost completely unknown to this barbarous land before, [Charlemagne] with God lighting the way returned the kingdom to brilliance and sight. But now, on the contrary, with learning in a state of decline, the light of wisdom, which is less loved, grows rarer by the day almost everywhere.

Thus it was that that little man—for his height seemed contemptible— worthily grew so great in glory, prudence, and goodness at the court of Charles, himself a lover of wisdom, that there was almost no one [else] among the many officials of his royal Majesty to whom the king, the most powerful and wisest [ruler] of his time, would impart his many intimate secrets. And in truth that [trust] was not misplaced, since not only in the times of Charles himself, but also—and this is the greater wonder—under those of the emperor Louis, when the state of the Franks was battered by many disturbances and was faltering in many places, [Einhard], with God's defense, protected himself by keeping a certain remarkable and divinely inspired distance [from affairs]. In this way, a reputation for loftiness, which earned him the jealousy of many and [also brought] misfortune, did not soon abandon him or deliver him up to dangers from which he could not escape.

I am relating these things, so that the reader will have little doubt about what Einhard says, inasmuch as he [now] knows [something] about him, about the special praise he recorded out of love for his patron, and about the evident truth he meant to convey to the interested reader.

I, Strabo, introduced titles and chapters in this little book, where they seemed appropriate, so that the reader looking for specific topics might find them more easily.

15. Hrabanus Maurus,
"Poem on the Martyrs Marcellinus and Peter"

Hrabanus wrote this poem of prayer at the request of Abbot Ratleig (840-854) who intended to have it inscribed in the finished nave of the church at Seligenstadt.

Source: translated from Hrabani Mauri Carmina, 83, ed. Ernst Dümmler, in Monumenta Germaniae Historica: Poetae Latini Aevi Carolini, vol.2 (Berlin: Weidmann, 1884; repr. Berlin: Hildebrand, 1964), pp.236-237.

You, O savior of the world, who control the scepters of heaven
    And rule with fitting command the kingdoms of the world,
May you be kind to your servants and hear their prayers,
    And full of mercy may you grant what your followers ask.
May you justly grant this with honor to your martyrs,
    So that they may return generous rewards to their servants.
That excellent man Einhard received these witnesses of Christ
    From the city of Rome and constructed this place [for them].
His successor, the priest Ratleig, placed this inscription
    For the saints in this finished nave.
O Christ [our] God, save them for all eternity,
    And, with your saints, deliver the reward of heaven to them.

16. Rudolf of Fulda, "Miracles of the Saints Translated into the Churches of Fulda"

Rudolf wrote this account before 847. Though the relics of Marcellinus and Peter were not deposited at Fulda, Einhard and his history of the translation of the martyrs were so famous and so much a part of the orbit of Fulda, that Rudolf could not but mention them.

Source: translated from Miracula Sanctorum in Fuldenses ecclesias translatorum, ed. Georg Waitz, in Monumenta Germaniae Historica: Scriptores, vol. 15.1 (Hanover: Hahn, 1887), pp.329, 331-332.

As well the bones of the blessed martyrs Marcellinus and Peter, of Protius and Hyacinth, and the relics of Saint Hermes shine daily with the great glory of the miracles brought about in curing the sick. Those bones were translated from Rome and brought by the Abbot Einhard to the village formerly called Mulinheim, but which is now known as Saligunstaat, which lies beside the Main River in Germany. There they are worthily venerated with [divine] services by the faithful. Concerning the translation of those saints and also the miracles that God brings about because of them, I shall omit to speak here, since they were carefully recorded [by Einhard]....

3. The deacon [Deusdona] began a journey which brought him into Francia [in 830, see 5.4.16]. First he looked in on Einhard [at Seligenstadt], about whom I spoke above, since they knew each other. After [Deusdona] had placed saints' relics under a seal to be kept there in the church of the blessed martyrs Marcellinus and Peter, he carried on to Mainz ...

17. Hrabanus Maurus, "The Epitaph of Einhard"

Einhard died on 14 March 840. Hrabanus composed these verses for his tomb in the church of Seligenstadt.

Source: translated from Hrabani Mauri Carmina, 83, ed. Ernst Dümmler, in Monumenta Germaniae Historica: Poetae Latini Aevi Carolini, vol.2 (Berlin: Weidmann, 1884; repr. Berlin: Hildebrand, 1964), pp.237-238.

> I beg of you, who enter this church, that you not refuse to know
>> What this place holds and, knowing that, what it instructs.
> Behold, a noble man lies resting in this very tomb,
>> To whom his father had given the name Einhard.
> He was prudent by nature, wise in deed, and eloquent in speech,
>> And he was skillful in the art of many things.
> Prince Charles raised him at his own court,
>> And by means of him [Charles] accomplished many fine works.
> He was committed to the fitting honor of these saints:
>> He sought out their bodies in Rome and brought them here,
> So that they might answer the many requests for cures
>> And grant the kingdom of heaven to the soul of that man.
> Christ, [our] kind God, savior, ruler and creator of humans,
>> Grant everlasting rest to this man in heaven.

2. Hrabanus Maurus is shown presenting a copy of his book *On the Praises of the Holy Cross* to the enthroned Pope Gregory IV. This illumination, painted at Fulda in the 830s, comes from Vienna, Österreichische Nationalbibliothek, Cod. 652, fol. 2v.

THE WORKS OF EINHARD

2. THE LIFE OF CHARLEMAGNE

Source: translated from Einhardi Vita Karoli Magni, 6th edition, ed. G. Waitz, in Monumenta Germaniae Historica: Scriptores rerum Germanicarum in usum scholarum (Hanover: Hahn, 1911; repr. 1965). See also Eginhard, Vie de Charlemagne, ed. and trans. L. Halphen, 5th ed. (Paris: Les Belles Lettres, 1981).

[Preface]

After I decided to describe the life and character, and many of the accomplishments, of my lord and foster father, Charles, that most outstanding and deservedly famous king, and seeing how immense this work was, I have expressed it in as concise a form as I could manage. But I have attempted not to omit any of the facts that have come to my attention, and [yet I also seek] not to irritate those who are excessively critical by supplying a long-winded account of everything new [I have learned]. Perhaps, in this way, it will be possible to avoid angering with a new book [even] those who criticize the old masterpieces composed by the most learned and eloquent of men.

And yet, I am quite sure that there are many people devoted to contemplation and learning who do not believe that the circumstances of the present age should be neglected or that virtually everything that happens these days is not worth remembering and should be condemned to utter silence and oblivion. Some people are so seduced by their love of the distant past, that they would rather insert the famous deeds of other peoples in their various compositions, than deny posterity any mention of their own names by writing nothing. Still, I did not see why I should refuse to take up a composition of this sort, since I was aware that no one could write about these things more truthfully than me, since I myself was present and personally witnessed them, as they say, with my own eyes. I was, moreover, not sure that these things would be recorded by anyone else.

I thought it would be better to write these things down [that is, his personal observations], along with other widely known details, for the sake of posterity, than to allow the splendid life of this most excellent king, the greatest of all the men in his time, and his remarkable deeds, which people now alive can scarcely equal, to be swallowed up by the shadows of forgetfulness.

There is still another reason, an understandable one, I believe, which even by itself might explain why I felt compelled to write this account; namely, the foster care [Charlemagne] bestowed on me and the constant friendship [I had] with him and his children after I began living at his court. Through his friendship he so won me over to him and I owed him so much both in life and death, that I might both seem and be fairly criticized as ungrateful if I forgot the many kindnesses he conferred upon me. Could I keep silent about the splendid and exceedingly brilliant deeds of a man who had been so kind to me and could I allow his life to remain without record and proper praise, as if he had never lived? But to write and account [for such a life] what was required was [an almost] Ciceronian eloquence, not my feeble talent, which is poor and small, indeed almost non-existent.

Thus [I present] to you this book containing an account of the most splendid and greatest of all men. There is nothing in it that you should admire but his accomplishments, except perhaps that I, a German with little training in the language of Rome, should have imagined that I could write something correct and even elegant in Latin. Indeed, it might seem [to you] that my headlong impudence is very great and that I have willfully spurned the advice of Cicero [himself], since in the first book of his *Tusculan* [*Disputations*], when speaking of Latin authors, he had said: "for people to set their thoughts down in writing when they cannot organize them, make them clear, or charm their readers with any style is a complete waste of time and energy." Indeed, this opinion of the famous orator might have stopped me from writing [this book, at all], if I had not decided in advance that it was better to risk the criticisms of people and to endanger my own small reputation by writing [this book], than to neglect the memory of so great a man and [instead] save myself.

[The Life of Charlemagne]

1. The family of the Merovingians, from which the Franks used to make their kings, is thought to have lasted down to King Childeric [III], whom Pope Stephen [II] ordered deposed. His [long] hair was shorn and he was forced into a monastery. Although it might seem that the [Merovingian] family ended with him, it had in fact been without any vitality for a long time and [had] demonstrated that there was nothing of any worth in it except the empty name of 'king'. For both the [real] riches and power of the kingdom were in the possession of the prefects of the palace, who were called the mayors of the palace [*maiores domus*], and to them fell the highest command. Nothing was left for the king [to do] except sit on his throne with his hair long and his beard uncut, satisfied [to hold] the name of king only and pretending to rule. [Thus] he listened to representatives who came from various lands and, as they departed, he seemed to give them decisions of his own, which he had [in fact] been taught or rather ordered [to pronounce]. Except for the empty name of 'king' and a meager living allowance, which the prefect of the court extended to him as it suited him, he possessed nothing else

of his own but one estate with a very small income. On that estate, he had a house and servants who ministered to his needs and obeyed him, but there were few of them. He traveled about on a cart that was pulled by yoked oxen and led, as happens in the countryside, by a herdsman to wherever he needed to go. In this way he used to go to the palace and so also to the public assembly of his people, which was held annually for the good of the kingdom, and in this manner he also returned home. But it was the prefect of the court [the mayor of the palace] who took care of everything, either at home or abroad, that needed to be done and arranged for the administration of the kingdom.

2. When Childeric was deposed, Pepin [III, the Short], the father of King Charles, held the office [of mayor of the palace], as if by hereditary right. For his father Charles [Martel] had brilliantly discharged the same civil office, which had been laid down for him by his father Pepin [II, of Herstal]. This Charles overthrew those oppressors who claimed personal control over all of Francia and he so completely defeated the Saracens, who were attempting to occupy Gaul, in two great battles – the first in Aquitaine near the city of Poitiers [in 733] and the second near Narbonne on the River Berre [in 737] – that he forced them to fall back into Spain. For the most part, the people [that is, the Frankish nobles] only granted the office [of mayor of the palace] to those men who stood out above others because of the nobility of their birth and the magnitude of their wealth.

For a few years Pepin, the father of King Charles, had held, as if under that [Merovingian] king, the office [of mayor of the palace], which was left to him and his brother Carloman by his grandfather and father. He shared that office with his brother in splendid harmony. [Then in 747] Carloman walked away from the oppressive chore of governing an earthly kingdom. It is not clear why he did this, but it seems that he was driven by a desire to lead a contemplative life. [Hence] he went to Rome in search of a quiet life and there changed his way [of dress and life] completely and was made a monk. With the brothers who joined him there, he enjoyed for a few years the quiet life he so desired in the monastery [he] built on Mount Soracte near the church of St-Sylvester. But since many nobles from Francia frequently visited Rome in order to fulfill their solemn vows and did not wish to miss [seeing] the man who had once been their lord, they interrupted the peaceful life he so loved by constantly paying their respects and so forced him to move. For when he realized that this parade [of visitors] was interfering with his commitment [to the monastic life], he left Mount [Soracte] and retreated to the monastery of St-Benedict located on Monte Cassino in the province of Samnium. There he spent what was left of his earthly life [until 755] in religious contemplation.

3. Moreover, Pepin, who had been mayor of the palace, was established as king [in 751] by the decision of the Roman pope [Zacharias] and he ruled the Franks by himself for fifteen years or more. When the Aquitainian war, which Pepin waged against Waifar, the duke of Aquitaine, for nine straight years, was over, he died of edema in Paris [in 768]. He was survived by two sons, Charles and Carloman, and upon them, by divine will, fell the succession of the kingdom. Indeed, the Franks at a general assembly solemnly established both of them as their kings, but on the condition, agreed to in advance, that they should divide up the entire territory of the kingdom equally. Charles was to take up and govern that part [of the kingdom] which their father Pepin had held and Carloman that part which their uncle Carloman had [once] governed. Both of them agreed to these conditions and each of them received the portion of the kingdom allotted to him by the plan. That peaceful agreement of theirs held fast, but with the greatest strain, since many on Carloman's side sought to drive the brothers apart. Some went so far as to plot to turn them [against each other] in war. But the outcome of things proved that the threat [of war] was more suspected than real in this case, and when Carloman died [in 771] his wife and sons, along with some of his chief nobles, took refuge in Italy. For no reason at all, she spurned her husband's brother and placed herself and her children under the protection of Desiderius, the king of the Lombards. In fact, Carloman had died [naturally] from disease after ruling the kingdom for two years with his brother. After his death, Charles was established as king by the agreement of all the Franks.

4. I believe it would be improper [for me] to write about Charles's birth and infancy, or even his childhood, since nothing [about those periods of his life] was ever written down and there is no one still alive who claims to have knowledge of these things. Thus, leaving aside the unknown periods [of his life], I have decided to pass straight to the deeds, habits, and other aspects of his life that should be set forth and explained. Nevertheless, so that I might not skip anything either necessary or worth knowing, I shall first describe his deeds inside and outside [the kingdom], then his habits and interests, and finally his administration of the kingdom and his death.

5. Of all the wars he waged, [Charles] began first [in 769] with the one against Aquitaine, which his father had started, but left unfinished, because he thought that it could be quickly brought to a successful conclusion. His brother [Carloman] was [still] alive at the time and [Charles] even asked for his help. And despite the fact that his brother misled him [by not delivering] the promised help, he pursued the campaign with great energy. He refused to

back away from a war already in progress or to leave a job undone, until he had by sheer determination and persistence completely achieved the goal he had set for himself. For he forced Hunold, who had tried to take possession of Aquitaine after Waifar's death and to revive a war that was almost over, to give up Aquitaine and seek [refuge in] Gascony. But [Charles], unwilling to allow him to settle there, crossed the River Garonne and through messengers commanded Lupus, the duke of the Gascons, to hand over the fugitive. If he did not do this quickly, [Charles] would demand his surrender by waging war. Lupus not only gave way to wiser counsel and returned Hunold, but he even entrusted himself and the territory he governed to [Charles's] power.

6. With things settled in Aquitaine and the war over, and since the co-ruler [of Francia, his brother Carloman] was now also dead, [Charles] took up war against the Lombards [in 773]. Hadrian [I], the bishop of the city of Rome, [had] asked and appealed to him to do this. Indeed, his father had previously taken up this war at the request of Pope Stephen [II], [but] with great trouble, since some of the chief Franks, whom he regularly consulted, were so opposed to his plan that they openly stated that they would abandon the king and return home. Despite that [threat], [Pepin] took up the war against King Haistulf and quickly finished it at that time. But, although [Charles] and his father seem to have had a similar or, rather, identical reason for taking up this war, all agree that the [actual] fighting and conclusion [of the two conflicts] were different. For in fact, after laying siege to King Haistulf for a short time [in 756] in Pavia, Pepin forced him to surrender hostages, to restore the cities and fortified places seized from the Romans, and to swear that he would not try to regain the things he had returned. But Charles after he had begun the war did not stop until he had, by means of a long siege [in 774], worn King Desiderius down and had accepted his complete surrender. He forced [Desiderius's] son Adalgis, on whom the hopes of all [the Lombards] seemed to rest, to depart not only from the kingdom, but also from Italy. [Charles] restored everything that had been seized from the Romans. He also overcame Rotgaud, the duke of Friuli, who was plotting new [uprisings in 776], and brought all Italy under his control. He set up his own son Pepin as the king of this conquered land.

I would relate here how difficult it was for one to enter Italy across the Alps and what a struggle it was for the Franks to overcome unmarked mountain ridges, upthrust rocks, and rugged terrain, were it not my intention in this book to record the manner of his life, rather than the details of the wars which he waged. Nevertheless, the end result of this war [against the Lombards] was that Italy was conquered, King Desiderius was sent into permanent exile, his son Adalgis was driven out of Italy, and the properties stolen by the Lombard kings were returned to Hadrian, the head of the Roman church.

7. At the conclusion of this campaign, the Saxon war, which had seemed merely postponed, was begun again. No war taken up by the Frankish people was ever longer, harder, or more dreadful [than this one], because the Saxons, like virtually all the peoples inhabiting Germany, were naturally fierce, worshiped demons, and were opposed to our religion. Indeed, they did not deem it shameful to violate and contravene either human or divine laws. There were underlying causes that threatened daily to disturb the peace, particularly since our borders and theirs ran together almost everywhere in open land, except for a few places where huge forests or mountain ridges came between our respective lands and established a clear boundary. Murder, theft, and arson constantly occurred along this border. The Franks were so infuriated by these [incidents], that they believed they could no longer respond [incident for incident], but that it was worth declaring open war on the Saxons.

Thus, a war was taken up against them, which was waged with great vehemence by both sides for thirty-three straight years [772-804]. But the damage done to the Saxons was greater than that suffered by the Franks. In fact, the war could have been brought to a close sooner, if the faithlessness of the Saxons had [but] allowed it. It is almost impossible to say how many times they were beaten and pledged their obedience to the king. They promised [on those occasions] to follow his orders, to hand over the hostages demanded without delay, and to welcome the representatives sent to them by the king. At different times, they were so broken and subdued that they even promised to give up their worship of demons and freely submit themselves to Christianity. But though they were on occasion inclined to do this, they were always so quick to break their promises, that it is not possible to judge which of the two ways [of acting] can be said to have come more naturally to them. In fact, since the start of the war with the Saxons there was hardly a single year in which they did not reverse themselves in this way. But the king's greatness [of spirit] and steadfast determination – both in bad times and good – could not be conquered by their fickleness or worn down by the task he had set himself. Those perpetrating anything of this sort were never allowed to go unpunished. He took vengeance on them for their treachery and exacted suitable compensation either by leading the army [against them] himself or by sending it under [the charge of] his counts. Finally, when all those who were in the habit of resisting had been crushed and brought back under his control, he removed ten thousand men who had been living with their wives and children along both sides of the Elbe river and he dispersed them here and there throughout Gaul and Germany in various [small] groups. Thus, that war which had lasted for so many years ended on the terms laid down by the king and accepted by the Saxons, namely that they would reject the worship of demons, abandon their ancestral [pagan] rites, take up the Christian faith and the sacraments of religion, and unite with the Franks in order to form a single people.

8. Although this war had been long and drawn out, [Charles] himself met the enemy in battle no more than twice, once near a mountain called Osning in the place known as Detmold and again at the River Haase. [Both battles occurred] within one month, with only a few days separating them [in 783]. His [Saxon] enemies were so destroyed and conquered in these two battles that they no longer dared to anger the king or to thwart his advance, unless they were protected by some fortified place. Nevertheless, in that war many Frankish and Saxon nobles, men holding high offices, were killed. Finally, that war ended in its thirty-third year [in 804], but in the meantime a great many serious wars had broken out against the Franks in other lands. The king managed these with such skill, that an observer might easily wonder which deserves more praise, [the king's] persistence or his successes under adverse conditions. For [the Saxon] war began two years before the Italian [conflict] and, although it was waged without interruption, no war that needed to be fought elsewhere was abandoned or [even] postponed in any way on account of that equally onerous war [against the Saxons]. For in wisdom and greatness of soul this king was the most surpassing of all the kings who ruled the peoples of his time. He abandoned no war that had been entered into and needed to be fought through to the end, because of the exertion [it demanded] or the danger it presented. But rather he had learned to meet and endure each circumstance as it presented itself. Thus, it was not his nature to give up in bad times or to be seduced by the false flattery of success in good times.

9. While he was vigorously pursuing the Saxon war, almost without a break, and after he had placed garrisons at selected points along the border, [Charles] marched into Spain [in 778] with as large a force as he could [mount]. His army passed through the Pyrenees and [Charles] received the surrender of all the towns and fortified places he encountered. He was returning [to Francia] with his army safe and intact, but high in the Pyrenees on that return trip he briefly experienced the treachery of the Basques. That place is so thoroughly covered with thick forest that it is the perfect spot for an ambush. [Charles's] army was forced by the narrow terrain to proceed in a long line and [it was at that spot], high on the mountain, that the Basques set their ambush. They fell

upon the last part of the baggage train and drove the men of the rear guard, who were protecting the troops in front, down into the valley below. In the skirmish that followed, they slaughtered every last one of those men. Once they had looted the baggage train, the Basques, under the cover of darkness, since night was then coming on, quickly dispersed in every direction. The Basques had the advantage in this skirmish because of the lightness of their weapons and the nature of the terrain, whereas the Franks were disadvantaged by the heaviness of their arms and the unevenness of the land. Eggihard, the overseer of the king's table, Anselm, the count of the palace, and Roland, the lord of the Breton March, along with many others died in that skirmish. But this deed could not be avenged at that time, because the enemy had so dispersed after the attack that there was no indication as to where they could be found.

10. [Charles] also conquered the Bretons, who live along the sea in the western most part of Gaul. Since they were not subject to him, he sent a force against them [in 786]. The Bretons were forced to surrender hostages and to promise that they would follow his orders.

Next he himself entered Italy with his army and traveled by way of Rome to Capua, a city in Campania. There [in 787], after securing his camp, he threatened to wage war against the Beneventans, unless they surrendered. Areghis, the duke of that people, sent his sons Rumold and Grimold along with a great amount of money to the king. He asked him to accept his sons as hostages and committed himself and his people to following [all the king's] orders, except for an order that would force him personally to appear before [the king]. The king, more concerned with the best interests of [Areghis's] people than with the stubbornness of the duke, accepted the hostages offered to him and granted that, in exchange for a great gift [of money], the duke would not have to appear before him. He kept the younger of the two sons as a hostage, but sent the older one back to his father. His representatives were sent to extract and receive oaths of fidelity from the Beneventans and from Areghis [himself]. [Charles then] returned to Rome and spent a few days visiting holy places before coming back to Gaul.

11. Then the Bavarian war suddenly broke out, but it was brought to a quick end. That war was a product of the pride and foolishness of Duke Tassilo. His wife, who urged him to it, was the daughter of King Desiderius and she thought that she could take revenge for [Charles's] expulsion of her father [from the kingdom of Lombardy] through her husband. Thus, after Tassilo had struck a deal with the Huns, who lived to the east of the Bavarians, he

attempted not only to disobey the king, but to provoke him to war. The king in his fury could not abide [the duke's] defiance, which seemed outrageous [to him], and so he gathered troops from all over [Francia] and prepared to invade Bavaria. He himself led that great force [in 787] to the River Lech, which separates the Bavarians from the Alemannians [or Germans]. Before entering the province [of Bavaria], he set up camp on the bank of the river [Lech] and sent representatives to learn the duke's intentions. But Tassilo [now] realized that holding out would benefit neither himself nor his people and so he humbly surrendered to the king. He submitted the hostages demanded, among whom was his own son Theodo, and he also swore with an oath that he would not [in the future] listen to anyone who advised him to rebel against the king's authority. And so this war, which [had] seemed likely to be the greatest conflict of all, was brought to the quickest end. But a little later [that was in 788] Tassilo was summoned before the king and not allowed to leave. The province, which he had [once] held, was not given to another duke to rule, but to [a series of] counts.

12. After [Tassilo's] insurrection had been settled in this way, [the king] declared war against the Slavs, whom we normally refer to as the Wilzi, but who are properly called the Welatabi in their own language. In that war the Saxons fought as auxiliaries alongside the other peoples who were ordered to march in the king's army, but the obedience [of the Saxons] was insincere and lacking in complete commitment. That war came about because [the Slavs] were constantly harassing and attacking the Abodrites, who had once allied themselves with the Franks. [The Slavs] were not inclined [in this matter] to listen to the [king's] commands.

A certain gulf [the Baltic Sea] with an unknown length and a width no more than a hundred miles wide and in many places [much] narrower runs from the western ocean towards the east. Many peoples live around this sea. In fact, the Danes and Swedes, whom we call Northmen, live along the northern shore [of the Baltic] and on all the islands located there. The Slavs, Estonians, and other peoples live along the southern shore [of the Baltic]. The Welatabi were the most prominent of these peoples and it was against them that the king now took up war. He beat them so [badly] and brought them under his control in the one and only campaign he personally waged [against them], that from that point on they never thought of refusing to obey his commands.

13. Aside from the war against the Saxons, the greatest of all the wars waged by [Charles] was the one against the Avars or Huns, which came next [in

791]. He managed that war with greater attention and preparation than his other wars. Even then, he still led one campaign himself into Pannonia, a province then occupied by the Avars. He turned the other campaigns over to his son Pepin, to the governors of the provinces, and to the counts and even their representatives. These men very vigorously conducted this war and finally brought it to a close in its eighth year [it actually ended in 803]. How many battles occurred in that war and how much blood was spilled is indicated by the utter depopulation of Pannonia and the desertion of the khan's palace; in fact, there is hardly a trace [now] that people once lived there. All the nobility of the Huns died out in this war and all their glory vanished. All the wealth and treasure they had collected over many years was seized. No one can recall any war against the Franks that left them richer or better stocked with resources. Until then they had seemed almost impoverished. So much gold and silver was found in the [khan's] palace and so many precious objects were taken in this war, that it might be fairly said that the Franks had justly seized from the Huns what the Huns had unjustly seized from other peoples. Only two Frankish leaders died in that war: Eric, the duke of Friuli, who was ambushed by the people of Tersatto, a seaside city in Liburnia, and Gerold, the governor of Bavaria. When Gerold was about to engage in battle with the Huns in Pannonia, he was setting out the line of his troops. [At this point] he was killed, it is not known by whom, along with his two escorts as they inspected the troops and urged them individually on. Besides those deaths, the Franks spilled little of their own blood in this war, which was brought to a successful conclusion; and that despite the length of time it took, which was a reflection of the importance of this war.

Then the Saxon [war] came to a [successful] end [in 804] as was [only] appropriate given its long duration. The Bohemian and Linonian wars [in 805 and 808-811] came next, but did not last long. Both of those wars were brought to quick ends under the leadership of the younger Charles [the eldest son of Charlemagne].

14. Charles's final war was the one taken up against the Northmen who are called Danes. First they had operated as pirates, but then they raided the coasts of Gaul and Germany with larger fleets. Their king, Godefrid, was so filled with vain ambition, that he vowed to take control of all Germany. Indeed, he already thought of Frisia and Saxony as his own provinces and had [first] brought the Abodrites, who were his neighbors, under his power and [then] made them pay tribute to him. He even bragged that he would soon come to Aachen, where king [Charles] held court, with a vast army. Some stock was put in his boast, although it was idle, for it was believed that he was

about to start something like this, but was suddenly stopped by death. For he was murdered by one of his own attendants and, thus, both his life and the war he had begun came to a sudden end [at the same time].

15. These [then] were the wars that that mighty king waged with great skill and success in many lands over the forty-seven years he reigned. In those wars he so splendidly added to the Frankish kingdom, which he had received in great and strong condition from his father Pepin, that he nearly doubled its size. Previously the so-called eastern Franks had occupied no more than that part of Gaul bounded by the Rhine, the Loire, the [Atlantic] ocean, and the Balearic Sea and that part of Germany bounded by Saxony, the Danube, Rhine, and Saal (the river that divides the Thuringians and Sorabians). In addition to these areas, the Alemannians and Bavarians fell under the control of the Frankish kingdom. Charles himself, in the wars just described, first added Aquitaine, Gascony, and the whole range of the Pyrenees until the River Ebro, which has its source in Navarre, passes through the fertile fields of Spain, and joins the Balearic Sea under the city walls of Tortosa. Next he conquered all of Italy, which runs more than a thousand miles from Aosta to lower Calabria, which forms the border between the Beneventans and the Greeks. Then, he subdued Saxony, which comprises a large part of Germany and is thought to be twice as wide as the land occupied by the Franks, but similar to it in length. After that he added both [upper and lower] Pannonia, Dacia on the far side of the Danube, and also Istria, Liburnia, and Dalmatia. However, for the sake of [maintaining] friendly relations and [preserving] the pact between them, he allowed the emperor of Constantinople to keep certain coastal cities. Then he subordinated and made tributary all the rough and uncivilized peoples inhabiting Germany between the Rhine and Vistula rivers, the ocean and the Danube. They almost all speak a similar language, but are very different from each other in customs and appearance. Among these peoples the Welatabi, Sorabians, Abodrites, and Bohemians are of special importance, and he came into armed conflict with all of them. Other peoples [living there], who far outnumbered them, simply surrendered.

16. He also increased the glory of his kingdom by winning over kings and peoples through friendly means. In this way he so completely won over Alfonso [II], the king of Galicia and Asturias, that when he sent letters or emissaries to Charles, he ordered that in Charles's presence he was only to be referred to as his subject. By his generosity he had so impressed the Irish kings with his goodwill, that they publicly declared that he was certainly their lord and they were his subjects and servants. Some letters they sent to

[Charles] still survive and testify to this sort of feeling toward him.

He had such friendly relations with Harun-al-Raschid, the king of the Persians, who held almost all the east except India, that [Harun] counted the favor of his friendship as more valuable than that of all the kings and rulers in the world and thought that only [Charles] was worthy of receiving his honor and generosity. Indeed, when [Charles's] representatives, whom he had sent loaded with gifts for the most Holy Sepulcher of our Lord and Savior [in Jerusalem] and for the place of his resurrection, came before [Harun] and informed him of their lord's wishes, he not only allowed them to complete their mission, but even handed over that sacred and salvific place, so that it might be considered as under Charles's control. [Harun] sent his own representatives back with [Charles's] and he sent magnificent gifts for him, among which were robes, spices, and other riches of the east. A few years before this he had sent an elephant, the only one he then possessed, to Charles who had asked him [for such an animal].

The emperors of Constantinople, Nicephorus [I], Michael [I], and Leo [V], who were also voluntarily seeking friendship and an alliance with Charles, sent many representatives to him. But when he took up the title of emperor, [it seemed] to them that he might want to seize their empire. Thus, [Charles] struck a very strong treaty [with them], so that no [potential] source of trouble of any sort might remain between them. For the Romans and Greeks were always suspicious of Frankish power; hence that Greek proverb which still circulates: "Have a Frank as a friend, never as a neighbor."

17. Despite being so committed to increasing the size of the kingdom and to subduing foreign peoples and being so constantly preoccupied with business of this kind, [Charles] still took up many projects in different places to improve and beautify the kingdom. He achieved some of them, but not all. Probably the most outstanding of these [projects] are the church of the Holy Mother of God in Aachen, which is a remarkable edifice, and the bridge spanning the Rhine River at Mainz, which was half a mile long, the width of the river at that point. But that bridge burned down the year before Charles died. Although he thought of rebuilding it, this time in stone rather than wood, his sudden death prevented that. He also began [to build two] splendid palaces, one not far from the city of Mainz, on the [royal] estate of Ingelheim, and the other at Nijmegen on the River Waal, which passes along the south side of the island of the Batavians. Even then, if he learned that sacred churches had fallen into ruin because of their age anywhere in his kingdom, he ordered the bishops and priests responsible for them to repair them and charged his representatives with insuring that his orders had been followed.

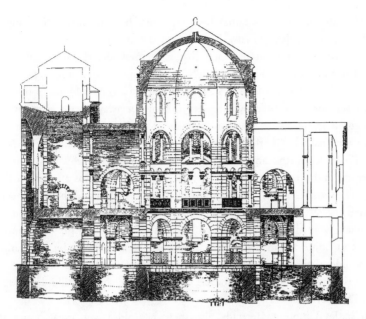

3. Cross-section of Charlemagne's chapel, called the Holy Mother of God or St-Mary's of Aachen, which was built between 792 and 815. It was dedicated by Pope Leo III in 805. After Clemen, *Die romanische Monumentmalerei in den Rheinlanden*, p. 9, fig.2.

He [also] constructed a fleet for use against the Northmen. Ships were built for this purpose near the rivers that flow from Gaul and Germany into the North Sea. Since the Northmen were constantly raiding and ravaging the coasts of Gaul and Germany, fortifications and guards were set up at all the ports and at the mouth of every river that seemed large enough to accommodate ships. With such fortifications he stopped the enemy from being able to come and go [freely]. He took the same [precautions] in the south, along the coasts of the province of Narbonne and Septimania and along the whole coast of Italy up to Rome, where the Moors had recently taken to plundering. Through these measures, Italy suffered no great harm from the Moors while [Charles] lived, nor did Gaul and Germany suffer from the Northmen. The Moors did, however, through betrayal capture and pillage Civitavécchia, a city of Etruria, and the Northmen raided some islands in Frisia not far from the German coastline.

18. It is widely recognized that, in these ways, [Charles] protected, increased the size of, and beautified his kingdom. Now I should begin at this point to speak of the character of his mind, his supreme steadfastness in good times and bad, and those other things that belong to his spiritual and domestic life.

After the death of his father [in 768], when he was sharing the kingdom with his brother [Carloman], he endured the pettiness and jealousy of his brother with such great patience, that it seemed remarkable to all that he could not be provoked to anger by him. Then [in 770], at the urging of his mother [Bertrada], he married a daughter of Desiderius, the king of the Lombards, but for some unknown reason he sent her away after a year and took Hildegard [758-783], a Swabian woman of distinct nobility. She bore him three sons, namely Charles, Pepin, and Louis, and the same number of daughters, Rotrude, Bertha, and Gisela. He had three other daughters, Theoderada, Hiltrude, and Rothaide, two by his wife Fastrada, who was an eastern Frank (that is to say, German), and a third by some concubine, whose name now escapes me. When Fastrada died [in 794], [Charles] married Liutgard, an Alemannian woman, who bore no children. After her death [in 800], he took four concubines: Madelgard, who gave birth to a daughter by the name of Ruothilde; Gersvinda, a Saxon, by whom a daughter by the name of Adaltrude was born; Regina, who bore Drogo and Hugh; and Adallinda who gave him Theoderic.

[Charles's] mother, Bertrada, also spent her old age in great honor with him. He treated her with the greatest respect, to the point that there was never any trouble between them, except over the divorce of King Desiderius's daughter, whom he had married at her urging. She died [in 783], not long after Hildegard's death, but [had lived long enough] to have seen three grandsons and the same number of granddaughters in her son's house. [Charles] saw to it that she was buried with great honor in St-Denis, the same church where his father lay.

He had only one sister, whose name was Gisela. She had devoted herself to the religious life from the time she was a girl. As he had with his mother, he treated her with the greatest affection. She died a few years before him [in 810] in the monastery [that is, the convent of Chelles where she was abbess] in which she had spent her life.

19. [Charles] believed that his children, both his daughters and his sons, should be educated, first in the liberal arts, which he himself had studied. Then, he saw to it that when the boys had reached the right age they were trained to ride in the Frankish fashion, to fight, and to hunt. But he ordered his daughters to learn how to work with wool, how to spin and weave it, so that they might not grow dull from inactivity and [instead might] learn to value work and virtuous activity.

Out of all these children he lost only two sons and one daughter before he himself died: Charles, his eldest son [who died in 811], Pepin, whom he had set up as king of Italy [died in 810], and Rotrude, his eldest daughter, who [in 781] was engaged to Constantine, emperor of the Greeks [she died in 810]. Pepin left behind only one surviving son, Bernard [who died in 818], but five daughters: Adelhaid, Atula, Gundrada, Berthaid, and Theoderada. The king displayed a special token of affection toward his [grandchildren], since when his son [Pepin] died he saw to it that his grandson [Bernard] succeeded his father [as king of Italy] and he arranged for his granddaughters to be raised alongside his own daughters. Despite the surpassing greatness [of his spirit], he was deeply disturbed by the deaths of his sons and daughter, and his affection [toward his children], which was just as strong [a part of his character], drove him to tears.

When he was informed [in 796] of the death of Hadrian, the Roman pontiff, he cried so much that it was as if he had lost a brother or a deeply loved son, for he had thought of him as a special friend. [Charles] was, by nature, a good friend, for he easily made friends and firmly held on to them. Indeed, he treated with the greatest respect those he had bound closely to himself in a relationship of this sort.

He was so attentive to raising his sons and daughters, that when he was home he always ate his meals with them and when he traveled he always took them with him, his sons riding beside him, while his daughters followed behind. A special rearguard of his men was appointed to watch over them. Although his daughters were extremely beautiful women and were deeply loved by him, it is strange to have to report that he never wanted to give any of them away in marriage to anyone, whether it be to a Frankish noble or to a foreigner. Instead he kept them close beside him at home until his death, saying that he could not stand to be parted from their company. Although he was otherwise happy, this situation [that is, the affairs of his daughters] caused him no end of trouble. But he always acted as if there was no suspicion of any sexual scandal on their part or that any such rumor had already spread far and wide.

20. Earlier I chose not to mention with the others [Charles's] son Pepin [the Hunchback] who was born to him by a concubine [named Himiltrude]. He was handsome in appearance, but hunchbacked. When his father had taken up the war against the Huns [in 792] and was wintering in Bavaria, [Pepin] pretended to be sick and entered into a conspiracy against his father with certain leading Franks who had enticed him with the false promise of a kingdom [of his own]. After the plot was uncovered and the conspirators were condemned, [Pepin] was tonsured and allowed to pursue the religious life he had always wanted in the monastery of Prüm [where he died in 811].

Another powerful conspiracy against Charles had arisen even earlier [in 785-786] in Germany, but all its perpetrators [led by Hardrad] were sent into exile; some blinded, others unharmed. Only three conspirators lost their lives, since to avoid arrest they had drawn their swords to defend themselves and had even killed some men [in the process]. They were cut down themselves, because there was [simply] no other way to subdue them. But it is [widely] believed that the cruelty of Queen Fastrada was the cause and source of these conspiracies, since in both cases these men conspired against the king because it looked as if [Charles] had savagely departed from his usual kind and gentle ways by consenting to the cruel ways of his wife. Otherwise, [Charles] passed his whole life with the highest love and esteem of everyone, both at home and abroad, and not the least charge of cruelty or unfairness was ever brought against him by anyone.

21. He loved foreigners and took great trouble to welcome them [to his court], but the large number [who came] truly seemed a drain both on his palace [resources] and also on the kingdom. But, because of the greatness of his nature, he considered the burden to be insignificant, since he was [more than] repaid for his great trouble with praise for his generosity and with the reward of a fine reputation.

22. [Charles] had a large and powerful body. He was tall [at slightly over six feet or 1.83 meters], but not disproportionately so, since it is known that his height was seven times the length of his own foot. The crown of his head was round, his eyes were noticeably large and full of life, his nose was a little longer than average, his hair was grey and handsome, and his face was attractive and cheerful. Hence, his physical presence was [always] commanding and dignified, whether he was sitting or standing. Although his neck seemed short and thick and his stomach seemed to stick out, the symmetry of the other parts [of his body] hid these [flaws]. [When he walked] his pace was strong and the entire bearing of his body powerful. Indeed, his voice was distinct, but not as [strong as might have been] expected given his size. His health was good until four years before he died, when he suffered from constant fevers. Toward the very end [of his life] he also became lame in one foot. Even then he trusted his own judgment more than the advice of his physicians, whom he almost loathed, since they urged him to stop eating roast meat, which he liked, and to start eating boiled meat [which he did not].

He kept busy by riding and hunting frequently, which came naturally to him. Indeed, there is hardly a people on earth who can rival the Franks in this skill. [Charles] also liked the steam produced by natural hot springs and the exercise that came from swimming frequently. He was so good at swimming that no one was considered better than him. For this reason [that is, the existence of the hot springs], he built his palace in Aachen and lived there permanently during the final years of his life until he died. He invited not only his sons to the baths, but also his nobles and friends. Sometimes he invited such a crowd of courtiers and bodyguards, that there might be more than a hundred people bathing together.

23. He normally wore the customary attire of the Franks. [Closest] to his body he put on a linen shirt and underwear, then a silk-fringed tunic and stockings. He wrapped his lower legs with cloth coverings and put shoes on his feet. In winter he covered his shoulders and chest with a vest made of otter or ermine skin, above which he wore a blue cloak. He was always armed with a sword, whose handle and belt were made of gold or silver. On occasion he bore a jeweled sword, but only on special feast days or if the representatives of foreign peoples had come [to see him]. He rejected foreign clothes, however gorgeous they might be, and never agreed to be dressed in them, except once in Rome when Pope Hadrian had requested it and, on another occasion, when his successor Leo had begged him to wear a long tunic, chlamys [a Greek mantle], and shoes designed in the Roman [that is to say, Greek] fashion. On high feast days he normally walked in the procession dressed in clothes weaved with gold, bejeweled shoes, in a cloak fastened by a golden clasp, and also wearing a golden, gem-encrusted crown. But on other days his attire differed little from people's usual attire.

24. [Charles] was moderate when it came to both food and drink, but he was even more moderate in the case of drink, since he deeply detested [seeing] anyone inebriated, especially himself or his men. But he was not able to abstain from food, and often complained that fasting was bad for his health. He seldom put on [large] banquets, but when he did it was for a great number of people on special feast days. His dinner each day was served in four courses only, not including the roast, which his hunters used to carry in on a spit. He preferred [roast meat] over all other food. While eating, he was entertained or listened to someone read out the histories and deeds of the ancients. He was fond of the books of Saint Augustine, particularly the one called the *City of God*.

He was so restrained in his consumption of wine and other drinks, that he seldom drank more than three times during a meal. After his midday meal in the summertime, he would eat some fruit and take a single drink. Then, after he had removed his clothes and shoes, just as he did at night, he would lie down for two or three hours. While sleeping at night, he would not only wake four or five times, but would even get up. [In the morning] while putting on his shoes and dressing, he not only saw friends, but if the count of the palace informed him that there was some unresolved dispute that could not be sorted out without his judgment, he would order him to bring the disputing parties before him at once. Then, as if he were sitting in court, he heard the nature of the dispute and rendered his opinion. He not only looked after cases such as this at that time, but also matters of any sort that needed to be handled that day or to be assigned to one of his officials.

25. [Charles] was a gifted and ready speaker, able to express clearly whatever he wished to say. Not being content with knowing only his own native tongue [German], he also made an effort to learn foreign languages. Among those, he learned Latin so well, that he spoke it as well as he did his own native language, but he was able to understand Greek better than he could speak it. Indeed, he was such a fluent speaker, that [at times] he actually seemed verbose.

He avidly pursued the liberal arts and greatly honored those teachers whom he deeply respected. To learn grammar, he followed [the teaching of] Peter of Pisa, an aged deacon. For the other disciplines, he took as his teacher Alcuin of Britain, also known as Albinus, who was a deacon as well, but from the Saxon people. He was the most learned man in the entire world. [Charles] invested a great deal of time and effort studying rhetoric, dialectic, and particularly astronomy with him. He learned the art of calculation [arithmetic] and with deep purpose and great curiosity investigated the movement of the stars. He also attempted to [learn how to] write and, for this reason, used to place wax-tablets and notebooks under the pillows on his bed, so that, if he had any free time, he might accustom his hand to forming letters. But his effort came too late in life and achieved little success.

26. With great piety and devotion [Charles] followed the Christian religion, in which he had been reared from infancy. For this reason he constructed a church of stunning beauty at Aachen and adorned it with gold and silver, with lamps, grillwork, and doors made of solid bronze. When he could not obtain the columns and marble for this bulding from any place else, he took the trouble to have them brought from Rome and Ravenna. As long as his health allowed him to, [Charles] regularly went to church both morning and evening, and also to the night reading and to the morning Mass. He was particularly concerned that everything done in the church should be done with the greatest dignity and he frequently warned the sacristans that nothing foul

or unclean should be brought into the church or left there. He made sure that his church was supplied with such an abundance of sacred vessels made of gold and silver and with such a great number of clerical vestments, that, indeed, in the celebration of the Mass not even those looking after the doors, who hold the lowest of all ecclesiastical orders, found it necessary to serve in their normal clothes. He very carefully corrected the way in which the lessons were read and the psalms sung, for he was quite skilled at both. But he himself never read publicly and would only sing quietly with the rest of the congregation.

27. [Charles] was so deeply committed to assisting the poor spontaneously with charity, which the Greeks call alms, that he not only made the effort to give alms in his own land and kingdom, but even overseas in Syria, Egypt, and Africa. When he learned that the Christians in Jerusalem, Alexandria, and Carthage were living in poverty, he was moved by their impoverished condition and used to send money. It was chiefly for this reason that he struck up friendships with kings overseas, so that the poor Christians living under their rule might receive some relief and assistance.

He loved the church of St-Peter the Apostle in Rome more than all other sacred and venerable places and showered its altars with a great wealth of gold, silver, and even gems. He [also] sent a vast number of gifts to the popes. During his whole reign he regarded nothing as more important than to restore through his material help and labor the ancient glory of the city of Rome. Not only did he protect and defend the church of St-Peter, but with his own money he even embellished and enriched it above all other churches. Despite holding it in such high regard, he only traveled there four times during the twenty-seven years he reigned [in 774, 781, 787, and 800-801] to fulfill his vows and pray.

28. The reasons for his last visit [to Rome] were not just those [that is, his religious vows and for prayer], but rather because residents of Rome had attacked Pope Leo [III]. They had inflicted many injuries on him, including ripping out his eyes and cutting off his tongue. This [attack] forced him to appeal to the loyalty of the king [in 799 at Paderborn]. Thus, [Charles] traveled to Rome to restore the state of the church, which was extremely disrupted, and he spent the whole winter there [until April 801]. It was at that time that he received the title of emperor and augustus, which at first he disliked so much that he stated that, if he had known in advance of the pope's plan, he would not have entered the church that day, even though it was a great feast day [Christmas 800]. But he bore the animosity that the assump-

tion of this title caused with great patience, for the Roman [that is, Greek] emperors were angry over it. He overcame their opposition through the greatness of his spirit, which was without doubt far greater than theirs, and by often sending representatives to them and by calling them his brothers in his letters.

29. After assuming the imperial title, [Charles] realized that there were many deficiencies in the laws of his own people, for the Franks have two sets of laws that differ tremendously at a number of points. He decided, therefore, to fill in what was lacking, to reconcile the disagreements, and also to set right what was bad and wrongly expressed. He did nothing more about this than to add a few items to these laws, but even those were left in an imperfect state. But he did direct that the unwritten laws of all the peoples under his control should be gathered up and written down.

[Charles] also [ordered] that the very old Germanic poems, in which the deeds and wars of ancient kings were sung, should be written down and preserved for posterity. He began [as well] a grammar of his native language. He even gave [German] names to the months, since before then the Franks were used to referring to them by a mix of Latin and Germanic names. He also assigned individual names to the twelve winds, since until then scarcely more than four of them had been named. About the months, he called them:

January	*Wintarmanoth*	[winter month]
February	*Hornung*	[antler-shedding or mud month]
March	*Lentzinmanoth*	[the month of Lent]
April	*Ostarmanoth*	[easter month]
May	*Winnemanoth*	[month of joy]
June	*Brachmanoth*	[plowing month]
July	*Heuuimanoth*	[hay month]
August	*Aranmanoth*	[month of ripening wheat]
September	*Witumanoth*	[wind month]
October	*Windumemanoth*	[wine month]
November	*Herbistmanoth*	[harvest month]
December	*Heilagmanoth*	[holy month].

He gave the winds these names:

Subsolanus	*Ostroniwint*	[the east wind]
Eurus	*Ostsundroni*	[the east-south wind]
Euroauster	*Sundostroni*	[the south-east wind]

Auster	*Sundroni*	[the south wind]
Austro-africus	*Sundwestroni*	[the south-west wind]
Africus	*Westsundroni*	[the west-south wind]
Zephyrus	*Westroni*	[the west wind]
Chorus	*Westnordroni*	[the west-north wind]
Circius	*Nordwestroni*	[the north-west wind].
Septentrio	*Nordroni*	[the north wind]
Aquilo	*Nordostroni*	[the north-east wind]
Vulturnus	*Ostnordroni*	[the east-north wind].

30. At the very end of his life, when he was already weighed down by poor health and old age, [Charles] summoned his son Louis [the Pious], the king of Aquitaine and the only one of Hildegard's sons still alive, to come to him. When all the leading Franks from the entire kingdom had solemnly assembled and had given their opinion, he established Louis as the co-ruler of the entire kingdom and the heir to the imperial title. Then [on 11 Septemeber 813] he placed a crown upon his [son's] head and ordered that he should [henceforth] be addressed as emperor and augustus. This decision of his was widely approved by all who were present, for it seemed to have been divinely inspired in him for the general good of the kingdom. This act [the elevation of Louis] enhanced his powerful reputation and filled foreign peoples with great fear.

[Charles] then sent his son back to Aquitaine and, despite being slowed down by old age, went hunting, as was his usual habit. But he did not travel far from the palace at Aachen and passed what was left of the autumn hunting. He returned to Aachen around the beginning of November [813]. While spending the winter there, he was overcome by a strong fever and took to his bed in January. He immediately decided to abstain from food, as he usually did when he had a fever, because he thought that he could overcome the sickness by fasting or, at least, relieve [its symptoms]. But on top of the fever he developed a pain in his side, which the Greeks call pleurisy. Still he continued his fast and sustained his body with nothing more than an occasional drink. On the seventh day after taking to his bed, he died after receiving Holy Communion. It was nine o'clock in the morning on 28 January [814]. He died in the seventy-second year of his life and in the forty-seventh year of his reign.

31. His body was washed and looked after in a solemn manner and was [then] carried into the church and interred while everyone there wept. At first there had been some uncertainty about where he should be laid to rest, since when

he was alive he had specified nothing about it. Finally everyone agreed that the most honorable place for him to be entombed was, in fact, in the very cathedral that he himself had built out of his own resources in Aachen, for the love of God and our Lord Jesus Christ and to honor his mother, the holy and eternal Virgin. He was buried in that church on the same day on which he died and a gilded arch with an image and inscription was erected above his tomb. That inscription ran as follows:

> UNDER THIS TOMB LIES THE BODY OF CHARLES, THE GREAT AND
> CATHOLIC EMPEROR, WHO GLORIOUSLY INCREASED THE
> KINGDOM OF THE FRANKS AND REIGNED WITH GREAT SUCCESS
> FOR FORTY-SEVEN YEARS. HE DIED IN HIS SEVENTIES, IN THE
> SEVENTH INDICTION, ON THE TWENTY-EIGHTH DAY OF
> JANUARY, IN THE YEAR OF THE LORD 814.

32. There were so many signs of his approaching death, that not only other people, but even he himself knew that the end was near. For three straight years near the end of his life there were frequent eclipses of the sun and moon and a dark mark was seen on [the face of] the sun for a space of seven days. The arcade that he had erected with great effort between the church and palace fell to the ground in unexpected ruin on the day of the Ascension of our Lord. Similarly, the bridge over the Rhine River at Mainz, which he built, had taken ten years to complete. Though it was built out of wood with such great labor and remarkable skill that it seemed that it might last forever, it accidentally caught on fire and burned down in three hours [in May 813]. In fact, not a single piece of the bridge's wood survived, except some that was below water.

He himself, when he was waging his last campaign [in 810] in Saxony against Godefrid, the king of the Danes, was leaving camp before dawn one morning, when he saw a brilliant meteor suddenly fall from the sky. It cut across the open sky from right to left. As everyone pondered what this sign meant, the horse on which [Charles] was sitting suddenly fell down headfirst and threw him to the ground with such a bang that the clasp holding his cloak snapped and his sword belt was ripped off. The attendants who were present rushed to his side and lifted him up without his weapons or mantle. Even the javelin that he had been grasping tightly in his hand had fallen and now lay twenty feet or more distant from him.

Added to these events, the palace at Aachen frequently shook [from earthquakes] and the [wooden] ceilings of the buildings in which he lived con-

stantly creaked. The church in which he was later entombed was hit by lightning and the golden apple that stood at the peak of the roof was struck by
lightning and landed on top of the bishop's house next door. In that same
church an inscription written in red letters that ran between the upper and
lower arches along the inside of the building [the inner octagon] gave the
name of the builder of the church. In the last line of that inscription [the
words] KAROLVS PRINCEPS were to be read. But it was observed by some
people that in the very year he died, a few months before his death, the letters
that formed PRINCEPS became so faint that they were almost invisible. Yet
Charles either rejected all these things or acted as if none of them had anything to do with him.

33. [Charles had] decided to draw up a will, so that he might make his daughters and illegitimate children heirs to some part of his estate. But the will was
left too late and could not be completed. Nevertheless, three years before he
died, he divided up his precious possessions, money, clothes, and other moveable goods in the presence of his friends and officials. He called on them to
insure that, with their support, the division he had made would remain fixed
and in force after his death. He described in a charter what he wanted done
with the goods he had [so] divided. The terms and text of this [division of
properties] are such:

In the name of the Lord God Almighty – the Father, Son, and Holy Spirit –
[this] inventory and division [of goods] was made by the most glorious and
pious Lord Charles, emperor and augustus, in the eight hundred and eleventh
year from the Incarnation of our Lord Jesus Christ [that is, 810], in the forty-
third year of his reign in Francia and thirty-sixth in Italy, [and] in the eleventh
year of his empire, and in the fourth Indiction.

With pious and prudent reflection he decided to make this inventory and
division of his precious possessions and the wealth that was located in his
treasury on that day and with God's support he accomplished it. In this division he particularly wanted to insure that not only the gift of alms, which
Christians solemnly provide for from their own resources, would be looked
after on his behalf out of his own wealth and in an orderly and reasonable
manner, but also that his heirs should be in no doubt as to what would come
to them and so that they might plainly know and divide without legal strife
or dispute those things among themselves in an appropriate partition [of
goods].

Therefore, with this intention and purpose in mind, he first divided all the
wealth and moveable goods (that is, all the gold, silver, precious stones, and
royal vestments), that were found in the treasury on that day, into three lots.

Then he subdivided two of those [three] lots into twenty-one parts, but kept the other lot whole. He divided those two lots into twenty-one parts because there are twenty-one metropolitan cities in his kingdom. In the name of charity his heirs and friends should pass one of those [twenty-one] parts to each metropolitan city. The archbishop then presiding over that church should receive the part given to his church and divide it among his suffragans in this way: one third should remain with his own church, two thirds should be divided among the suffragans [of his diocese]. Each of these divisions, which was made from the first two lots according to the recognized existence of the twenty-one metropolitan cites, has been separated off from the others and lies individually stored in its own repository under the name of the city to which it should be carried. The names of the metropolitan cities to which these alms or gifts should be given are: Rome, Ravenna, Milan, Cividale del Friuli [Aquiliea], Grado, Cologne, Mainz, Salzburg, Trier, Sens, Besançon, Lyons, Rouen, Rheims, Arles, Vienne, Moutiers-en-Tarantaise, Embrun, Bordeaux, Tours, and Bourges.

He wished the third lot to be kept intact so that, while the [the other] two lots had been stored under seal in the [twenty-one] parts described, this third lot might serve his own daily needs as if it were property which he was under no obligation to part with or see alienated from his direct possession. This [arrangement] should hold for as long as he lived or he deemed the use [of the property] necessary for his well-being. But after his death or voluntary withdrawal from the world [into a monastery], this [third] lot should be divided into four parts and one of them should be be added to the already [allotted] twenty-one parts. Another [the second] part should be taken up and divided by his sons and daughters, and by the sons and daughters of his sons in a fair and reasonable partition [of goods]. The third part, in keeping with Christian practice, should be set aside for the poor. The fourth part should, in like charitable fashion, be set aside to support the male and female servants of the palace itself. It was his wish to add to the third lot of his complete wealth, which also consists of gold and silver, everything else that was found in his treasury and wardrobe on the day [of his death]: namely, all the vessels and utensils of bronze, iron, and other metals, along with the arms, garments, and other moveable goods, both precious and ordinary, used for various things, such as curtains, bedspreads, tapestries, woolen goods, leather articles, and saddles. [He hoped] in this way that the size of the parts of the third lot would increase and that the distribution of charity would reach more people.

He arranged that his chapel, that is to say its church property, both that which he himself had provided and gathered together, and that which had come by way of family inheritance, should remain whole and not be divided up in any way. If, however, any vessels, books, or other objects should be found in the chapel which he had not indisputably given to the chapel, these could be purchased and retained by anyone who wished to have them after a fair price was determined. He similarly stipulated that the books that he had collected in great number in his personal library could be sold for a fair price to people who wished to own them and that the money [so raised] should be distributed among the poor.

Among his other possessions and riches, it is known that there are three silver tables and a gold one of great size and weight. He arranged and ordered that one of the silver tables, a square-shaped one containing an outline of the city of Constantinople, was to be sent to Rome to the church of St-Peter the Apostle along with the other gifts assigned to the saint. Another [silver table], this one having a round shape and bearing a likeness of the city of Rome, was to be transported to the episcopal seat of Ravenna. The third [silver table], which far surpasses the others in the beauty of its workmanship and its weight, contains a delicate and fine line drawing of the whole universe set within three linked circles. He stipulated that it and the gold table, which is referred to as the fourth, should be used to increase the third lot among his heirs and to increase the share of charity to be distributed from it.

[Charles] made and established this disposition and arrangement [of his goods] in the presence of the bishops, abbots, and counts who were able to be present at that time. Their names are inscribed here. The bishops [were] Hildebald [archbishop of Cologne], Richolf [archbishop of Mainz], Arn [archbishop of Salzburg], Wolfar [archbishop of Rheims], Bernoin [archbishop of Clermont], Leidrad [archbishop of Lyons], John [archbishop of Arles], Theodulf [bishop of Orléans], Jesse [bishop of Amiens], Heito [bishop of Basel], [and] Waltgaud [bishop of Liège]. The abbots [were] Fridugis [of St-Martin of Tours], Adalung [of Lorsch], Angilbert [of St-Riquier], Irmino [of St-Germain-des-Prés]. The counts were Wala, Meginher, Otulf, Stephen, Unruoc, Burchard, Meginhard, Hatto, Rihwin, Edo, Ercangar, Gerold, Bero, Hildigern, Hroccolf.

After examining this same charter his son Louis, who succeeded by divine right, saw to it that [this division of properties] was fulfilled as quickly and faithfully as possible after his [father's] death.

3. THE CHARTERS

The documents collected below are of various sorts. Aside from the description of the property of Michelstadt [11], which he personally supervised and, perhaps, dictated, Einhard cannot be considered 'the author' of these documents, but then land charters don't have authors; they have actors, witnesses, and recorders. Einhard may be said to be a participant and actor in these documents, acting sometimes as notary or scribe, sometimes as enactor, and sometimes as one of the principals. In the case of the Fulda charters the reader cannot be absolutely certain that the Einhard mentioned is the famous Einhard, but it seems highly likely. Those early charters not only supply us with evidence of Einhard's presence and activity at Fulda before he moved to court, but also of his family's ties to the monastery. The charters after 814 testify, as Einhard's letters do, to the properties he received after Charlemagne's death and to how he wished to administer, document, and dispose of his holdings.

1. A Charter Written by Einhard at Fulda on 19 April 788

While resident at Fulda, Einhard occasionally acted as a scribe or notary recording land transactions of the monastery. Here he recorded a gift of land to the monastery of St-Boniface by the brothers Matto and Megingoz. Since for our purposes the charter is chiefly significant for placing Einhard at Fulda at a specific date, only the dating and subscription clauses have been given.

Source: translated from Urkundenbuch des Klosters Fulda, vol.1, part 2: Die Zeit des Abtes Baugulf, no.175, ed. Edmund E. Stengel (Marburg: N.G. Elwert, 1956), p. 269; and also in the older edition, Codex Diplomaticus Fuldensis, no.87, ed. E.F.J. Dronke (1850; repr. Aalen: Otto Zeller, 1962), p.53.

Enacted at the monastery of Fulda on the thirteenth day [before] the Kalends of May [19 April] in the twentieth year of the reign [that is, 788] of Charles, king of the Franks and Lombards and patrician of the Romans.

I, Einhard, having been asked, wrote [out this charter].

2. A Charter Written by Einhard at Fulda on 12 September 791

Einhard recorded a gift of property to Fulda by Hiltrih and his wife Hruadun. Again only the dating and subscription clauses have been translated.

Source: translated from Urkundenbuch des Klosters Fulda, vol.1, part 2: Die Zeit des Abtes Baugulf, no.189, ed. Edmund E. Stengel (Marburg: N.G. Elwert, 1956), p. 286; and also in Codex Diplomaticus Fuldensis, no.100, ed. E.F.J. Dronke (1850; repr. Aalen: Otto Zeller, 1962), p.60.

Enacted at the monastery of Fulda on the day before the Ides of September [that is, 12 September] in the twenty-third year of the reign [that is, 791] of Charles, king of the Franks.

I, Einhard, wrote [out this charter].

3. Another Charter Written by Einhard at Fulda, 790-791

Einhard here recorded a gift to Fulda by Folcwin. Again only the dating and subscription clauses have been translated.

Source: translated from Urkundenbuch des Klosters Fulda, vol.1, part 2: Die Zeit des Abtes Baugulf, no.191, ed. Edmund E. Stengel (Marburg: N.G. Elwert, 1956), p. 288; and also in Codex Diplomaticus Fuldensis, no.102, ed. E.F.J. Dronke (1850; repr. Aalen: Otto Zeller, 1962), p.61.

Enacted at the monastery of Fulda in the twenty-third year of the reign [that is 9 October 790 to 8 October 791] of Charles, the most glorious king of the Franks.

I, Einhard, wrote [out this charter].

4. Another Charter Written by Einhard at Fulda

Einhard here recorded a gift to Fulda during the abbacy of Baugulf (780-802) by Gundherus. The dating clause in this charter lacks a specific indication of the year.

Source: translated from Urkundenbuch des Klosters Fulda, vol.1, part 2: Die Zeit des Abtes Baugulf, no.234, ed. Edmund E. Stengel (Marburg: N.G. Elwert, 1956), p. 338; and also in Codex Diplomaticus Fuldensis, no.183, ed. E.F.J. Dronke (1850; repr. Aalen: Otto Zeller, 1962), p.103.

Enacted at the monastery of Fulda on the third day [before] the Kalends of March [that is, 27 February].

I, Einhard, wrote [out this charter].

5. Another Charter Written by Einhard at Fulda

Einhard here recorded a gift to Fulda during the abbacy of Baugulf (780-802) by Hartger and his son Hruadmunt. The dating clause in this charter again does not specify the year.

Source: translated from Urkundenbuch des Klosters Fulda, vol.1, part 2: Die Zeit des Abtes Baugulf, no.235, ed. Edmund E. Stengel (Marburg: N.G. Elwert, 1956), p. 338; and also in Codex Diplomaticus Fuldensis, no.184, ed. E.F.J. Dronke (1850; repr. Aalen: Otto Zeller, 1962), p.103.

Enacted at the monastery of Fulda on the sixth [day before] the Ides of March [that is, 10 March].

I, Einhard, wrote [out this charter].

6. Einhard's Parents Grant Land to Fulda

Einhard also recorded a gift of land to Fulda during the abbacy of Baugulf (780-802) by a certain Einhard and his wife Engilfrit. It has long been assumed that these two people were Einhard's own parents, though there is little corroborating evidence. The dating clause in this charter is once again unspecific. The complete charter is translated below.

Source: translated from Urkundenbuch des Klosters Fulda, vol.1, part 2: Die Zeit des Abtes Baugulf, no.240, ed. Edmund E. Stengel (Marburg: N.G. Elwert, 1956), p. 346; and also in Codex Diplomaticus Fuldensis, no.185, ed. E.F.J. Dronke (1850; repr. Aalen: Otto Zeller, 1962), p.103.

In the name of Christ, I, Einhard, and my wife Engilfrit give and leave to [the monastery of] St-Boniface, where a venerable man, Abbot Baugulf, is known to rule over the monastery with its great crowd of monks, that is, that we give whatever property we hold in Urithorpfe with the exception of [five] *haftunnae* [measures of land] and one dependent [a serf]. Whatever else I possess I leave with this condition, that while I am still alive I should [continue to] hold that. Likewise if that wife of mine should outlive me, she should enjoy [the benefits of] that place. But, with that stipulation attached, after the death of both of us, you and your successors should possess the aformentioned things on a permanent basis.

Enacted on the eighth day [before] the Ides of June [that is, 6 June].

I, Einhard, wrote [out this charter].

7. Louis the Pious grants Michelstadt and Mulinheim [Seligenstadt] to Einhard and his wife Emma on 11 January 815.

In January 815, just a little under a year after Charlemagne's death, the new emperor granted Einhard and Emma the substantial properties of Michelstadt and Mulinheim [Seligenstadt; see Map 3].

Source: translated from Codex Laureshamensis, vol. 1: Einleitung Regesten Chronik, ed. Karl Glöckner (Darmstadt: Verlag des historischen Vereins für Hessen, 1929), pp. 299-300 and also in Chronicon Laureshamense, ed. K.A.F. Pertz, in Monumenta Germaniae Historica: Scriptores, vol. 21 (Hanover: Hahn, 1869; repr. Leipzig: Karl W. Hiersemann, 1925), pp. 359-360.

In the name of the Lord God and our Savior, Jesus Christ, Louis, august emperor by the design of divine providence, [proclaims the following:]

It is the custom of imperial Highness to honor those faithfully serving it with many gifts and to elevate them with great honors. Therefore, [since] we follow the custom of our ancestors, that is, the kings preceding us, it pleased our Highness to honor a certain faithful man of ours by the name of Einhard with some of our property and to confer by the gift of our generosity [this property] into his personal possession. Not unjustly [did we do this], since by his faithful sevice and devoted obedience to our Serene Highness he worthily deserves to acquire this [property], for with every effort and at every moment he has striven faithfully to submit to our service and our demands.

Thence, [by] knowledge and practice all our faithful people, both those alive now and those to come in the future, should know that we have granted to that same faithful man of ours, Einhard, and also to his wife, Emma, a place in Germany called Michelstadt in the forest called Odenwald. In the middle of that place there is a small wooden church and the two leagues, that is, one *rasta* [or three Roman miles], of fields and woods around the church belong to that same place. Within the boundary of this measure [of land], there remain at the present time fourteen of our own servants, with their wives and children. Besides these, there are in that same place forty dependent men and women. [We grant to Einhard] this place with its demarcated area in its entirety and with its dependents.

[We also grant] the village called Mulinheim [later, Seligenstadt], which is in the Maingau, and situated upon the banks of the Main River, which was once held by Count Drogo. It has a small church built with a [stone] wall. In that village there are nineteen homesteads (*mansi*) and at the present time there are thirteen dependents living there with their wives and children. As well, at another village which goes by the same name, [being] called Lower Mulinheim, upon the same river, there are four homesteads and the same number of dependents [that is, four] living there with their wives and children, who belong to the village mentioned above [Upper Mulinheim]. We have granted through this charter of our gift this village, that is, Upper Mulinheim, with the things that belong to it and those dependents belonging to it, and all those things described above in churches, estates, houses, dependents, woods, lands, meadows, pasture lands, [standing] waters, running waters, cultivated and uncultivated lands, with all adjacent and attached things, whole and entire, to our aforementioned faithful Einhard and to his wife Emma as their own.

Thus, from today into the future let them possess the power to do whatever they wish to according to hereditary right, that is, with respect to the aforementioned things and places, or concerning those things that pertain to them. No one subject to the holy church of God and to us should be tempted to remove or diminish any of those aforementioned things granted by us to our mentioned faithful man and his wife. Rather, let them be permitted to have and hold those things in peace and to leave them by hereditary right to whomever they choose.

And that this charter of our gift might attain an inviolable and uncontested permanence perpetually through the years and that it might be believed certainly and truthfully by our subjects now alive and those in the future, and even by our own successors, that this was done by us, we signed it below with our own hand and we ordered it to be impressed with the seal of our signet-ring.

The sign of the most serene emperor Louis.

I, Helisachar [the emperor's archchancellor], certified [this]. Dated on the third [day before] the Ides of January [11 January] in the first year, with Christ's blessing, of the empire of Lord Louis [that is, 815], the most pious and august emperor, in the seventh Indiction. It was enacted at Aachen in the royal palace, in the name of God. Amen.

8. The *Liber Traditionum* of the Monastery of Blandin [St-Peter], Ghent

The Liber Traditionum *is a miscellany of texts on the early history of Blandin or St-Peter [see Map 1] written down in 941. It seems likely that portions of the document, which recount the early history of the abbey and various donations to it, depended on a document or materials compiled during Einhard's abbacy. Here, however, only those parts that directly refer to him or in which he participated have been translated. 1. comes from the very end of the short history of the monastery which concludes with Einhard's abbacy. 2. is the charter in which Louis the Pious renewed the monastery's immunities in 815. 3. is an undated charter issued by Einhard, probably in 815. 4. comes from the start of the list of holdings Einhard apparently ordered compiled. 5. contains some of the donations made to Blandin while Einhard was its abbot.*

Source: translated from Diplomata Belgica ante annum millesimum centesimum scripta, ed. M. Gysseling and A.C.F. Koch (Brussels: Belgisch Inter-Universitair Centrum, 1950), pp. 125-128, 130.

1. *An Account of the Foundation and Building of the Monastery of Blandin*

...From then until the time at which Louis of divine memory, son of the Emperor Charles the Great, acquired the imperial government, that place [Blandin] was reduced almost to nothing, until, with the help of the prayers of Saint Amand, the distinguished bishop, there arose in that monastery an abbot by the name of Einhard. Like ancient Zorobabel [1 Esdras 3:2-3], who had led the Israelites, he began, with God's inspiration, to think about how he could lift that monastery, which was entrusted to his care, from its impoverished state by restoring it in some small way. And so he pondered this matter for many days and finally, inspired by divine mercy, restored to that place certain possessions that could support its twenty-four clerics, who were serving Christ continuously in that monastery. He willingly restored alms to them, which according to the needs of the previous abbots [had been] received in an inappropriate way, for they [had] paid no attention to what the Lord said about priests: that they devour the sins of the people [see Ps. 5:5]. Therefore, the alms that are given by the people as if for the redemption of their souls [lead to] the even greater ruination of those removing them, unless because of various prayers the Lord forgives the sins of those whose alms they took away. Therefore that very Einhard devised a wise plan about all the things that seemed to belong by law to the monastery he ruled. In a charter of the aforementioned emperor, Louis, he confirmed [these things] by means of a written document [3.8.2] and signed it with his signet-ring.

2. The Grant of Blandin's Immunities, 2 June 815

In the name of the Lord God and our Savior Jesus Christ, Louis, august emperor by divine providence. If we bestow useful benefices upon places devoted to holy religion on account of [our] love of God and his servants in those places, we do not despair that the Lord will repay us with the reward of eternal recompense.

Therefore, all our faithful subjects, both present and future, should know that the venerable man, Einhard, abbot of the monastery of Blandin, which was built in honor of the holy apostles Peter and Paul in the district of Tournai upon the Scheldt River, presented for our consideration the [charter of] immunity of our lord and father, Charles of good memory, the most pious emperor. In it we found inserted how our father and the preceding kings had, out of divine love and their respect for divine religion, always held the said monastery under the fullest protection and defense of immunity. Nevertheless, in order to be certain in this matter, the aforementioned Abbot Einhard also asked us, for the love of God and out of reverence for the holy apostles Peter and Paul, to confirm the original charter with our own. We have freely granted his request and have ordered this charter of our judgment about that monastery to be made. By it we order and command that none of our subjects or anyone holding judicial powers should presume to claim those things listed or dare in our time or in the future to infringe upon the churches, places, fields or other possessions of the said monastery, which in our time it fairly and reasonably holds under the power of our authority, or [upon] those things which were granted over time to the same monastery by religious men. Nor [should judges or *missi* infringe] in order to hear cases, to impose fines or tribute, to obtain overnight dwelling or supplies, to lodge people prepared to pledge, to engage unjustly [in a case] the people of the same monastery, whether free or unfree, who live constantly on the same land of that [monastery], or to ask for any restitution or illegal taxes.

But let it be permitted to the aforesaid abbot [Einhard] and to his successors to hold the things of the said monastery in peaceful order under the defense of our immunity, and whatever then the imperial purse allows we ourselves grant on behalf of [our] eternal recompense entirely to the said monastery so that in the support of the poor and in allowances for the clergy continuously serving God there it should be of use and increase, in so far as it pleases those servants of God, who serve God in that same place, to beseech the Lord constantly for us, for our wife and children, and for the stability of the entire empire granted to us by God and to be safe-guarded by us.

And so that this charter might be more truly believed and more carefully kept by the subjects of the holy church and our own subjects, we signed below with our own hand and we ordered it to be confirmed with the impression of our signet-ring.

The sign of the most serene emperor Louis.

I, Helisachar [the emperor's archchancellor], certified [this]. Dated on the fourth [day before] the Nones of June [that is, 2 June], in the second year [that is, 815] of the empire, with Christ's blessing, of the most pious emperor, Lord Louis, in the eighth Indiction. Enacted at Aachen in the royal palace, in the name of God. Amen.

3. A Charter of Abbot Einhard

Einhard called abbot, although a sinner and unworthy, [sends his greetings] to the holy and venerable priests in Christ, to the deacons, and to the remaining congregation serving God in the monastery of Blandin.

Since it is known to you that your allowances were not fully supplied by our predecessors and on account of this that you have frequently suffered a dearth of necessities and penury, it pleases me on account of the love and honor of our Lord God, Jesus Christ, and the blessed apostle Peter, and on account of the fraternal love between us, which we have mutually acknowledged has existed up until the present with the Lord's help and which will always exist into the future with his help, to bestow from the things of this monastery, which we [the abbot and monks] have hitherto held together, a special portion upon you. And so I assign it to your power, so that it be turned to your needs according to the determination of your approrpriate arrangements and it should remain in this state forever. That is to say that I have determined to set aside your allowances for you. [These consist] of arable land in the place called Cranaberga in which twenty-five modia [dry measures of grain] can be sown, and in another place which is called Heminga in which six modia [can be sown], and in a third place which is called Farnoth [suitable for sowing] twelve modia, and [to support] one herd of cattle a meadow called Foraria, and another meadow near the sea that can support 120 wethers [rams], and near the monastery itself five dependent homesteads, and in the village that is called Fredingahem one homestead in which two people live, and in the place that is called Olfne one serf's holding and what belongs to it, and one meadow that is called Rodum or Hubela, and in the village called Hrokingahem two homesteads and whatever belongs to them, which until now the priest Baderic held in benefice.

And I especially grant for your benefit a part of the alms that are accustomed to come to the monastery, which up until now were received for my [the abbot's] benefit, and so [also] the precarial tenures that are freed up from this present moment forward should be taken into your portion. I even grant to you a part of the vineyard located below the monastery, as has now been settled, so that it may be cultivated by you and the fruit of that part be received for your use. As well I have decided to give to you a portion of my forest in the woods called Scheldeholt, in which forty pigs, more or less, can be fattened in the fall.

All these things I have decreed should be granted to you, so that you may always hold them under your power and control, and at no time and in no way should this [arrangement] made by my free will be transformed either by us or our successors into another arrangement, but with the help of the almighty God, let this grant and our arrangement remain strong and unbroken forever. So that it might acquire even greater strength I have decided to sign [this charter] with my own hand.

4. Einhard's Memorandum on Blandin's Properties

I [the compiler of the *Liber Traditionum*] thought to add to this work a memorandum just as the lord and venerable abbot Einhard fittingly arranged it.

Of the homesteads that the brothers possess near the monastery.

First concerning allodial land where [one] can sow ninety-five modia [of grain] and collect fifty cartloads of hay in one meadow and forty in another and of land in which to sow fifteen modia of oats in the third year, of woods in which fifty pigs, more or less, can be fattened in the fall....

An account of the properties that freemen handed over to Saint Peter at the monastery of Blandin, with the taxes Einhard ordered the brothers to hold, and to receive those same properties after the deaths of them [the freemen]....

5. Notice of the Things that the Donors of St-Peter Gave to the Monastery of Blandin

...3. In the time of the emperor Louis and Abbot Einhard, Wicbertus and his wife Hildeberga gave to the monastery of St-Peter, Blandin, in the district of Tournai in the place near the river called Scheldt and the stream Rugge Bacceningahem, a manor...

...5. When Emperor Louis reigned and Abbot Einhard governed the monastery of Blandin, Hereger gave to St-Peter for the table of the brothers in the district of Tournai beside the River Leie near the village called Mahlinum in a place called Flaswereda arable land where [one] can sow three and a half modia, and in another place called Fuouinga a field fit for sowing two modia, and in Mantingalanda [a field] fit for sowing one and a half modia. The charter of that man lays out everything....

...18. The donations recorded above were handed over [to Blandin] in the time of Emperor Louis and Abbot Einhard.

9. Louis the Pious's Grant of Immunities to St-Bavo in Ghent

On 13 April 819 Louis the Pious reconfirmed, at the request of Abbot Einhard, the immunities of the monastery of St-Bavo in Ghent [see Map 1].

Source: translated from Diplomata Belgica ante annum millesimum centesimum scripta, ed. M. Gysseling and A.C.F. Koch (Brussels: Belgisch Inter-Universitair Centrum, 1950), pp. 222-223.

In the name of the Lord God and our Savior Jesus Christ, Louis, august emperor by divine providence. If we bestow useful benefices upon places devoted to holy religion on account of [our] love of God and his servants in those places, we do not despair that the Lord will repay us with reward of eternal recompense.

Therefore, all the faithful subjects of the holy church of God and our subjects, both present and future, should know that the venerable man, Einhard, abbot of the monastery called Ghent, which is located in the district of Brabant and built in honor of Saint Peter, the prince of the apostles, and in which the remains of Saint Bavo, the confessor of Christ, also rest, presented for our consideration the charter of immunity of the lord and our father, Charles of good memory, the most outstanding emperor. In it is found inserted how he himself, for the love of God and the security of the brothers living in that same monastery, had always held [that monastery] under the fullest protection and defense of immunity.

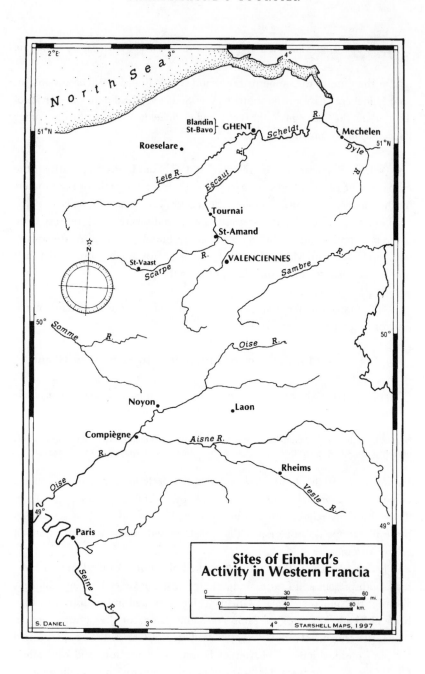

Sites of Einhard's Activity in Western Francia

Map I

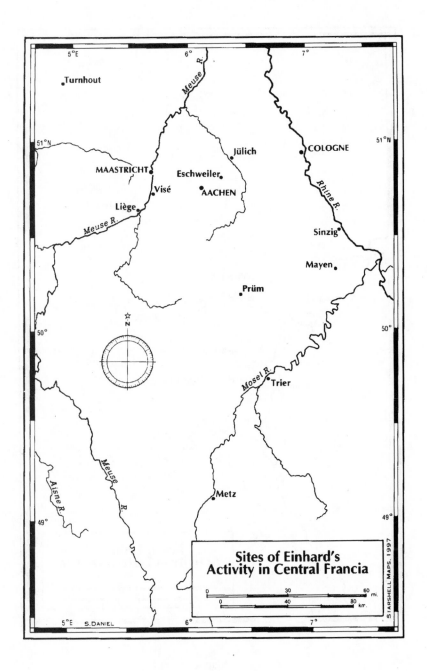

Sites of Einhard's
Activity in Central Francia

Map 2

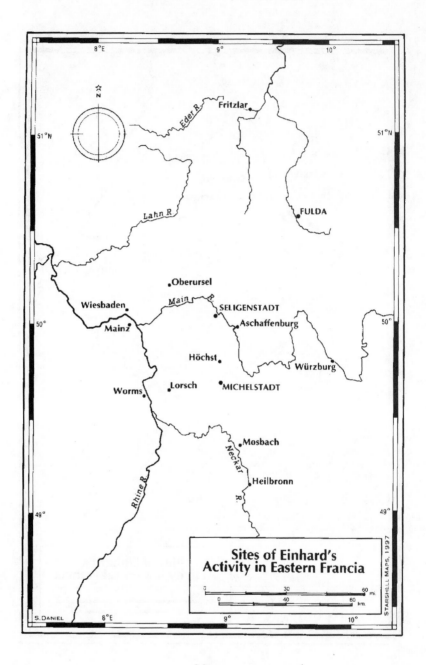

Sites of Einhard's
Activity in Eastern Francia

Map 3

The aforementioned Abbot Einhard, in pursuit of certainty [in this matter], also asked us to add our charter to this paternal charter for the sake of confirmation. We have freely assented to this request, and we have decreed that this charter of ours is to be granted to the aforesaid monastery and to its rectors for the sake of immunity and defense. By means of it we order and command that no public judge or anyone holding judicial power should presume to claim those things listed or dare in our time or in the future to infringe upon the churches, places, fields or other possessions of the said monastery, which in our time it fairly and legally holds under the power of our authority in whatever districts or territories, or which the divine feeling [of donors] wished to add to the possession of that same holy place over time. Nor [should judges or *missi* infringe] in order to hear cases, to impose fines, to obtain overnight dwelling or supplies, to lodge people prepared to pledge, to engage unjustly [in a case] the people of the same monastery, whether free or unfree, who live constantly on the same land of that [monastery], nor to ask for any restitution or illegal taxes.

But let it be permitted to the aforesaid abbot [Einhard] and to his successors to hold the things of the said monastery in peaceful order under the defense of our immunity, with all its taxes granted, just as is set out in the charter of our lord and father, and to obey our order faithfully, in so far as it pleases those servants of God, who serve God in that same place, to beseech the mercy of the Lord constantly for us, for our wife and children, and for the stability of the entire empire granted to us by God and to be safe-guarded by us.

So that this charter might be more truly believed and more carefully kept, and so that it might obtain greater permanence in God's name and by the faithful of the holy church and by our own subjects, we signed below with our own hand and we ordered it to be stamped with the impression of our signet-ring.

The sign of the most serene emperor Louis.

The seal.

The deacon Durandus certified and signed in place of Helisachar. Dated on the Ides of April [that is, 13 April], in the sixth year, with Christ's blessing, of our empire [that is, 819] in the twelfth Indiction. Enacted at Aachen in the royal palace, in the name of God. Amen.

10. Einhard and Emma grant Michelstadt to the Monastery of Lorsch

On 12 September 819 Einhard and Emma granted Michelstadt, as was permitted by Louis the Pious's original grant, to the monastery of Lorsch.

Source: translated from Codex Laureshamensis, vol. 1: Einleitung Regesten Chronik, ed. Karl Glöckner (Darmstadt: Verlag des historischen Vereins für Hessen, 1929), pp. 301-302 and also in Chronicon Laureshamense, ed. K.A.F. Pertz, in Monumenta Germaniae Historica: Scriptores, vol. 21 (Hanover: Hahn, 1869; repr. Leipzig: Karl W. Hiersemann, 1925), p. 360.

Our Lord and Redeemer having lived physically here on earth, thought it worth admonishing humankind, which was much defiled by the stain of sin, and so said: "Give alms and behold all things are clean unto you" [Luke 11:41] and again, "Make unto you friends of the mammon of iniquity… who may receive you into everlasting dwellings." [Luke 16:9] For that reason, we, Einhard and Emma, in the name of that omnipotent God who commands those things, thinking together of the salvation of our souls and about the abolition of our sins, and considering with equal devotion the rewards of the blessed and eternal life to follow, decided to make this deed. By it with free and unimpaired will we grant, [and] we want to be granted from this very day, the cell that is legally ours with the name Michelstadt located in the region of Phlumheim, in the forest that is called Odenwald, upon the River Mümling, which the most glorious ruler, the lord and emperor, Louis, granted to us by his very great generosity. He passed [this cell] from his own legal possession into our legal possession by a solemn donation and he confirmed that transfer of property to us with a charter containing his command [3.7].

We grant and hand over to the church or monastery of the venerable martyr of Christ Nazarius, which is called Lorsch, this aforementioned cell in its entirety with all its attached things and its demarcated area, and with all things pertaining to it, that is, churches, houses, other buildings, lands, meadows, woods, fields, pasture lands, [standing] waters, running waters, cultivated and uncultivated lands, moveable and immoveable things, creatures, and dependents of both sexes and all ages, [who are] one hundred in number. That place [Lorsch] was built in the Rhineland on the bank of the river called Weschnitz, where at the present time the venerable man, Abbot Adalung [804-837], is known to be the abbot and rector of the congregation serving God.

We are making this donation and transfer [of lands] on this condition, namely that for as long as we are, by divine disposition, still alive in this mortal life, we should hold that aformentioned cell under our own power and under our command without challenge or impediment from any person or any power. [This should apply to us] either together or individually, [that is] by succession if one of us should predecease the other and there be but one of us left. Also if it should happen that we have sons, one of them should succeed us in that same possession by precarial law. But after our deaths that aformentioned cell in its entirety should be guaranteed to that previously named and venerable monastery [of Lorsch] without challenge by anyone, and should remain under its power and perpetual control.

And if anyone wishes to speak against this deed of our donation or if anyone attempts to overthrow or cancel it, let him first perceive that Christ and his holy martyr Nazarius are opposed to this foul effort, and let him under compulsion open his purse and pay damages from his own property to the party of the aforesaid venerable monastery, namely one pound of gold, twelve [pounds] in silver weight. And let this deed and this donation of ours remain firm and unbroken. And if another document at any time should be brought forth in our name by any person that is contrary to this deed of ours and possessing an indication of dates either before or after [ours], even if it should seem to be in our own hand or is said to have been signed [by us], let it remain empty and invalid and may it achieve no success. But, as we said above, let this grant of ours, with the attached stipulation, remain forever firm and unbroken. And, so that this deed, according to the custom of the law, might be accepted as wholly confirmed, we decided to confirm it by signing it below with our own hand, and we insured that it was signed by suitable witnesses who observed the donation itself.

This donation was made in the monastery of Lorsch, on the second [day before the] Ides of September [12 September] in the sixth year of the reign [that is, 819] of our Lord Louis, the most glorious emperor, in the name of God.

I, Einhard, a sinner and the donor, approved and signed below with my own hand. I, Emma, consented and signed below. † the sign of Rabangarius. † the sign of Warboto. † the sign of Wolfbert, and of others.

I, Hirminmar, a deacon and imperial notary, at the request of Einhard, wrote out this deed and signed below.

11. A Description of Einhard's Michelstadt Estate

In order to transfer the land to Lorsch, Einhard himself surveyed the property and his notary wrote up this description of the land. One should note that Einhard was not claiming to hold all of this property, since he recognized that various monasteries had claims on parts of it and that local lords held benefices all around it. Also the boundaries themselves seem vague, since the reference points are rivers, villages, and oak trees.

Source: translated from Codex Laureshamensis, vol. 1: Einleitung Regesten Chronik, ed. Karl Glöckner (Darmstadt: Verlag des historischen Vereins für Hessen, 1929), pp. 302-304 and also in Chronicon Laureshamense, ed. K.A.F. Pertz, in Monumenta Germaniae Historica: Scriptores, vol. 21 (Hanover: Hahn, 1869; repr. Leipzig: Karl W. Hiersemann, 1925), p. 361.

There are some people who, being full of worldly pride and loving themselves, seize things donated by Christ's faithful to his holy churches and monasteries, either so that they might retain them for themselves by hereditary right or distribute them by their secular power in benefice. Therefore, lest the hand of the iniquitous prevail over [and] divert these things in the place [called] Michelstadt which I received from the royal hand of Emperor Louis [himself], I, Einhard, beseech that, in the recollection of both the living and future faithful, these things be gathered into one and described in these words. Afterwards, when I had decided to subject that said place to the control of Lorsch, and it was learned that this decision was acceptable, I carefully investigated its boundaries and placenames, and based on my refreshed memory I ordered my notary Luther to record [this description]; [but] with this caution, namely that the estates of many monasteries are joined together with those [properties] and the benefices of various lords are found all around them.

The locations of the boundaries and names of the places [in question] are designated as follows: [these places] begin from Mount Mamenhart [near the village of Momart] and include the whole of the same mountain until the [Roman] road; from the road until the double oak; from there between Ulenbuch [Eulbach] and Rumpheshusen to the oak; from the oak to the River Bramaha; through the descent of this [river] into Vullinebach [Günzbach], through its ascent [upstream] to the stony brook [Steinbach]; from there to Vullineburch [Hainhaus], through one gate [is] the inside [of the property], through the other [is] the outside. From there into the bank of the Euterun [Euterbach], through the descent [downstream] of this [river] to Langenvirst [Langeforst], where the Langenvirst is divided. Upon the Langenvirst to Breitensol [Breitung]; from there through Eichendal [Rindengrund] to the river Urtella [Sensbach]. Through the ascent [upstream] of this [river] into Vinsterbuch; from there to the Phaphenstein [Pfannestein] of Einhard. From Phaphenstein above Richgeressneitten [Rickersgrund]; from there to the summit Clophendales to Clophenberk [Klafterberg]; from there into Cuningesbrunnen. Through the descent [downstream] of this [river] into the Mümling [river]; through the ascent [upstream] of this [river] to Manegoldes-cellam [Klosterbrunnen]; from here into the River Mosaha [Marbach]. Through the ascent [upstream] of this [river] to Ellenbogen into the river Branbach [Brombach]. Through the descent of this [river] into the Mümling; from there to the oak tree between Grascapht [Grafschaft] and Munitat; then again [back] to Mount Mamenhart.

12. Einhard's Manumission of Meginfrid at St-Servais of Maastricht

There is a problem with the dating clause, in which the imperial year and Indiction do not agree, so it is not clear whether this manumission occurred in 819 or 821. A copy of this charter written in Tironian notes survives.

Source: translated from Formulae Imperiales, no. 35, ed. Wilhelm Schmitz, in Monumenta Germaniae Historica: Formulae Merowingici et Karolini Aevi, ed. Karl Zeumer (Hanover: Hahn, 1886), p. 313.

Ecclesiastical authority openly recommends and royal majesty, in addition, with its constant religious devotion agrees with the canonical decrees, that [if] any church chooses to advance someone from its own household into sacred orders, the one who is at that time the rector of that church should, in the presence of the priests and the other clerics living there according to canonical rule, and also [in the presence] of noble laymen, release this man with solemn manumission from his yoke of servitude and should confirm with a charter of manumission the freedom granted to him in the presence of those witnesses.

For this reason and in the name of God, I, Einhard, the venerable abbot of the monastery of St-Servais, the confessor of Christ, declare, by the authority of ecclesiastical and imperial decree, as stipulated above, this servant of our church, Meginfrid by name, [who has been] lifted to holy orders by the general agreement of our venerable congregation at the side of the altar in the presence of priests and noble men, to be a Roman [that is, free] citizen. By means of the transmission of this page, which was drawn up by me in order to confirm his free status, I release him from the bonds of servitude. And so from this day or time let him remain fully free and safe from all bonds of servitude as if he had been conceived by and born to free parents.

In short let him advance to that place, which the honor of canonical freedom will grant to him, finding the doors open to his [advancement] just as [they are for] other Roman [free] citizens. Thus, neither to us nor to our successors in turn should he owe any service of a detrimental or servile character, nor [should there be] any loosening of his free status; but [rather he should] live for all the days of his life under sure and complete freedom, just as other Roman citizens do, always truly free and safe by means of this legal title of manumission and freedom. And from the special [condition] that he holds, or whatever can follow from it, let him, according to canonical authority, freely do whatever he wishes.

And that this charter of manumission and freedom should obtain an undisturbed and unbreakable permanence, I signed below with my own hand, and I asked the priests and also the clergy of our church and also the noble laymen, who were present at this release, also to sign below.

Enacted at Maastricht in the monastery of St-Servais on the Nones of March [7 March] in the sixth year, with Christ's blessing, of the imperial reign of Lord [Louis], in the fourteenth Indiction.

I, Abbot Einhard, confirmed [this charter] by signing below with my own hand.

13. An Exchange of Dependents in 824

Since Egisharius was the deputy or vicedominus of Blandin, it is possible, that this exchange of dependents in 824 concerned Blandin and Notre-Dame of Argenteuil. Einhard did not apparently sign this contract.

Source: translated from Einhardi Chartae, ed. A. Teulet in Einhardi omnia quae exstant opera, vol.2 (Paris: Jules Renouard, 1840), pp.423-425.

With the assistance of the Lord Jesus Christ, it has pleased and suited Theodrada, the most noble abbess of the monastery of Notre-Dame of Argenteuil [near Paris], and also Einhard, the venerable abbot, together with the consent and approval of those depending upon the servants of God in the same place, to agree, in consenting to good people [that is, local nobles], that they ought to commute and exchange dependents between themselves, and so they did. Therefore, that very distinguished abbess Theodrada gave from the number [of the dependents] of Notre-Dame to the side of Abbot Einhard, a certain man, the priest Gulfolcus. Similarly [and] in compensation for this [grant], Lord Einhard, the venerable abbot, for his part, gave to the side of Notre-Dame two dependents with these names, Imbold and Vulfram, so that from this very day whatever each of us receives from this [exchange], each chose to do this for their own advantage and according to their own free will in all things. And to set down that agreement permanently between us and for the sake of our successors, we were inclined to write up and make two identical written accounts of this business, and this we did.

Neither we nor our successors should dare to raise any dispute [about] or go back on [this deal] at any time in dispute with the other party over that which he received from that party. Who[soever] will do that shall lose the thing received and, on top of that, shall be forced to open his purse and pay one pound of gold, six pounds of silver, to the other party. And this going back [on the deal] shall have no effect, but these present exchanges [of dependents] should remain firm and enduring.

Enacted at Argenteuil in the basilica of Notre-Dame, in the eleventh year of the reign [that is, 824] of Lord Louis, the most pious emperor.

† signed by Egisharius, vicedominus. † signed by Theotbald. † signed by Derulf. † signed by Berharius. † signed by Anelonus. † signed by Anseluc.

14. A Lease of Land Overseen by Einhard in 830

On 21 January 830 Abbot Einhard of Blandin approved a lease of land to a certain Nordbert. Some scholars believe that the original of this document survives [see Fig. 4].

Source: translated from Diplomata Belgica ante annum millesimum centesimum scripta, ed. M. Gysseling and A.C.F. Koch (Brussels: Belgisch Inter-Universitair Centrum, 1950), pp. 139-140.

Einhard, the venerable abbot in Christ, [declares].

It is not unknown that you purchased your properties and transferred them to our monastery and assigned and confirmed [them] for the work of the brothers, but afterwards you requested and we voluntarily agreed to provide that property with that land, which Thiodsumda [once] held through our benefice, to you Nordbert, and so we did. Since at certain times [of the year] you were accustomed to come to our monastery out of duty, we decided to give a prebend to you, and [in exchange] for the agricultural use [of the land] you raised the tax [paid] to us for that property, so that in each year you are obliged to pay two denarii on the feast of Saint Martin [11 November] and the brothers should receive that same tax [from you]. And so it seemed proper and right to us that you should not sell, give, estrange, or exchange that property, nor should you have the right of placing it in a state of disrepair, but rather that, as long as you shall live, you should determine to use and improve [it]. And, after your death, since you purchased [this property] and held [it] in benefice from us, and you previously transferred it [to us] in [the form of] an allod [or free hold], from that day [that is, the day of your death] the brothers ought to hold it for their own sustenance and work. And let

4. Charter 3.14 from 21 January 830 found in Ghent. Some scholars believe that this is an original charter and carries Einhard's own signature. After L.A. Warnkönig, *Flandrische Staats- und Rechtsgeschichte bis zum Jahr 1305*, facsimile III.

Odbertus be allowed to pay two solidii to this clergy and the brothers, who are [living] in the monastery, should receive that same tax [rent] on the anniversary of [your death] for the sake of your soul.

This lease [of land] was made in public in the monastery of Blandin on the twelfth day [before] the Kalends of February [21 January] in the sixteenth year of the reign of our Lord Louis, the most glorious emperor [that is, 830].

I Einhard abbot confirmed [it] and signed below.

Signed by Egisharius, the deputy [of Blandin]. Signed by Baduricus, keeper [and] priest. Signed by Winegarius, deacon [and] priest. Signed by Fletuuald, priest. Signed by Ermenland, priest. Signed by Regenmund, priest. Signed by Thegenland, priest. Signed by Hrodgarius, deacon. Signed by Johannes, subdeacon. Signed by Odric, subdeacon. Signed by Teutmund, cleric. Signed by Folcuuinzus, cleric. Signed by Sigebertus, cleric. Signed by Brunhard, cleric. Signed by Adalgarius, deacon. Signed by Egelmund, priest. Signed by Erchenmarus, priest.

I Rinhadus, a priest, wrote [out this charter].

15. A Lease of Land Confirmed by Abbot Einhard, 7 September 839

A lease was issued by Einhard in the interests of Blandin. Here although the monastery claimed the land and established its ownership, the right to live and work on the land was granted to Engelhard's family far into the future.

Source: translated from Diplomata Belgica ante annum millesimum centesimum scripta, ed. M. Gysseling and A.C.F. Koch (Brussels: Belgisch Inter-Universitair Centrum, 1950), p. 141.

From Einhard, the venerable abbot in Christ of the monastery of Blandin, to our beloved friend Engelhard.

It is not unknown that you transferred and bestowed on our monastery a certain allod of yours in the district of Rhodes, in a place called Vake [near Meldegem in Belgium] near the small river, Absencia. There is in that same place a house with some land, other buildings and a canal, and a field of arable land in Facharia [the area associated with Vake] able to produce fifteen modia [of grain] and a small meadow able to produce four cartloads of hay, and in Wieleghem a meadow able to produce twelve cartloads of hay. You transferred and bestowed all these things, [that is,] whatever is seen from that same house, on our monastery.

But afterwards you requested, and we agreed, to provide that same allod through our benefice to you Engelhard and to your wife Hiltrude, and so we did. And we released Hiltrude and your sons, safe and without service and rent; and instead of your inheritance [they received] that property, which

Engelramnus gave and confirmed to the monastery of Blandin, though our benefice. That [property] is in that district of Rhodes, and in that village called Vake near the small river Absencia, [and] there is in that same place a house with land, other buildings, and in the area which is called Facharia there is a field which can produce eleven modia, and a small meadow from which three cartloads of hay can be gathered, and in Wieleghem [land] able to produce twelve cartloads of hay. We provide all these things, whatever can be seen from the house, to you, Engelhard and Hiltrude, for your use and you should raise the rent from these two properties, so that each year you ought to pay on the feast of Saint Martin [11 November] four denarii. And whichever [of you] survives is allowed to hold both properties and to pay that same rent. And, after the deaths of them, their sons are permitted to pay this [rent] of six denarii; and after the demise of their sons, their nearest relatives are permitted to pay this.

This lease [of land] was made on the seventh day [before] the Ides of September [that is, 7 September], in the twenty-seventh year of the reign of our Lord Louis, the most glorious emperor.

† I, Einhard, the abbot, confirmed [this].

[Written out by] Barduin the monk.

4. ART AND ARCHITECTURE

Einhard's patronage of art and architecture may be the side of his career that we can know least well. His reputation as a Bezaleel or master craftsman was once considerable, but today we can associate very few objects with him. He may have been centrally involved in the design and production of objects that one can still see in Aachen today – bronze doors, grillwork, and pine-cones – but one cannot know what part he played in their production, for those marvelous and enduring objects are shrouded in the anonymity of church art. Photographs of the interior and exterior of Einhard's basilica at Steinbach can be found in most of the art books listed in the bibliography above. Perhaps, some day the script and manuscripts of Seligenstadt's scriptorium under Einhard will be identified, which would open one door to the identification of more Einhard materials.

Below the reader will find a few things that can be connected to Einhard with confidence.

5. The dedicatory panel inscribed in square capitals on Einhard's small triumphal arch said:

> EINHARD, A SINNER, STROVE TO SET UP AND DEDICATE TO
> GOD THIS ARCH TO SUPPORT THE CROSS OF ETERNAL VICTORY

6. This drawing of the arch was made by some unknown seventeenth-century antiquarian or engraver in Paris, Bibliothèque Nationale, fr. 10440. He preserved a surprising amount of information as to both the structure and iconography of the piece. Although his drawing consists of a single sheet, it has been broken into two sides here for better presentation on the facing pages. The front side should properly be this one with Christ as the central figure in the top register flanked by the twelve apostles. The second level presents the four evangelists with their writing stands. Their symbols are set in medallions; Mark with his lion symbol is the one our left; Luke with the symbol of the ox is on the right. The scene on the left end of the second register depicts John the Baptist beside a stream of water watching Christ approach and testifying that he is the Son of God [John 1:29-36]. Two of John's disciples are witnesses to his testimony [John 1:34-36]. Below that on the left side of the bottom register are two haloed standard-bearers. Two haloed soldiers with shields and lances turn toward the opening of the arch. The mounted warrior without halo on the inner panel of the arch spears a serpent which his horse tramples upon.

7. The back side of the arch contains the dedicatory inscription prominently displayed and perhaps raised in the top register [see Fig. 5], flanked by two angels. Above the arch in the second level is the Chi-Rho symbol of Christ and the two evangelists, Matthew with his symbol of a man to the left and John with the symbol of an eagle to the right. The left side panel contains a small scene of the Annunciation [Luke 1:26-38]. The bottom level contains not only the haloed standard-bearers on the left side, but holy warriors with shields and lances each facing toward the opening of the arch. The panel inside the arch contains a mounted warrior without halo who is spearing the serpent or dragon his horse is trampling upon.

8. Reconstruction of the arch. In order to show all aspects of the decoration of the arch, except for any design that may have been found on the horizontal piece at the top, the man who drew the arch distorted some of the angles, specifically the inner archway, and the cube base for the cross at the top of the arch. An attempt has been made in the computer reconstruction above to restore these angles and perspective to the arch.

9. The original, as is known from another drawing of the arch's dimensions, was eleven inches in height. The arch consisted of a wooden form overlaid with silver plate. The decorated front and back sides of the arch were roughly square and the round arch had dimensions not unlike those found on monumental ancient arches such as the Arch of Constantine. The decorative design on the ceiling of the arch and the lattice design of the cube on top of the arch remind one of some of the decorative effects achieved in bronze in Charlemagne's chapel.

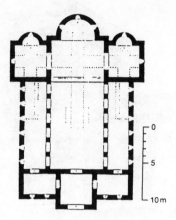

10. Plan of Einhard's basilica at Steinbach outside Michelstadt. The church was built between 815 and 827. After Otto Müller.

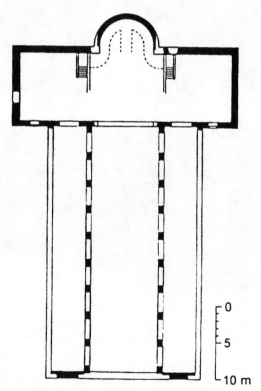

11. Plan of Einhard's church at Mulinheim [Seligenstadt]. The church was built between 830 and 836. After Otto Müller.

5. THE TRANSLATION AND MIRACLES OF THE BLESSED MARTYRS, MARCELLINUS AND PETER

Source: translated from Translatio et miracula sanctorum Marcellini et Petri auctore Einhardo, ed. G. Waitz, in Monumenta Germaniae Historica: Scriptorum, vol. 15.1 (Hanover: Hahn, 1888), pp.239–264.

[Preface]

Einhard, a sinner, [sends greetings] to the true worshippers and genuine lovers of the true God, of our Lord Jesus Christ, and of his saints.

Those who have set down in writing and recorded the lives and deeds of the just [that is, the saved] and of people living according to divine commands, seem to me to have wanted to accomplish nothing but to inspire by means of examples of this sort the spirits of all people to emend their evil ways and to sing the praises of God's omnipotence. These [writers] did this, not only because they lacked envy, but because they were completely full of charity, which seeks the improvement of all. Since their praiseworthy intention was so obviously to accomplish nothing other than those [goals] I described, I do not see why their [plan] should not be imitated by many other [writers]. Therefore, since I am aware that the books I have written, with what skill I could, concerning the translation of the bodies of the blessed martyrs of Christ, Marcellinus and Peter, and concerning the signs and miracles the Lord wished to bring about through them for the salvation of believers, were composed with the same wish and purpose [in mind], I have decided to disseminate these books and to offer them to the lovers of God to read. For I suppose that this book will not only seem deep and meaningful to the faithful, but I also assume that I will have worked productively and usefully if I am able to move the spirit of [even] one person reading these things to rise up in praise of its Creator.

[Book 1]

1. When I was resident at the palace and occupied with the business of the world, I used to give much thought to the retirement I hoped one day to enjoy. Due to the generosity of Louis, the ruler whom I then served, I [had] obtained a certain remote piece of property that was well out of most people's way. This estate is in Germany in the forest that lies halfway between the

Neckar and Main rivers [see Michelstadt on Map 3], which in these days is called Odenwald by both its inhabitants and those living nearby. I had constructed there, as far as my resources would allow, not only permanent houses and dwellings, but also a well-built church that was suitable for holding divine services. Then I became very concerned, wondering in whose name and honor – to which saint or martyr – that church should be dedicated.

After I had passed quite some time unsure what to do, it [so] happened that a certain deacon of the Roman church by the name of Deusdona came to the palace to appeal to the king for help in some pressing problems of his own. He remained there for some time and, when he had finished the business for which he had come, he was preparing to return to Rome. One day, to show courtesy to the traveler, I invited him to share a meager meal with us. Then, after we had spoken of many things over dinner, we came to a point in our conversation where the translation of the body of the blessed Sebastian was mentioned [Hilduin of St-Denis had acquired the relics of Sebastian in 826]. [We also spoke] of the neglected tombs of the martyrs, for there are many of those in Rome. When the conversation came to the [question of the] dedication of my new church, I began to inquire how I might arrange to obtain some particle of the genuine relics of the saints buried in Rome. At first, in fact, he hesitated, and stated that he did not know how it could be done. Then, when he saw that I was both distressed and intrigued by this business, he promised that he would respond to my inquiry on another day.

After that I invited him [to my place] again and he [then] produced a document from his purse and handed it to me. He asked me to read it thoroughly when I was alone and to be sure to tell him whether I liked what it said. I took the document and, as requested, read it carefully when I was alone. It said that he possessed many saints' relics at home and that he wished to give them to me, if [only] I could help him return to Rome. He knew that I had two mules [and said that], if I gave one to him and sent along one of my faithful men to receive the relics from him and bring them back to me, he would immediately send those [relics] to me. The plan he suggested was very appealing to me, and I hastily decided to check out the truth of his uncertain claim.

As a result, after giving him the animal he requested and even adding [some] money for his daily expenses, I ordered my notary, Ratleig, who had made a vow to travel to Rome to pray, to accompany him. Therefore, they set out from the palace at Aachen, where the emperor [Louis] was then holding court, and traveled to Soissons. There they spoke with Hilduin, the abbot of the monastery of St-Médard, because the deacon [Deusdona had] promised him that he could arrange for the body of the holy martyr Tiburtius to come into his possession. Seduced by these promises, [Hilduin] sent a certain priest, a cunning man by the name of Hunus, with them and ordered him to bring him back the body of the martyr [Tiburtius] once he had received it from [Deusdona]. And so having started out on their journey, they made their way as quickly as they could toward Rome [see Map 4].

2. After they had entered Italy, however, it happened that my notary's servant, whose name was Reginbald, was seized by a tertian fever [malaria]. His sickness led to a serious delay in their progress, since during those times when he was gripped by bouts of fever they could not continue their journey, for their number was small and they did not want to be separated from each other. Although their journey had been considerably delayed because of this trouble, they nevertheless tried to hurry as fast as they could. Three days before they reached [Rome], the feverish man had a vision in which a man in a deacon's clothes appeared to him and asked him why his master was rushing to Rome. When [Reginbald] revealed to him, as much as he knew, about the deacon's promises to send saints' relics to me and about what he had promised Abbot Hilduin, [the figure] said: "[Events] will not turn out as you think [they will], but quite differently, and yet the goal of your mission will [still] be achieved. For that deacon, who asked you to come to Rome, will bring about few or none of the things he promised you. For that reason, I want you to come with me and to pay careful attention to the things I am about to reveal and describe to you."

Then grasping him by the hand, which is how it seemed to him, he made him ascend with him to the peak of an extremely high mountain. When they stood on the summit together, he said: "Turn to the east and look down upon the landscape before your eyes!" When he had done that and had seen the landscape [the figure] had mentioned, he saw buildings of immense size rising up there like some great city. When he was asked if he knew what that was, he answered that he did not. Then [the figure] said, "That is Rome you see." He also added: "Direct your gaze to the more distant parts of the city and see if any church is visible to you there." And when he had said that, [Reginbald] did [in fact] see a certain church, and [his guide] said: "Go and tell Ratleig that in the church you just saw is hidden the very thing that he should carry to his lord. Let him strive to acquire it as soon as possible and then return to his lord." When he said that none of his companions would believe an account of this sort, [his guide] answered, saying: "You know that everyone making this journey with you is aware that you have stuggled with a tertian fever for many days [now] and that you have not yet been released from it." He said: "It is just as you say." His [guide] said, "For that reason, I wish [to

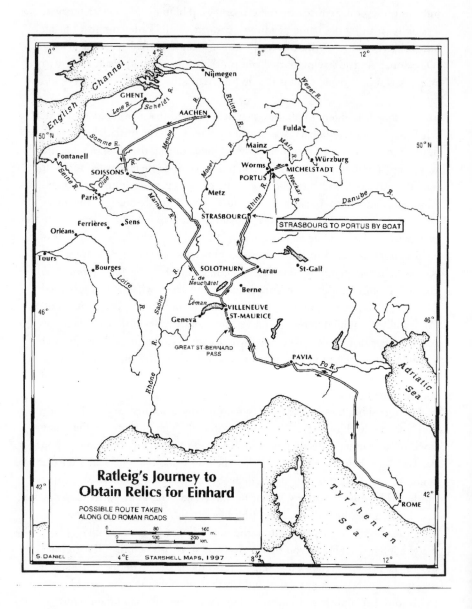

Map 4

provide] a sign to you and to those to whom you will recount what I have said, for from this [very] hour you will be so cured, by the mercy of God, from the fever that has gripped you until now, that it will no longer bother you on this journey." [Reginbald] awoke at these words, and made sure to recount everything he thought he had seen and heard to Ratleig. When Ratleig had revealed these things to the priest traveling with him, it seemed [prudent] to both of them to accept [as true] the experience of the dream if [Reginbald regained] his health as promised. On that very day, according to the usual nature of the fever he was suffering from, the one who had seen the dream should have become feverish [again]. But [the dream] was shown to have been a true revelation rather than a vain illusion, since he perceived no sign of the usual fever in his body on that day or on the ones that followed. Thus, they came to believe in the vision and [now] had no faith in the promises of the deacon [Deusdona].

3. When they arrived in Rome, they took up residence near the church of the blessed Apostle Peter that is called [St-Peter] in Chains, in the house of the very deacon with whom they had come. They stayed with him for some time, waiting for him to fulfill his promises. But that man, like those not able to carry out their promises, concealed his inability by procrastinating. Finally, they spoke to him and asked him why he wished to deceive them like that. At the same time they asked him not to detain them any longer by trickery or by delaying their return home with false hopes. When he had heard them out, and realized that he could now no longer take advantage of them with cunning of this sort, he first let my notary know that he could not [at present] obtain the relics I had been promised, because his brother, to whom he had entrusted his house and all his possessions while he was away, had left for Benevento on business and he had no idea when he would return. He had given him those relics to watch over, along with his other moveable property, but he was entirely unable to determine what he had done with them, since he had not found them in the house. Hence he did [not] see what he could do, since there remained nothing on his part that he could hope for.

After he said that to my notary, [Ratleig] complained that he had been deceived and badly treated by him. I do not know with what empty and meaningless words [Deusdona] spoke to Hilduin's priest, [but] he sent him away filled with little hope. The very next day, when he saw how sad they were, he urged them all to come with him to the saints' cemeteries, for it seemed to him that something could be discovered there that would satisfy their desires, and that there was no need for them to go home empty-handed. Since this plan appealed to them, they wanted to begin what he had urged them to do as soon as possible, [but] in his usual manner he neglected the matter and threw those men, whose spirits had been high a short while before, into such a state of despair by this postponement, that they gave up on [Deusdona] and resolved to return home, even though their business had not been accomplished.

4. But my notary, recalling the dream his servant had seen, began to press his partner [the priest Hunus] to go [with him] to the cemeteries without their host. [Deusdona had] promised that he wanted to take them there to see those [cemeteries]. Thus, after they had found and hired a guide to the [holy] places, they first traveled three miles outside the city to the church of the blessed martyr Tiburtius on the Via Labicana. There they investigated the tomb of the martyr with as much care as they could, and cautiously inspected whether it could be opened in such a way that others would not detect [it]. Then they descended into the crypt connected to the same church, in which the bodies of the blessed martyrs of Christ, Marcellinus and Peter, were entombed. After they had also examined the condition of this monument, they departed. They thought that they could hide their activity from their host, but it turned out otherwise than they supposed. Word of their activity quickly reached him, though they were unsure how. Since [Deusdona] was worried that they might achieve their goal without him, he was determined to thwart their plan and so rushed to them. He spoke to them seductively and advised them that, since he had a complete and detailed knowledge of those holy places, they should visit them together and, if God chose to answer their prayers, they would do [together and] as agreed upon by all whatever they thought they needed to do. They gave in to his plan and together set a time for carrying out [this business].

Then, after a fast of three days, they traveled by night to that place without any Roman citizens noticing them. Once in the church of St-Tiburtius, they first tried to open the altar under which it was believed his holy body was located. But the strenuous nature of the job they had started foiled their plan, for the monument was constructed of extremely hard marble and easily resisted the bare hands of those trying to open it. Therefore, they abandoned the tomb of that martyr and descended to the tomb of the blessed Marcellinus and Peter. There, once they had called on our Lord Jesus Christ [for help] and had adored the holy martyrs, they were able to lift the tombstone from its place covering the top of the sepulcher. Once it had been lifted off, they saw the most sacred body of Saint Marcellinus set in the upper part of that sepulcher and a marble tablet placed near his head. It contained an inscription clearly indicating which martyr's limbs lay there. They lifted up the body, treating it, as was proper, with the greatest reverence. After they had wrapped it in a clean linen shroud, they handed it over to the deacon [Deusdona] to carry and hold for them. Then they put the tombstone back into place, so that no trace of the body's removal would remain, and they returned to their dwelling place in Rome. The deacon, however, asserted that he could and would keep the body of the most holy martyr, which he had received, in that house where he lived, [which was located] near the church of the blessed Apostle Peter that is called [St-Peter] in Chains. He entrusted it to the care of his own brother Luniso. [Deusdona] thought that this [relic] would satisfy my notary [and so] began to urge him to return to his own country, now that he had obtained the body of the blessed Marcellinus.

5. But [Ratleig] was contemplating and considering something very different. For, as he told me later, it seemed wrong to him to return home with only the body of the blessed Marcellinus. [Indeed] it would almost be a crime for the body of the blessed martyr Peter, who had been his companion in death and who had for more than five hundred years rested with him in the same sepulcher, to remain there after his [friend] had left. Once this thought had occurred to him, his mind labored under such great anxiety and torment that he could neither eat nor sleep with any pleasure until the martyrs' bodies were joined together again on the trip they were about to make far from home, just as they had been joined together in death and in their tomb. He was in great doubt, however, about how this [reunification of the relics] could be achieved. For he realized that he could not find any Roman to help him in this affair, nor in fact was there [a Roman] to whom he dared reveal his secret thoughts. While wrestling with this worry in his heart, he happened to meet a foreign monk by the name of Basil who two years before had traveled from Constantinople to Rome. He resided in Rome with four of his students on the Palatine hill in a house occupied by other Greek [monks]. [Ratleig] went to him and revealed the [nature of the] anxiety troubling him. Then, encouraged by [the monk's] advice and confident of his prayers, he discovered such strength in his own heart that he was determined to attempt the deed as soon as he could, despite the danger to himself. He sent for his partner, Hilduin's priest, and suggested to him that they should return in secret to the church of the blessed Tiburtius, just as they had before, and try once again to open the tomb in which the body of the martyr was thought to be buried. This plan pleased [them] and [so], in the company of the servants they had brought with them [to Rome], they set out secretly at night. Their host had no idea where they were going. After this band had come to that place and prayed for success in their mission before the doors of the church, they

entered. The group [then] split up. The priest stayed with some of them to search for the body of the blessed Tiburtius in his church. Ratleig [descended] with the rest into the crypt connected to the church and approached the body of the blessed Peter. They opened the sepulcher with no trouble and [Ratleig] removed the sacred limbs of the holy martyr without any resistance and carefully placed the recovered [bones] on the silk cushion he had prepared for this purpose.

In the meantime, the priest who was looking for the body of the blessed Tiburtius had expended a great deal of energy without success. When he saw that he could accomplish nothing [there], he abandoned his efforts and descended into the crypt [to join] Ratleig. He started to ask him what he should do. [Ratleig] answered that he thought that the relics of Saint Tiburtius had [already] been found, and showed him what he meant by this. Not long before the priest had joined him in the crypt, he had discovered [something] in the very tomb in which the sacred bodies of the saints Marcellinus and Peter lay. For a hole, which was round in shape, almost three feet deep and one foot wide, had been excavated there and a substantial quantity of fine dust had been stored in it. It seemed to both of them that this dust could have been left there by the body of the blessed Tiburtius, if his bones had been removed from there. Perhaps, [at one time] his body had been placed in that tomb between the blessed Marcellinus and Peter to make it more difficult to discover. They agreed that the priest should collect that dust and take it away as the relics of the blessed Tiburtius. When they had settled and arranged things in this way, they returned to their dwelling with the objects they had discovered.

6. After this, Ratleig spoke to his host and asked him to return the sacred ashes of the blessed Marcellinus that he had entrusted to his care. He also requested that, since he wished to return to his own country, that [Deusdona] not detain him with any unnecessary delay. He not only restored immediately what was demanded, but also presented [Ratleig with] a substantial quantity of saints' relics collected together in a parcel that was supposed to be carried to me. When he was asked the names of these saints, he said that he would supply them to me after he had visited me. Nevertheless, he advised [Ratleig] that these relics should be cherished with the same veneration as the other relics of the holy martyrs, since they were worthy of the same respect before God as the blessed Marcellinus and Peter, and that I would realize this as soon as I knew their names. [Ratleig] accepted the gift he was offered and, as he had agreed, placed it alongside the bodies of the holy martyrs. After hitting upon a plan with his host [for secreting away the relics], he arranged for that

sacred and deeply desired treasure to be sealed and hidden in chests and for them to be carried as far as Pavia by Luniso, [Deusdona's] brother, whom I mentioned before, and also by Hilduin's priest with whom he had come. [Ratleig] himself stayed with his host in Rome, waiting and listening for seven consecutive days to determine whether any news of the removal of the bodies of the saints had come to the attention of the people [of Rome]. After he observed that no mention was made of this deed by any stranger and he judged that this business was still unknown, he started out [see Map 4] after those whom he had sent in advance and took along his host [Deusdona]. They found them awaiting their arrival in Pavia in the church of the blessed John the Baptist that is commonly called Domnanae and that was then under my possession through a benefice of the kings [Louis and Lothar]. They too [Ratleig and company] decided to stop there for a few days, in order to give the horses on which they were riding a rest and to ready themselves for the longer journey ahead.

7. During this delay, a rumor arose that representatives of the holy Roman church, sent by the pope to the emperor, would shortly arrive there. Since [Ratleig and company] feared that, if they were found there when [the papal party] arrived, they might experience some inconvenience or even some obstacle [to their return], they decided that some of their party by leaving at once could depart [with the relics] before their arrival. The rest of the party, [however], would remain there and after the business they were concerned about had been carefully investigated and those representatives [of the pope] had departed, they would hurry to follow their companions, whom they had sent on in advance. After they had agreed upon [this plan] among themselves, Deusdona and Hilduin's priest departed before the representatives from Rome arrived. They traveled with as much speed as they could to Soissons, where Hilduin was believed to be. But Ratleig stayed in Pavia with the treasure he was holding, waiting for the representatives of the Apostolic See to come and go, so that when they had crossed the Alps he could make his own way with more safety. Still he feared that Hilduin's priest, who had gone ahead with Deusdona and who had a full and complete knowledge of everything they had done and decided, and who seemed so cunning and slimy, had probably plotted to place some obstacle for him along the route by which he had chosen to travel. [So Ratleig] decided to travel by a different route. First he sent the servant of my steward Ascolf to me with a letter apprising me of his own return and of the treasure that he had discovered with divine assistance and was [now] carrying to me. After calculating the number of stops made ready for the [other party], he thought that they must have already

crossed the Alps and [so] he left Pavia and reached St-Maurice in six days [a distance of approximately 240 kms or 150 miles]. There he purchased the things he needed [to construct a bier] and placed the sacred bodies, which were enclosed in a reliquary, upon the bier. From that point on, and with the help of the people flocking to them, he began to carry the relics publicly and openly.

8. When, however, he had gone by that place known as the Head of Lake [that is, Villeneuve in Switzerland], he reached the point where the way leading into Francia splits into two. He took the path to the right and came via the territory of the Alemannians to Solothurn, a town of the Burgundians. There he encountered the people I had sent from Maastricht to meet him after word of his return had reached me. For when the letter of my notary was brought to me by my steward's servant, the one I mentioned before, I was at the monastery of St-Bavo on the Scheldt River. After reading that letter I learned about the approach of the saints and I immediately ordered a member of my household to go to Maastricht to collect priests, other clergymen, and also laymen there, and then to hasten to meet the oncoming saints at the first possible place. With no delay, he and the group he brought with him met up in a few days with those who were carrying the saints at the place I mentioned above [Solothurn]. They joined forces at once and were accompanied from that point on by an ever increasing crowd of chanting people. Soon they came, to the great joy of everyone, to the city of Argentoratus, which is now called Strasbourg. From there they sailed down the Rhine until they came to a place called Portus [the port at Sandhofen] where they disembarked on the eastern shore of the river, and, after a trip lasting five days and with a great crowd of people reveling in the praise of God they came to that place called Michelstadt. It lies in the German forest known today as Odenwald and is located about six leagues from the Main River. In that place they found the church I had recently built, but had still not dedicated, and they carried those sacred ashes into it and deposited them as though they were destined to stay there forever.

9. When that news reached me, I immediately hurried to that place as quickly as I could. Three days after my arrival, at the end of the evening service, a certain servant of Ratleig, who was acting on his [master's] orders, remained alone in the church, which was empty and had its doors closed. He took up a position on a small stool next to those holy bodies, as though he would keep watch [over them]. Suddenly he fell asleep and seemed to see two doves fly through a choir window on the right side [of the church] and come to rest

on the top of the bier above the saints' bodies. One of the doves appeared to be entirely white, the other to be variously colored grey and white. After they had walked back and forth on the top [of that bier] for a long time and had made again and again the cooing sound normally made by doves, as if they were talking to each other, they [finally] flew out through the same window and were not to be seen [any more]. Then, all at once, a voice spoke above the servant's head: "Go and tell Ratleig to announce to his master [Einhard] that these holy martyrs of his do not want their bodies to rest in this place, because they have selected another place to which they intend to move very soon." He could not see the one who spoke in this way, but when the sound stopped he awoke. Now awake, he told Ratleig, who had returned to the church, what he had seen. [Ratleig] was anxious to relate to me the very next day, as soon as he could see me, what his servant had reported to him. For my part, although I did not dare to spurn the sacred secret of this vision, I nevertheless decided to await evidence of some more certain sign [of its truth]. In the meantime I arranged for those sacred ashes to be removed from the linen shroud in which they had been bound up and carried and to be sewn up in new silk cushions. Upon inspecting them, I noticed that the relics of the blessed Marcellinus were smaller in quantity than those of Saint Peter. I thought that [perhaps Saint Marcellinus] had been of smaller size than Saint Peter in the stature of his body. But the discovery of a theft later on proved that this was not so. Where, when, by whom, and how this theft was committed and [finally] uncovered I shall describe at the proper time. For now the sequence of the story as I have begun to relate it must be laid out and consistently followed.

10. After I had inspected that great and wonderful treasure, which was more valuable than gold, the reliquary in which it was held began to displease me a great deal, because of the poorness of the material out of which it was made. I wanted to improve it, [and so] one day at the end of the evening service I directed one of the sacristans to find out for me the dimensions of the reliquary as measured by a ruler. When he was about to do this he lit a candle and raised the cloth covering the reliquary; then he noticed that the reliquary was dripping all over in an amazing fashion with a bloody liquid. Frightened by the strangeness of this phenomenon, he immediately made sure to tell me what he had seen. I went there at once with the priests who were present and I [too] with wonder observed that awesome and true miracle. For just as columns, tiles, and marble statues commonly sweat and drip when rain is coming on, so that reliquary containing those most sacred bodies was drenched with blood and was dripping all over. The unusual nature of this

miracle, which had never been heard of before, terrified us. Thus, we devised a plan and decided to spend three days fasting and praying, in order to be worthy of learning by a divine revelation what that great and ineffable sign meant and what it wanted done. When the three days of fasting had passed and twilight was coming on, that liquid of frightening blood suddenly began to dry up. It was amazing, but that liquid, which had dripped for seven straight days without stopping like some incessant stream, dried up so quickly in a few hours that when the bell called us to the night service, for it was Sunday and we celebrated before dawn, and we entered the church, no trace of blood could still be found on the reliquary. But I ordered that the linen cloth hanging around the reliquary, which had been splashed with that liquid and so was stained with bloody spots, should be saved. To this day considerable evidence of that unique portent remains on those linens. Indeed, it is agreed that that liquid had a somewhat salty taste similar to that of tears and had the consistency of water, but that it possessed the color of real blood.

11. On that same night, in a dream, one of our servants by the name of Roland saw two young men standing at his side. They commanded him, as he himself reported, to tell me many things about the necessity of translating the bodies of the saints. They revealed to him both to what place and how this transfer ought to take place. They menaced him in frightening ways, demanding that this must be announced to me at once. As soon as he could, he carefully told me everything that he had been ordered to tell me. When I had learned of these things, I was very troubled and began to wonder what I should do. Should I again order fasts and prayers and should God once again be asked to resolve my doubt? Or should I seek out some individual serving God with perfect devotion, to whom I could reveal the worry in my heart and the plaintive nature of my troubles, and whom I could ask to pray to God to reveal the meaning of this thing to us? But where and when could I find such a servant of the Lord Christ, particularly in this region? For although it was known that some monasteries had been founded not far from us, nevertheless, because of the crude regulation of [religious] life in those places, there was no one, or few men, about whose holiness anything, even the slightest rumor, was spoken. In the meantime, while I was troubled by these worries and had prayed for the intercession of the holy martyrs and had eagerly advised everyone around me to do the same, it happened that for twelve straight days no night passed in which it was not revealed in dreams to one, two, or even three of our companions that the bodies of the saints should be transferred from that place [Michelstadt] to another.

On the last night, a certain man in the dress of a priest, who was distinguished by the venerable whiteness of his hair and who was dressed all in white, appeared in a vision to a certain priest from our church by the name of Hiltfrid. He himself reported that [this man] addressed him in words like these: "Why is Einhard so hard-hearted and so stubborn that he refuses to believe these many revelations and supposes that he should scorn these many warnings sent to him from heaven? Go and tell him that what the blessed martyrs want done with their bodies cannot remain undone, even though until now he has put off satisfying their wishes in this matter. But let him now hurry, if he does not want the reward for this deed to pass to another, to fulfill their command and not fail to transport their bodies to the place they have selected."

12. After these and other warnings of various kinds had been brought to my attention, it seemed to me that the translation of the sacred ashes should not be postponed any longer. And so, after we had devised a plan, I decided to try to achieve [the transfer] as quickly as possible. Therefore, after everything that seemed necessary for transporting [the relics] was rapidly and with greatest care readied, we lifted up that sacred and priceless treasure at dawn after the completion of the morning Mass and started on our way. There was great sadness and grief among those who were to remain behind [at Michelstadt], as we started on our journey. As we began to carry [the relics] we were accompanied by a throng of poor people, who had gathered there from one place or another at that time to receive charity. The people who lived nearby were entirely ignorant about what we were doing. The sky was full of dark clouds that could soon turn into a heavy rain unless divine power prevented it. Indeed, it [had] rained so hard without stopping the [previous] night, that it had almost not seemed possible for us to begin our journey that day. But that doubt of ours sprang from the weakness of our faith, for divine grace, because of the saints' merits, arranged something very different from what we had expected. We found that the way through which we were traveling had been changed into another condition than the anticipated one. For we found that there was little mud and that the streams that usually rise after so much and such steady rain as there had been that night had hardly risen at all. When we left the forest and approached the nearest villages, we were intercepted by constant crowds of people praising God. These people accompanied us for a distance of almost eight leagues. They were committed to helping me and my party carry the sacred burden and they actively joined with us in singing divine praises.

13. But when we saw that we could not reach our destination that day, we stopped at a village called Ostheim, which we could see from the road. With night now falling, we carried those holy bodies into the church of St-Martin

located in that village. While our companions were left there to act as guards [of the relics], I and a few others hurried on toward our final destination. During the night, I prepared those things that ritual stipulates for the reception of saints' bodies.

But a partially paralyzed nun by the name of Ruodlang was brought to the church in which we had left that very holy treasure. She belonged to the convent of Mosbach that lies about one league from that church and had been brought there on a cart by her friends and relatives. After she had spent the entire night along with others awake and praying beside the bier of the saints, health was restored to all her limbs. With no one helping her or propping her up in any way, she walked the next day on her own feet all the way back to the place she had come from.

14. Now we rose at daybreak and went out to meet our approaching companions. We had with us a huge throng of our neighbors, who were excited by the rumor of the arrival of the saints. For this reason, they had gathered before our [church] doors at the first light of dawn, in order to travel out with us to meet the saints. We encountered them at the spot where the small river Gersprinz flows into the Main River [near Aschaffenburg]. From there we traveled on together and, praising in unison the mercy of our Lord Jesus Christ, we carried, to the great happiness and joy of all who were there, the sacred remains of the most blessed martyrs to Upper Mulinheim [later renamed Seligenstadt], for that is how that place is called in our day. But, because a great throng of people preceded us and had blocked every way [forward], we were unable to reach the church or to carry the bier into it. And so in a nearby field, which was on higher ground, we erected an altar in the open air. After depositing the bier behind the altar, we celebrated the solemn rights of the Mass. When the service was finished and the crowd had gone home, we carried those most sacred bodies into the church [as] specified by the blessed martyrs [themselves]. There we placed the bier beside the altar and celebrated the Mass once again.

While the Mass was being celebrated there, a boy about fifteen years old by the name of Daniel, from the Portian region, who had come there with other poor people to beg and who was so bent over that if he did not lay on his back he could not see the sky, approached the bier. Suddenly he collapsed as if he had been struck by someone. After he had lain there a long time like someone sleeping, all his limbs were made straight and he regained the strength of his muscles. He got up before our eyes and was healthy. This happened on the sixteenth [day before the] Kalends of February [17 January 828] and the light that day was so great and so clear that it rivaled the brilliance of the summer sun and the air was so calm and gentle that it seemed, along with the warming sunshine, milder than spring.

15. The next day [18 January] we placed the sacred bodies of the blessed martyrs, now enclosed in a new reliquary, in the apse of the church, and, as is the practice in Francia, we erected over it a wooden structure and, in order to beautify it, covered it with linen and silk cloth. Beside it, we placed an altar and erected on either side the two standards of the Lord's passion that had been carried before the bier on its journey. I tried within the extent of my limited means to make that place suitable and appropriate for the celebration of divine services. Clerics were appointed to keep permanent watch there and to devote themselves constantly and willingly to chanting the praises of the Lord. These men were summoned [to this task] not just by me, but by a royal charter that reached me on the road. The Lord made my journey a successful one and I returned to the palace [at Aachen] in an extremely joyful spirit.

[Book Two]

1. Quite a few days later after arriving at court, I went to the palace early one morning, since it was the habit of courtiers to rise very early. After entering, I found Hilduin there, of whom I had spoken in the previous book. He was sitting before the doors of the royal bedchamber waiting for the ruler to come out. After greeting him in the usual way, I asked him to get up and come over to a certain window with me, from which one could look [down] into the lower parts of the palace. Standing side by side while leaning on the window, we spoke with great wonder of the translation of the holy martyrs Marcellinus and Peter and also about the miracle revealed by the stream of blood with which, as I recorded, their reliquary sweated for seven days. When we had reached that point in our conversation where the subject of the garments found with their bodies was raised, I observed that the garment of the blessed Marcellinus was remarkably fine. [Hilduin], like one who had observed the same thing I had, responded that I had spoken the truth about that garment. I was astonished and surprised at this, [and so] I began to ask him how he had acquired his knowledge of garments he had never seen. He stared at me, but remained silent for a time. Then he said, "I suppose it would be better for you to hear this from me, since [even] if I don't tell you, you will soon learn of it from others [anyway]. I myself should be the direct betrayer of this [news], since should anyone else betray it, he would not report [it to you] as directly [as I can]. Nor, indeed, could he [report it], since it is only

natural that no one can tell the whole truth about something if he gained his knowledge of it not by himself, but from the stories told by others. Thus, I am counting on your good faith as to how you will act toward me after you have heard from me the whole truth about this incident." When I had responded briefly that I would not act other than as we had agreed, he said: "That priest, who traveled to Rome on my orders to bring back the relics of the blessed Tiburtius, discovered that he could not accomplish the goal for which he had come. So, after your notary had taken up the relics of the holy martyrs we have been talking about and had decided to return home, [Hunus] devised a plan with him whereby [Ratleig] would remain in Rome for a short time. He himself and Luniso, Deusdona's brother, along with the men who were assigned to carry those sacred ashes would proceed to Pavia and wait there for the arrival of [Ratleig] and Deusdona. This agreement suited both of them, and so, while [Ratleig and Deusdona] remained in Rome, my priest along with Luniso and the servants carrying the relics started out for Pavia. After they arrived there, they placed the cases containing the sacred ashes behind the altar. These were watched with constant attention by vigilant clerics and laymen. But one night while the priest himself was on watch along with others in the church, it happened, as he himself maintains, that around the middle of the night sleep gradually stole over every single person who had gathered in the church to guard [the relics], except the priest. Then the thought occurred to him that it was unlikely that sleep would have so suddenly overcome so many people without some powerful cause. He thought that he should seize the opportunity offered [to him] and so he arose and by candlelight proceeded quietly to the cases [containing the relics]. Then he burned the strings of the seals with the candle's flame and hurriedly opened the cases without [using] a key. He removed what seemed to him a [moderate] portion of each body and [then] he refastened the seals with the ends of the burned strings as though they were intact. Since no one was aware of his action, he returned to his place. Later on, after he had returned to me, he presented me with the saints' relics he had removed by this theft. At first he claimed that they were not the relics of Saint Marcellinus or Peter, but of Saint Tiburtius. Then, although I don't know what he was afraid of, he spoke to me in secret and fully disclosed to which saints the relics belonged and also how he had acquired them. I am holding those collected relics honorably at St-Médard in a prominent place where they are cherished with great veneration by all the faithful. But whether it is right for us to keep them [or not] is for you to decide."

After I heard this, I recalled what I had heard from a certain host of mine on my recent trip to the palace. Among the other things he told me, he said,

"Have you not heard the rumor about the holy martyrs Marcellinus and Peter that is spreading throughout this area?" When I said that I was unaware of it, he said, "Those coming from Saint Sebastian say that some priest of Abbot Hilduin traveled to Rome with your own notary. While they were returning from there and were sharing lodgings at a certain spot, all your people were overcome with drink and sleep and were entirely unaware of what happened. For [that priest] opened the cases containing the saints' bodies and removed them. When he returned [home], he delivered [the relics] to Hilduin, and now they are at St-Médard. Apparently little of the sacred dust was left in your own cases, the ones carried to you by your notary." When I had remembered this story and compared it to the one related by Hilduin, I was extremely upset, particularly since I have not as yet found a way to do away with that horrible rumor that was spread everywhere by the cunning of the devil or to drive it out of the hearts of the deceived masses. Nevertheless, I thought it best to ask Hilduin to restore to me what had been removed from my cases. After his voluntary confession, he could not deny that the relics had been brought to him and that he had received them. In fact I tried to bring about this [recovery] as quickly as I could. And although [Hilduin] was slightly more stubborn and difficult in agreeing to this than I might have wished, he was eventually won over by my persistent request. [Hilduin] had a little while before proclaimed that in this matter in particular he would submit to the judgment of no one, but he [finally] gave in to my censure.

2. In the meantime I sent a letter to Ratleig and Luniso, who were in the place [Seligenstadt] where I had deposited the bodies of the martyrs. I made sure to inform them of the sort of rumor about those holy martyrs that was spreading throughout most of Gaul. And I urged them in the strongest possible terms to ponder whether they could remember or identify some such event or something like those events that Hilduin claimed were committed on their journey by his priest. They immediatley came to me at the palace and told a story very different from Hilduin's. They especially declared that everything that the priest had told Hilduin was false. After they had left Rome, there had never been an opportunity for that priest or for anyone else to commit a crime of that sort. But they agreed that the [theft] of the sacred ashes of the martyrs had occurred in another way, for it had happened in Rome at the house of Deusdona through the greed of Luniso and the trickery of Hilduin's priest. For it had occurred during that time when the body of the blessed Marcellinus, after it had been lifted from its tomb, was being kept in the house of Deusdona. They said that it had happened in this way. That priest of Hilduin had been so thwarted in his hope of gaining the body

of Saint Tiburtius, that he was determined, in order not to return to his lord with nothing, to acquire by fraud what he had not been able to acquire honorably. Since he knew that Luniso was poor and, consequently, greedy, [Hunus] approached him and offered him four gold coins and five silver pieces, [and so] lured him into committing this act of betrayal. After receiving the proffered money, [Luniso] opened the chest in which the body of the blessed Marcellinus had been laid and locked up by Deusdona, and he gave that worthless rascal [Hunus] permission, just as he had hoped he would, to take from it what he wanted. He was not moderate in his theft, for it seemed that he removed as much of the sacred ashes of the blessed martyr as a pint container could hold. That the theft was committed in this way, Luniso himself, who had engineered the scheme with the priest, confessed in tears and threw himself at my feet. With the truth of the matter now known, I ordered Ratleig and Luniso back to the place they had come from [that is, Seligenstadt].

3. After I had spoken with Hilduin and we had reached an agreement about when the sacred relics would be returned to me, I sent two clerics from my household, Hiltfrid and Filimar – one was a priest and the other a subdeacon – to Soissons to receive the relics. I sent along with them 100 gold coins as a gift to the place from which the relics were to be carried away. After [my men] had arrived on Palm Sunday [29 March 828] at the monastery of St-Médard, they stayed there for three days. Once they had received that incomparable treasure they had been sent [to retrieve], they returned to the palace as quickly as they could in the company of two monks from the same monastery. But they gave the relics not to me, but to Hilduin. When he received them, he arranged for them to be held in the chapel of his house, until after the many engagements of Easter [which fell on 5 April] were over and he would have the free time in which to show me what was to be returned before he [actually] returned it. When eight days or even more had passed after holy Easter and the king had left the palace to go hunting, Hilduin, according to what we had agreed, removed those relics from his oratory where they had been held, and carried them into the church of the Holy Mother of God [Charlemagne's chapel at Aachen], and set them down upon the altar. He arranged for me to be summoned to receive those relics. Then he opened the box containing the relics and showed them to me, so that I could see what it was that he was returning and what it was that I was receiving. Next he lifted up that same box from the altar and set it in my hands. Once a fitting prayer had been given, he even took on the role of choirmaster and called upon clerics, who were skilled in singing psalms, to sing an

appropriate antiphon for the praise of the martyrs. And so, with everyone singing, he followed us to the door of the church as we withdrew with that priceless treasure. Praising the mercy of God, we moved slowly from [the church] with crosses and candles [in front of us] to the chapel that had been crudely constructed in my house. I carried the sacred relics into that [chapel], since no other [suitable] place was available there.

4. But on that procession we made, as I said, from the church to my chapel, something of a miracle occurred that I don't think I should neglect to mention. For as we were leaving the church and singing with raised voices to our Lord God, a great and sweet smell filled that part of the city of Aachen that lies west of the church. Almost all the residents of that part [of the city] and also everyone who happened to be there for some reason or for some business were so divinely affected by that fragrance that they dropped the work they were doing and all quickly raced first to the church and, then, as if [by following] the smell, to my chapel, for they had heard that those relics had been carried there. A great crush of people who were both full of joy and wonder gathered within the walls [of my house]. Although a great part of the crowd that collected there didn't know what was happening, they were nevertheless filled with great excitement and together they praised the mercy of almighty God.

5. After the rumor had spread far and wide that the relics of the martyr, Saint Marcellinus, had been carried [into my chapel], a huge crowd [of people] constantly collected there. They came not only from the city of Aachen itself and the neighboring and nearby towns, but also from more distant places and districts. Indeed, there was no easy way for us to enter that chapel to celebrate a divine service except during the evening or night hours. Sick people were brought there from all parts and friends and relatives deposited those suffering from various illnesses near the walls of the chapel. You would have seen there that almost every kind of infirmity, affecting both sexes and people of all ages, was cured by means of the power of the Lord Christ and the merit of that most blessed martyr. Sight was restored to the blind, the ability to walk to the lame, hearing to the deaf, and speech to the speechless. Even the paralyzed and those who had completely lost control over their bodies were carried forward by the hands of strangers. Once cured, they returned home on their own [two] feet.

6. When Hilduin brought these things to the attention of the king, [Louis] at first planned, after he had returned to the palace, to come to my chapel, in

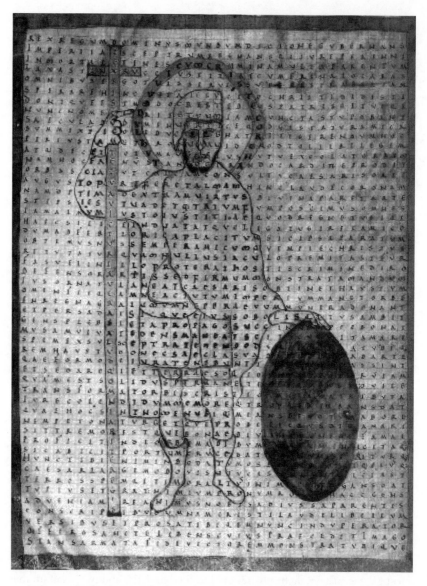

12. An image of Louis the Pious from a tenth-century copy of Hrabanus Maurus's *On the Praises of the Holy Cross*. Paris, Bibliothèque Nationale, lat. 2421, fol. 1v.

which these [miracles] were occurring, to venerate the martyr. But he was stopped from doing that by Hilduin himself who suggested that [the king should instead] order the relics brought to the larger church [of St-Mary]. When they had been carried there, he venerated them and prayed humbly. After the solemn celebration of the Mass, he granted to the blessed martyrs, Marcellinus and Peter, a small estate named Ludolvesthorp [near Sinzig] located close to the River Ahr; it has fifteen homesteads and nine arpents [an arpent was 120 square feet] of vineyards. And the queen [Judith] presented a belt made of gold and jewels that weighs three pounds. After the conclusion of these events, the relics were returned to their own place, namely in my chapel, and there they stayed for forty days or more until the emperor left the palace to go hunting in the forest, as was his annual practice. After that, I too, after purchasing the things needed for our journey [to Seligenstadt], left the town of Aachen with the relics.

7. At the very point of our departure, however, a certain old woman well-known around the palace, who was around eighty years old and suffering from a tightening of her tendons, was cured in front of us. I learned from her own account that she had suffered from this affliction for fifty years and had managed to walk by crawling around like a four-legged animal on her hands and knees.

8. After that we began our journey and, thanks to the merits of the saints, we came at last on the sixth day, with the Lord's help, to the village of Mulin-heim [Seligenstadt], where I had left the sacred ashes of the blessed martyrs when I had departed for court [in January]. I must report how much joy and happiness the arrival of those relics brought to the people living along [our] route, but it cannot be related or described in all its richness. Nevertheless, I must try to describe it, so that it not seem that something that brought forth so much praise of God was buried in silence because of my laziness. To begin with, I am anxious to report what I and many others remember having seen after we left the palace. A stream called the Wurm [which flows into the Ruhr] lies about two miles from the palace of Aachen and has a bridge across it. When we reached it, we stopped for a short time so that the crowd that had followed us all the way from the palace and now wanted to turn back might have an opportunity to pray. One of the men who was praying there approached the relics with another man and, turning to his companion, said, "For the love and honor of this saint, I release you from the debt you know you owe me." For he owed him, as that man admitted, half a pound of silver. Likewise, another man led a companion by the hand to the relics, and said,

"You killed my father and for that reason we have been enemies. But now, for the love and honor of God and this saint, I want to end our feud and to make and enter into an agreement with you that henceforth we shall maintain a lasting friendship between us. Let this saint be a witness to the reconciliation we have promised each other and let him punish the first person tempted to destroy this peace."

9. At this point the crowd that had left the palace with us, after adoring and kissing the sacred relics and after shedding many tears, which they could not restrain because everyone was filled with so much joy, returned home. Then another crowd met us and these people joined us in singing the *Kyrie eleison* without stopping until we reached another place where we were overtaken by others also hurrying to meet us. Then, just as before, the [second] crowd said prayers and returned home. In this way, we were joined every day from dawn to dusk by crowds of people praising the Lord Christ, and, with the Lord watching over our journey, we traveled from the palace at Aachen to Mulinheim [Seligenstadt]. Then we placed those relics [of Marcellinus], which were stored in a bejeweled box, upon the altar behind which was the reliquary containing the [rest of the] sacred ashes of the martyrs.

10. The relics remained in that position until November [828], when, as I was getting ready to travel to the palace, I was warned by a vision not to leave there before I had rejoined those relics to the body from which they had been removed. But how it was revealed that this should be done must be related, since it was made manifest not only through a dream, where it normally occurs, but even through some signs and frightening incidents experienced by those guarding [the relics] that the blessed martyrs wanted their commands followed down to the last detail in this business.

11. One of the clerics assigned to stand guard in the church was a man by the name of Landulf. His bed was near the eastern door of the church and he was in charge of ringing the bell. [Once] he had risen as usual and had solemnly rung the bell as usual for the evening and morning services, but then with his duty done before dawn, he wished to go back to sleep. He closed the doors of the church and prostrated himself in prayer before the holy ashes of the martyrs. Then, as he himself claims, when he had begun to say the fiftieth Psalm, he heard close to him the sound of footsteps on the ground, as if a man was walking back and forth there. He was very afraid and raised himself up a little onto his knees and began to look all around, thinking that one of the poor had stayed behind after the doors had been closed and was [now]

lurking in some corner of the church. When he realized that he was the only person inside the church, he kneeled down again in prayer and resumed the psalm that he had begun earlier. But before he could complete even one verse of it, the box containing the sacred relics of the blessed Marcellinus, which had been set upon the altar, suddenly began to shake and make such a loud noise that it was as if it had flown open after being struck by a hammer. Two of the church's doors, the western and the southern ones, also made a similar racket, as though someone was shaking and pounding them.

He was so terrified and shocked by this, not knowing what to do, that he got up from the altar and threw himself trembling upon his bed. Almost immediately he was overcome by sleep and saw a man whose face he didn't recognize standing beside him. He addressed him with words like these: "Is it the case," he said, "that Einhard wishes to rush so quickly to the palace that he may not first restore the relics of Saint Marcellinus, which he brought here, to the place from which they were removed?" When he answered that he did not know anything about this, he said, "Get up at dawn and command him on the authority of the martyrs not to dare to leave here or to go anywhere before he has returned those relics to their proper place." Startled from his sleep he arose and, as soon as he could, he saw me and urgently told me what he had been ordered to relate. Indeed, I did not think that a matter of this [importance] should be acted upon slowly, but rather I judged that what the saints had ordered must be carried out at once. In fact, on that very day I ordered the preparation of those things that seemed necessary [for the task]. On the following day, I delicately joined those sacred relics to the body from which they had been removed.

That the blessed martyrs were grateful for this is proved by the clear evidence of the following miracle. For the very next night, while we were solemnly seated in the church for the morning service, an old man, who was not able to walk, came forward with great difficulty to pray, crawling on his hands and knees. Before all of us and within an hour of entering the church he was so completely cured by God's power and the merits of the blessed martyrs that in fact he no longer required the support of a crutch in order to walk. He also stated that he had been deaf for five straight years, but that his hearing had been restored to him at the same time as his ability to walk.

After these events had transpired, I proceeded to court, as I said before I had intended to. I would spend the winter there thinking over these many events.

[Book Three]

[Preface]

I am about to write of the remarkable things and miracles that those most blessed martyrs of Christ, Marcellinus and Peter, brought about in various places after their most sacred bodies had been transported from Rome into Francia. Rather [I should say] that it is through their holy merits and pious prayers that God himself, our Lord Jesus Christ, the king of martyrs, deigned to bring about these [miraculous] cures for people. I think it is necessary to mention in this brief preface that most of the things I have decided to record were brought to my attention by the accounts of others. But I was entirely convinced to trust these accounts, because of the things I myself had seen and knew personally. Thus I was able to believe without the slightest doubt that these events, which were reported to me by those who said that they themselves had witnessed them, were true, even though I might, up until then, have had little or no [personal] knowledge of the individuals from whom I had heard these things.

Still, it seems [best to me] to record first of all those [miracles and cures] I myself saw and that happened in the place [Seligenstadt] to which those most blessed martyrs had said their sacred ashes should be translated. After that those [miracles] that occurred in the palace at Aachen under the very eyes of the courtiers should be recalled. Then I thought I should record those things that were reported to have happened in various places to which, at the request of religious men and by my permission, the sacred relics were carried. If I stick to this plan in my account, none of the various signs and miracles that came to the attention of my Smallness should be left out.

But now that the preface is complete, let me set forth the miracles themselves, for they need to be described.

1. As already set out above [in the previous books], the sacred bodies of the blessed martyrs were brought to the great joy of the faithful to that place in which they now rest. They had themselves ordered [this translation] and we had complied. After a Mass had been solemnly celebrated in a field [see 5.1.14], the relics were carried in the hands of priests, for a large number of them had gathered there at that time, into the church. The bier on which the [relics] were carried was set down near the altar. Another service had just begun there, when suddenly a young man, who was suffering from kidney failure and so was bent over and supporting himself on crutches, burst forth from the middle of the crowd of people standing around. He wanted to bow down in adoration and [so] fell forward onto his knees, but [this happened] in

a remarkable way, for it was as though someone had pulled him away or, rather, pulled him back, so that he fell on his back and lay there like someone sleeping for a very long time. Then, as if he were waking up, he lifted himself into a sitting position and, a little while later, got up with no one's help. He stood in the middle of the crowd surrounding him and praised the mercy of God and gave thanks along with the others for the restoration of his health. He told me, when I asked, that he had come there [to Seligenstadt] from the Portian district with other poor people and pilgrims, and that his name was Daniel.

2. At almost the same hour and, indeed, at the exact same moment, if I may put it so, at which [Daniel], about whom I was just speaking, regained his health within the church before the altar by means of the power of Christ and the intercession of the martyrs, a certain woman who was paralyzed and almost entirely without the use of her limbs was lying outside the doors of the church. She called upon the holy martyrs to help her. Very soon, before all those who were present, her stomach began to heave as if she were about to be sick, and then she began to vomit a great quantity of phlegm and bile. After that, she drank a small amount of cold water and asked to be lifted up from the spot where she was lying. Leaning on her crutch she entered the church. After she had prayed to the martyrs and had recovered the power of her limbs, she returned home on foot.

3. At about the same time a man by the name of Willibert, who owned a house not far from the church in which the bodies of the blessed martyrs now lie [in Seligenstadt], approached the bier with others who had also gathered to venerate the saints. He presented forty silver coins as a gift [to the saints]. When I asked him who he was and what he hoped to get for himself from offering this sort of gift, he replied that he had been overcome by intense fatigue a few days earlier and had sunk so low that everyone who saw him thought he was near death. He was urged to bequeath all his property right away for the salvation of his soul, and so he did. But when the bequest of all his things had been decided and to which holy places his property should be given, [he said that] one of his servants had complained loudly that they had handled things very badly and carelessly, since none of his property had been conferred upon the saints who had recently arrived from Rome. Then he had asked those standing nearby if they knew whether any of his possessions remained that could be sent to the martyrs. In fact [the martyrs] were still in Michelstadt at that time and it had not yet been revealed by any signs that they should leave that place. [He said] that someone had then informed him that only a single pig remained from all his [former] posses-

sions and that it had not [yet] been decided to which [holy place] it should be given. It pleased him a great deal [to learn that] and he ordered them to sell the pig and send the money, after his death, [to purchase] candles for the marytrs. As soon as he had finished giving [this command], he claims, he felt so suddenly cured that he was immediately free of all pain and even had a desire to eat [again]. After he had eaten, he felt strong so soon that the very next day he was easily able to go about managing and accomplishing all the work that his affairs demanded. After those [events] the pig was sold for the estimated price [forty silver coins], which he presented to the blessed martyrs to honor his vow.

4. I have decided that the other remarkable things and miracles that the Lord brought about in order to cure people should be described as they occur to my memory, since I see nothing of significance to report in the order in which they are set out. What must be considered more [significant] in the description of these miracles is what happened and why something happened rather than when it happened.

After the relics of the blessed martyrs had been solemnly installed in that church, it happened one day that a Mass was in progress, since according to standard ecclesiastical practice the sacred rites of the Mass were celebrated daily [there]. I had taken my place in the upper parts of the same church and was looking down upon the people gathered below in the lower parts [of the church]. I saw a half-naked cleric who had come with others to the same service. He was standing in the middle of the crowd when suddenly he collapsed so hard that he lay for a very long time on the floor as though he were dead. When some of the people standing nearby attempted to raise the man, who was breathing heavily, into a standing position, such a great flow of blood poured from his mouth and nostrils that the entire front of his body from his chest and stomach right down to the clothes covering his groin was drenched with this overflow [of blood]. He revived after he took some water and, with his strength restored, he spoke clearly. A little while later I questioned him. He informed me that he had neither been able to hear anything nor to speak from infancy right up until the present. He said that his native land was Britain and that he himself was English. In order to see his mother, who was undertaking a pilgrimage to Rome, he had hastily started upon this journey. In this way, he and other pilgrims who wanted to travel together to Rome had come to that place. But, when his companions departed, he had remained behind. He had been cured on the seventh day after coming there. When I asked him his name, he responded that he was completely ignorant of it, because he had never heard his name spoken while he was deaf.

5. A few days later, when we had solemnly gathered together in the church for the evening service, a deaf and mute girl from the region of Bourges was at long last brought there and made to stand with the others in that church. Her father and brother had taken her to many shrines of the saints in search of a cure. Suddenly, as if overcome by madness, she slammed together as hard as she could the tablets by whose noise she used to seek alms and threw [them] with a fury into the [crowd of] people assembled in front of her. Then she ran to the church's left wall and leaped three or more feet into the air, as if she was about to climb it. Then she fell down flat on her back. After she lay there for a little while more like someone dead than someone sleeping and was almost entirely covered with blood that was pouring from her mouth and nostrils, people standing nearby picked her up and carried her into the middle of the church. After she had laid there for a short time, she sat up like someone who had just awakened from a deep sleep. Then she extended her hands to the people beside her and pleaded [with them] with nods [of her head] to lift her onto her feet. Once she had been lifted up, she was led to the altar. When she saw that Ratleig was standing there near the altar with other clerics and that he was looking at her, she at once blurted out these words: "You are Ratleig," she said. "You are known by this name and you are the servant of these saints." When he asked her how she knew this and who had told her his name, she said: "Those saints of yours, who lie here, approached me while I lay there like someone sleeping and they thrust their fingers into my ears and said to me: 'When you arise and approach the altar, you should know that the young cleric you will see standing before you looking at you is named Ratleig and that he is our servant. For he was the very one who carried our bodies to this place.'" That was the case, of course, since [Ratleig] was the man, as I recorded in the first book, whom I had sent to Rome to receive the relics of the saints from a certain deacon and to carry them to me. Indeed, it was in this way and in my presence that the spirit of sickness was driven out by the power of the blessed martyrs and this girl regained her complete health. Her father and brother, who had led her there, declared that she had been deaf and mute since birth.

6. Although I myself did not see the miracle I am about to describe, I am able to believe the account of those who told it to me no less than if I had seen it with my own eyes. Thus, without any hesitation or doubt, I have decided to present it not as if I had [just] heard it, but rather as if I myself had actually seen it.

Some merchants from the city of Mainz, who were in the habit of purchasing grain in the upper parts of Germany and transporting it by the Main

River to their city, brought to the church of the blessed martyrs a blind man, an Aquitanian by the name of Alberic. They had taken him on board their boat, as he himself had requested, in order to win God's favor. After he had disembarked [at Seligenstadt] and was admitted as a guest in the house of church's guardian, he stayed there for seven days or more. Besides being blind, which seemed natural to him since he lacked eyes, he suffered from a horrible and vile disease of his entire body. For all his limbs shook so violently that he was entirely incapable of passing food to his mouth with his own hands.

One day, in the morning, when [Alberic] had fallen asleep while lying in his lodgings, he saw in his sleep a man approach him. He urged him to get up at once and hurry to the church. He said that the time had arrived when, though the power of the saints, he was sure to be released from his wretched suffering. After he awoke and was led to the church, he sat upon a stone in front of the [church] doors. At that very moment a divine service was being solemnly celebrated within the church. After the prayers that come before the sacred reading of the Gospel were finished, the Gospel itself was read out. Scarcely two verses of the reading had been completed, when, all of a sudden, it was as if [Alberic] was struck by a blow and trembling he screamed out loud, saying: "Help me, Saint Marcellinus!" Although everyone in the church was greatly alarmed by the commotion and clamor, most, because of their respect for the reading of the Gospel, stayed where they were, but many rushed over to see what the noise was all about. As they declared later on, they found [Alberic] in that place where he had been sitting, but now he was lying stretched out flat on his back and his chin and chest were covered with blood that was pouring from his nostrils. After they had lifted him onto his feet and he had taken a little cold water, he came around. He said that it had seemed to him, at the point at which he cried out, that someone had punched him in the neck, and so he had begged for the help of the blessed martyr. Still all agree that this blow was so beneficial to him that from that moment on no further evidence of that vile shaking was seen in his body.

After that he remained for almost two years in the same place [Seligenstadt], and, as he himself declared, there was no night in that two-year period in which he did not see the very martyrs who had cured him in his dreams. He also learned many things from them that he was ordered to tell others. I now see that many of the things that he then predicted would happen are coming true [see 6.41, a letter from 830].

7. A few days later we saw another man suffering from a similar disease who was cured in the same church in the same way by the merits of those same

saints. For on a certain night when I was sitting in the church to celebrate the morning service and to listen to the reading of the divine law [the Bible], a man in clerical habit entered [the church]. With his limbs trembling and leaning on a crutch, he [could only] control his faltering steps with difficulty. While he was leaning up against a wall in order to pray, he let forth a loud scream and fell in a sudden collapse onto his face. After a short delay, he rose up cured of the disease that had held him. I sought [to learn] from him if anything had appeared to him at the moment when he was cured other than what all of us could see. He said that not long before he had entered the church he had gone to pray at the old church [in Seligenstadt], which lay a short distance to the west of the new church [built between 830 and 836] where the martyrs were then resting. But since he had come upon it when it was locked up, he had prayed outside its doors. After that, when he had arisen [from praying] and had begun to move toward the [new] church, he had seen a cleric with venerable white hair, dressed in a white robe, preceding him to the place he himself wished to go. He said that he followed him as far as the church door. When both of them had arrived there, the [figure] in front moved to the side and stood against the left doorpost, as if he wanted the man he had just been in front of to enter first. When he was reluctant [to enter], [the figure] ordered him with a nod of his head to enter before he did. After he had entered and kneeled down to pray, [the white-haired figure] stood behind his back and hit him on the neck with his fist, knocking him down. [The figure] then immediately vanished. But, no one except the man who was cured was able to see him.

8. At almost the same time, when I had arisen one night and gone to church, I discovered a boy lying in the narthex before the [inner] doors of the church. He was so miserably deformed that his knees were touching his chin. He asked one of the men following us to carry him into the church. Moved by pity, [that fellow] lifted him up and arranged for him to lie down near the choir in the church. Drowsiness immediately overcame the boy and he fell asleep where he was lying. He did not wake up completely until he was entirely cured of that wretched tightening [of his limbs] because of the interecession of the saints. Then he awoke on his own, got up from the place into which he had been carried by someone else, and approached the altar to give thanks to God. When it was light outside and I was able to talk to him, he said that he had been summoned and warned three times before the church bell had sounded by a cleric he did not know to let nothing stand in the way of him going to church for the morning service. He had just done

that and afterwards, as I myself saw, he had received a complete cure of his body while he slept in the church. [This boy] seemed to be around fifteen years old.

9. I also saw another person cured in the same place in a similar way at about the same time. He was not a boy, as this one had been, but a very old and decrepit man who had been afflicted with a similar disease. One night when we had come to the door of the church to celebrate the morning service, we found him in the doorway. He was holding himself up on two canes while struggling forward on his knees. His extremely slow pace delayed our entrance [into the church]. While we were stuck behind him and waited for his slow advance, such a powerful fragrance of the most alluring kind poured forth from the church and filled our noses that it exceeded in its effect all artificial combinations of spices and thymes. Finally he entered [the church] and, before our eyes, lay down near the choir as if he was about to go to sleep. We too entered the church and took our places, and sang along with the others the psalms that were being sung in a solemn fashion. But when the first reading had begun, we heard that old man moan and beg for help as though he were being attacked. A little later we saw him lift himself into a sitting position and right after that he took up the crutches he had used to walk, and then stood up on his feet. In fact, I myself saw these things, but he told me that it had seemed to him as if two men had grabbed hold of him while he lay there. One had seized him by his shoulders and arms, the other by his knees and feet. It seemed as if by pulling him that they had stretched out his tendons, which had been very tight. He said that, aside from the problem with his tightened tendons, he had also been deaf, but when he had lifted himself into a sitting position it was as if an extremely powerful punch had landed on the top of his head. At the same moment he had heard someone's voice commanding him to hear from that point on. The old man declared that he had been cured in this way. He said that he had come from the land of the Swiss which is now called Aarau and that he was of German stock.

10. Another man also suffered similarly from a tightening of his tendons. He said that he had come from the town of Liège where the body of Saint Lambert rests. One Sunday night after the morning service was over and I had already returned from church, a priest was as usual celebrating the sacrament of the eucharist for the benefit of those who had come from far away and were anxious to return home. That man fell onto the hard ground in the presence of everyone there and he laid there for a little while as if he were fast asleep. Then, as if he had been awakened from sleep, he got up without

any help. One of the bystanders picked up the crutches he had used until then, since when he fell they had slipped out of his hands and lay some distance away. This bystander offered them to him, but he refused, saying: "May I never handle those [crutches] again!" And so he was cured and walked back on foot to the land from which he had come – more by crawling than walking – to the church of the martyrs.

11. A little later, in the month of November, I was as usual about to spend the winter at the palace and had arranged to travel to court. Once the journey had begun and I had crossed the Rhine River, I came to stay at a royal manor called Sinzig [see Map 2]. After dinner there, which had occupied a good portion of the evening, I had withdrawn with my servants into the privacy of the bedroom where I was to sleep, when suddenly the household servant who was assigned to supply me with drink entered in a rush as though he was about to announce some news. I looked at him and said, "What do you want to tell me, for I see that you want to bring something – I don't know what – to my attention?" Then he said, "Two miracles just occurred in our presence [that is, of the household servants], which I have come to tell you about." After I had directed him to tell me whatever he wished, he said, "A little while ago, while you were rising from supper and entering this bedroom, I descended with my companions into the cellar that lies below the dining-room. When we had started to serve beer to the household servants wanting it, a boy came forward carrying a small barrel in his hand. He had been sent by one of our companions and he demanded that it be filled up for him. After it had been filled, he also asked for a small amount of that beer to drink himself. [The beer] was given to him in a cup that happened to stand empty on top of the barrel containing the beer. But when he was about to drink it and had raised the cup to his mouth, he cried out in amazement that this drink was wine, not beer. The man who had filled up the small barrel and who had [also] drawn the drink from the opening [in the large barrel] that was given to the servant began to accuse him of lying. [The servant] said, 'Take it and try it yourself, and then you will know that I haven't lied, but rather told the truth.' The man took [the drink] and tasted it. He declared that to him it tasted like wine, not beer. After that a third person, a fourth, and the others gathered there, one by one tasted it in amazement and [so] drank up everything that was in the cup. Everyone who drank from that cup agreed that it tasted like pure wine, not beer."

"In the meantime, while they stood thunderstruck in amazement and admiration at the wonder of this sign, a candle, whose light they needed there, was attached to the wall near the [large] barrel and it illumined [the cellar]. Although no one touched it, the candle fell onto the floor, which was wet, and was so completely extinguished that not even the tiniest spark remained. One of the [servants] picked [the candle] up and ran to the door. But he was very afraid of the dark and before he went through, while [still] standing in the doorway, he said, 'May the holy martyrs Marcellinus and Peter help us.' With that appeal, the candle that he was holding in his hand began to burn."

When I heard these things I immediately praised and thanked almighty God, as was appropriate, for he always and everywhere glorifies his saints and he [had also] deigned with such great miracles to please us, his servants, for we then had the sacred relics with us. I ordered the [servant] who had told me these things to return to his place of rest. For my part, once I had settled down in bed to sleep, I began to ponder many things and to wonder what that transformation of beer into wine, that is, of an inferior drink into a superior one, meant or what it might portend. [Indeed,] why had a miracle of this sort occurred in that place, that is, in a royal house, rather than in the place where the most sacred bodies of the blessed martyrs, who accomplished these remarkable things through Christ's power, were stored away [in a reliquary]? But although I was not able after long and careful reflection to reach [a conclusion] in my determined investigation of this question, I was nevertheless certain and shall always remain certain that the divine and heavenly power through which these and other miracles of this kind are believed to occur never does anything without a reason or [permits] anything to happen by accident among his creatures; for I do not doubt that [all created things] fall under his providence and control.

12. Then, after this delay, as just described, I continued on to the court, for the emperor Louis was at that time [in 828] staying at the palace of Aachen and had issued orders for a general assembly of his chief nobles to be held there in the middle of the winter. I along with others had been orderd to be present there, but since I was forced to be absent from the company of the blessed martyrs, my stay at the place was a less than happy one.

Precisely one month after I arrived there, I dispatched a certain member of my household, a man by the name of Elleanhard, with orders to hurry with as much speed as he could manage to the church of the blessed martyrs. After he had visited with our brothers there, the ones whom I had on my departure left behind to celebrate the divine service and after he had carefully found out everything that had been happening there, he was to return quickly to me. When he had arrived there, he stayed for three days. But on the fourth day, when he was already preparing to return to me, that blind man by the name of Alberic, of whom I made mention above, detained him as he was getting ready to leave. He claimed that [Elleanhard] would not commence his journey before he had seen a sign that would make me happy and completely pleased when I heard of it. Moreover, he went on to say that the most blessed martyrs had appeared to him the previous night while he was sleeping and had ordered him to find a certain poor man by the name of Gisalbert, who was weighed down by a large hump [on his back] and, as a consequence, was bent over and leaned upon short crutches. He was to take him once he had been found to the room above the narthex of the church at the hour of the morning service and set him down near the relics which were there, because it was there that he would be freed of the deformity of the hump and the aggravation of being bent over through the merits and power of the saints whose relics those were. [Elleanhard] complied with Alberic's recommenda- tion and postponed until the next day the journey he had been ready to make. The blind man looked for the poor man he had been commanded to find, found him, and, as he had been ordered, situated him in the upper part of the church near the relics at the time of the morning service. But those relics, and we did not know that at this time, were those of the blessed martyr Marius, his wife, and sons, that is Martha, Audifax, and Habakkuk. In fact, they had been carried to us together with the bodies of Saints Marcellinus and Peter and in the same reliquary. The person who carried them [that is, Ratleig] did not know whose relics they were, for the one [Deusdona] who had sent them to me promised that he himself would visit me and would himself give me the names of the saints whose relics those were. That did happen later on. When the second reading of the night service was as usual being recited, the poor man who had been positioned near those relics by the blind man [Alberic] let forth a scream that greatly frightened those who heard it. Some clerics and the man charged with watching [the poor man] ran up to him and found him lying face down, spread out beside the altar. They saw that the floor below his mouth was drenched with blood. They lift- ed him up and brought water to revive him; [then] congratulating the cured man, they led him down[stairs] into the lower part of the church. He [now] walked upright and did not retain any indication of his [former] camel back. After the miracle had occurred in this way, the one I had sent there hurried back to me with the greatest possible speed. When he reported what he had seen, I was filled with great joy and happiness.

13. A little while later Ratleig, who had transported the sacred ashes of the martyrs from Rome, as I related above, arrived [at court]. He came as ordered, as he himself said, bearing a small book that contained a number of

edicts [*capitula* here in the sense of legal and binding pronouncements]. He told me that the reason for this was as follows. The blind man [Alberic], of whom I have just been speaking, had commanded him on the authority of the martyrs to write down and carry those edicts to me. He was to tell me that I should accept them and [then] present them to the emperor for him to read. I did receive that small book from him and examined it thoroughly. Once it had been corrected and newly inscribed, I presented that small book, as ordered, to the emperor. And, in fact, he did receive it and read it though-out, but of the things that he was ordered or urged to do by this small book he took the trouble to fulfill very few. But what the edicts said, either what was to be done by him or what was to be left undone, should be told in another place rather than here. But how it was revealed and ordered that that small book should be made and given to the king I think should not only not be bypassed, but rather should be openly and clearly set down.

Ratleig reported that it had happened in this way. He said that "A few days before when we had gathered together in church to celebrate the evening service as usual, that blind man whom you know approached me and asked me to withdraw with him into some more private place. I did as he wished and entered along with him into the small room where I normally sleep. Then he spoke first: 'This very night, a short time before we were awakened by the sound of the bells, a venerable, grey-haired man appeared to me in a vision. He was dressed in a white robe and was holding a golden rod in his hand. He addressed me in these terms. "Make sure, Alberic," he said, "that you completely understand everything that I am about to tell you. Hold it tight in your memory, so that you can repeat it clearly to others who will write these things down. For I want these things to be written down and shown by your lord [Einhard] to the emperor Louis who is to read them. But they are not just for him to know, but to act upon, for these things are extremely impor-tant to that ruler into whose kingdom these martyrs have come by divine command."

'Then he [the figure in white] started to dictate in sequence twelve or more edicts and he ordered me to relate them and explain them to you and to four others whom I shall name for you. After this, you should make a small book and take it to your lord, who is at this time resident in the palace. You should command him, on the authority of the martyrs, to present that book as quickly as he can to the emperor. After that, [the figure in white] added, "Do you know who I am, I who command you [to do] these things?" With no hesitation I then answered that he was Saint Marcellinus. But he said to me: "It is not as you think, for I am the archangel Gabriel and I have assumed the identity and appearance of Marcellinus because the Lord God has placed me in charge of all things and matters that concern those martyrs. I have come forward now to reveal these things to you that I want written down, because God wants those things to be brought immediately, with the saints' influence, to the attention of the king. Proclaim these things you have learned, as I have ordered you to, at dawn after the end of the morning service, to those men to whom I have ordered you to announce them." Then I said, "No one will believe that an angel spoke to me or commanded me to announce these things." [Gabriel] answered and said: "That is not so, for I shall give you a sign that you can demonstrate in their presence, and, once they have seen it, they will no longer doubt the things you have told them on my orders. I want you, therefore, to tell Ratleig to supply you with two new candles that have never been lit. While holding one of those in your right hand and the other in your left, stand before the altar. When you have finished relating everything that I commanded you to tell them, inform your listeners that they should believe that these things are true and that what you said was commanded by an angel of God if those candles in your hands should spontaneously catch fire before their very eyes.'"

Once this [miracle] had occurred, that small book was written down and brought to me, and I presented it to the king. He, for his part, received the book and read it throughout. It seemed appropriate for me to mention this small book among the other miracles [of the saints], because at the moment when [Gabriel] ordered it written down that remarkable and unheard of lighting of the candles happened. The angel, who lit the candles, foretold that it would happen because of the merits of the blessed martyrs.

14. At about the same time, after Ratleig had left us and returned to the martyrs' church, another small book was carried to me from that place. It contained the words and thoughts of a certain demon who called himself Wiggo. His [statement] was given in the presence of many witnesses before the altar near the site of the martyrs' sacred ashes; it arose from questions posed by a priest performing a rite of exorcism upon a possessed person. It is said to have happened in the following way.

There is an estate in the distict of Niedgau called Höchst [see Map 3] that belongs to the monastery of St-Nazarius [Lorsch]. A girl there, who was around sixteen years old, was possessed by that errant spirit [Wiggo]. Her parents brought her to the church of the martyrs. When she had come before the tomb containing the sacred bodies and the priest had, according to custom, recited the exorcism over her head, he then started to question the demon about how and when he had entered into her. [The demon] answered the priest not in German, which was the only language the girl knew, but in

Latin. The priest was amazed and asked how she knew Latin, since her parents, who were with her there, were utterly ignorant of the language. [The demon] said, "You have never seen my parents." Then the priest said, "Then where are you from, if those are not your parents?" The demon [speaking] through the girl said: "I am an assistant and disciple of Satan, and I was for a long time a gate-keeper in the infernal regions, but for the last few years I and eleven of my companions have wreaked havoc upon the kingdom of the Franks. We have destroyed and utterly ruined grain, wine, and all the other crops that come from the earth for human use, just as we had been orderd to; we killed off herds [of cattle] with disease; [and] we let plague and pestilence loose among those people of yours. Indeed, all the misfortunes and evils, that people have been suffering from for a long time now, as they so deserved, fell upon them because of our actions and our assault." When the priest asked at this point why such a power had been granted to them, he said, "Because of the wickedness of this people and because of the various sins of those appointed [to rule] over them. For they love rewards, not justice; they fear [other] humans more than God; they oppress the poor and refuse to hear the widows and orphans crying out to them; and they render justice only to those who pay for it. Besides these, there are many other, [indeed] almost an endless number of sins committed every day both by the people themselves and by their rulers: perjury, drunkenness, adultery, murder, theft, and rapine. No one prohibits these [crimes] and, once done, no one punishes them. The powerful are slaves to filthy lucre and, because of pride and vainglory, they abuse the higher station they received in order to govern the people below them. Hatred and envy are directed more toward neighbors and relatives than against distant peoples. Friends do not trust friends, brothers hate brothers, and fathers do not love their sons. Those who faithfully and devoutly pay tithes are rare and rarer still are those who give alms. This is the case because [people] think that whatever they are supposed to give to God and the poor is lost to themselves. Nor do they fear, though it is against God's command, to use crooked measures and false weights [on scales]. They trick one another with fraud and are not ashamed to bear false witness [against each other]. They do not observe Sundays and feast days, but on those days work just as hard as they do on other days, as their own interests dictate. Because of these things and many others that God either commanded people to do or prohibited them from doing, and since this people because of its stubbornness remained disobedient to his commands, we were allowed or, rather, were ordered to do those things among humans that I just related, so that they might pay the penalty for their lack of faith. For those people are faithless liars, since they do not bother to hold to what they promised in baptism." The demon said all this in Latin through the mouth of that German girl.

When the priest started to order [the demon] to come out [of her], [Wiggo] said, "I shall leave not because of your order, but because of the power of the saints who will not allow me to remain in that girl any longer." After he said this, he threw the girl down onto the ground and he forced her to lie there, face down, for a short time as though she were sleeping. But a little while later, after [Wiggo] had departed, the girl like someone waking from sleep rose up and was cured, because of the power of Christ and the merits of the blessed martyrs. All who were present observed this and were amazed. After the demon had been forced to leave her, she could no longer speak Latin, so that it can be understood clearly that it was not that girl who spoke on her own, but the demon who spoke through her mouth. What a miserable state of affairs, that our times have fallen so low that it is not good people, but evil demons who now instruct us. And those who [normally] incite us to vice and encourage us to commit crimes are now advising us to reform ourselves.

15. At almost the same time a nun by the name of Marctrude, from the district of Wetterau, had been so cruelly gripped for ten years with a bad case of paralysis, that throughout that time her body could hardly carry out any human activities. Her relatives had begun to despair that she would ever recover, since they had taken her to all the churches of the saints to which they could travel. But finally they brought her to the church of the martyrs and set her down near the choir at the time of the night service. By means of the merits and intercession of the saints she immediately regained the [good] health she had wanted for so long. It was restored to her so completely and perfectly that, once the strength had returned to all her limbs, this woman who had come [to Seligenstadt] on a litter went back to her own land on foot. But on her journey home, she was again seized by the same condition from which she had been [so] happy to be released. Thus she did penance for her return [home] and asked to be taken back again to the martyrs' church. As soon as she was brought back, she received at once the good health she had lost by leaving. She made a vow, in light of this, that she would never again depart voluntarily from her service to the saints. She constructed a small cell for herself not far from the church and, after that, having piously committed herself to the service of the blessed martyrs, she stayed there with the greatest devotion.

16. It is also well known that another woman, not long afterwards, was released from a severe disorder by those same blessed martyrs. This incident is known to have happened in this way. In the district of Niedgau there is an estate called Oberursel [see Map 3] that lies about six leagues from the church of the martyrs. A certain woman awoke there one morning from sleep

and sat up in bed. As people do when they awake to dispel their drowsiness she stretched her arms and yawned repeatedly. But she opened her mouth a little wider than she should have and the joints of her jaw, which are located near the ears, were dislocated and her open mouth became fixed in a [permanent] yawn. Now unable to close her mouth, she looked more like [someone wearing] a mask than a human being and so paid a very heavy price for her careless yawn. When this [ailment] came to the attention of some common women living on the estate, they hurried to her and attempted to help alleviate her suffering with herbs and useless incantations. But their empty and superstitious audacity accomplished nothing, for whatever their ignorant hands applied to her in the name of a cure actually distressed and harmed the suffering woman [even more]. In the meantime, the brother of that woman's husband came over and wisely recommended that she be taken at once to the martyrs' church. He said that if she could ever be cured anywhere, she would be cured there. They immediately began to lead her [there], mounted on a horse. But when they were approaching the church, they made her dismount from the horse and walk on her own feet. When she arrived at the spot where the bell-tower of the church could be seen, those who had brought her there told her to lift up her eyes to look at it. She looked up, saw [the tower], and all of a sudden she recovered her health. Everyone who was with her fell down onto the ground together there and praised the mercy of God with whatever words of praise they could find. They [then] arose and hurried to the church. After they had adored the holy martyrs and made offerings according to their means, they returned home in a spirit of great joy. I myself saw that very woman and spoke with her, and I learned of the things that happened to her from her own lips.

17. Now I want to relate what I myself saw happen on the feast day of the blessed martyrs [that is, 2 June]. A certain deaf and mute boy had arrived there three years earlier and had been appointed a door-keeper in the house of the guardian of the church. After the feast day was over and the evening service had been completed, the boy was sitting beside the door. Suddenly he arose and entered the church. He fell flat on his face beside the right side of the altar. When the sacristan, who was placing a candelabrum with candles before the altar, found the boy lying there, he made sure to tell me at once. I and those who were with me at that time quickly went to the church and we discovered the boy lying there just as he had been found by the sacristan. When I ordered him to get up, he could not be roused, for it seemed as if he had been overcome by a very deep sleep. But at last, like one awaking, he raised himself up. When he saw us standing around him, he stood up and

spoke Latin to those closeby. Some of our people say that about six months earlier, when that boy had been asleep one night in the house of one of my men, he had spoken two words in his sleep. At that very moment he had recovered his hearing, which he had lacked up until then just as he had lacked [the power of] speech. They inferred that this had happened, since after he arose from that [particular] sleep he was careful to do everything that people ordered him to do, as if he now understood [them]. But what seems peculiar about this miracle is that [at that time] he understood those who spoke to him in German, not Latin; but once cured he spoke the Latin language, not German. He even told us that he had seen the blessed martyrs and had heard them [say] many things that he was supposed to relate to others. But when he had put off passing along those things immediately, as if he would relate them the next day, he so completely forgot them that he could recall nothing of what he had certainly heard. Since he did not know his own name, I myself ordered that he should be called Prosper, because of the prosperous outcome of that miracle. [Prosper] is still alive and retains the same position he held before with the guardian of the church.

18. On the day before the one on which Prosper gained [the power of] speech, that is, on the eve of the saints' feast day, a certain young man who was also deaf and mute, entered the church. While he was begging for the saints' help through humble signs he was deemed worthy, with God's help, to be completely cured of both his afflictions. Just as I had named the other man, I called this man Gottschalk, since he had never heard his name [spoken]. Yet, once the power of speaking had been granted to him, because of the merits of the saints, he did not speak Latin as Prosper did, but German, since it was his native tongue.

19. Now when necessity forced me, as usual, to travel to the king's court in the month of December on the Kalends [1 December 829], if I recall correctly, I left the place of the martyrs [at Seligenstadt] and on the next day reached the fortified city that is today called Wiesbaden where I could rest [for the night]. Since that place is surrounded by a forest, in order to pass through it more easily we had arisen earlier than normal. The servants who were assigned to precede us with the baggage started out first. But after they had departed and had started to travel away from the town where we remained, such an immense cloud of darkness enshrouded them that they could not determine where they ought to turn. On top of that, it was dreadfully cold and the earth was so covered with frost that they could not see the road. As well the mountain peaks by which they had to travel were [so] socked in

with a blanket of clouds that it could not [even] be determined how far or how close they were. A thick fog lying in the valleys rose up those [mountain tops] and blocked their sight, [thus] delaying those who wanted to continue their journey. When they realized that they were hindered by all these difficulties and that it was not clear what they should do, they got off their horses and attempted to find the road by touch, since they could not see it. But when this didn't really work, they once again mounted their horses and decided it would be better to get lost, a prospect that horrified them, rather than to delay. Therefore, they carried on for a short time in the dark and came to a cross in honor of blessed Marcellinus that had been erected along the road they were traveling. Now, the reason that cross had been placed there was that two years before when I had been returning from the palace the residents of the town where I had spent that night had come out to meet me at that spot, since I was carrying the relics of the blessed martyr Marcellinus, which had just been returned to me. To mark this meeting, they took the trouble to erect a [cross] as if in place of an inscription or monument in veneration of the blessed martyr. After those servants had arrived there more by accident than by carefully planned journey, they decided to wait there for their companions who were on the way. So that they might not [also] get lost, they assembled everyone by blowing a horn. Once they were all together, they called upon the blessed martyrs to help them and they raised their voices and loudly chanted the *Kyrie eleison* three times.

After this, a great flash of light shone upon them, shimmering forth from the heavens for so long that it matched the brightness of daylight. That lightning was of such great help to them in continuing their journey, that once the cloud had lifted, the darkness had been dispelled, and their way forward was clear, they continued their journey without getting lost throughout the night, although they were traveling through woods and mountains darkened by forests. In fact, such a great amount of heat had been produced by that first flash [of lightning] and by [all] that light, that they said they felt that it was like the heat of a furnace. By that blast not only the cloud, but also the frost that was then covering the mountains and the entire forest was so burned off that by the time a third flash [of lightning] happened almost no trace of the [previous] cold could be detected. Those who saw and experienced these things reported them to me on the evening of the same day after we stopped for the night. I believed their account and praised and gave thanks for the mercy of the almighty God, because he had deigned to help and console us in our time of need because of the merits of his saints.

20. Although all [these miracles] are great and should be attributed to divine power, and I know that they were brought about for the health of people

from the merits of the blessed martyrs, nevertheless in the miracle that I have decided to commit to writing next the power of the almighty God is so clearly apparent that no one should doubt but that he can easily do whatever he wishes to do throughout his entire creation.

In the district of Niedgau there is a village called Suntilinga, in which a certain priest by the name of Waltbert held a church. His relatives brought him with great sadness to the church of the martyrs, [because] he was deranged. Three of the people who brought him [there] were his brothers; one was a priest and two were laymen. The fourth one, a close relative of his, was a monk of the monastery of Hornbach, in which the priest himself had been trained from a young age. I asked them if he had been treated by a physician. They said, "Once we learned that he had been seized by this affliction, we took him to the monastery in which he had been raised. When the physicians there had tried many things according to the knowledge of their art and were unable to dislodge the disease from him, our friends advised us to guide him to the mercy of these saints. For we are confident that they can save him, since we have heard that many others have been cured here." After this, they stayed with us for four days, leading him each day to the church and arranging for him to lie down in the presence of the sacred ashes of the martyrs. On the fifth day, however, his brother, the priest, and the monk who had traveled with him asked me to arrange for him to stay there along with his two brothers, the laymen, until they themselves returned. They said that they would return three days later. I did as they asked and entrusted him to a priest of ours by the name of Hiltfrid. After [Waltbert] had been received by the priest, he was led to the cell where [Hiltfrid] himself lived. That evening the madness that gripped him grew more violent and in a rage he picked up a knife that happened to be lying around and tried to kill one of his own brothers, who was keeping watch over him. But that man escaped death by fleeing and told my men, who were close by, about his brother's insanity. Then the priest, upon whom I had entrusted the responsibility of guarding him, suggested to me and, in fact, persuaded me to allow him to bind [Waltbert]. Thus, he was bound with iron chains and was placed in bed; the doors were locked and he was left alone in that small room. His [lay] brothers stood on guard outside his door and carefully kept watch on him as though he might try to break out. But the chains with which he was bound were attached in such a way that while he was in them he could not turn himself to the right or left, nor could he lie in any other way than on his back.

He slept in this manner, as he himself declared, and did not wake until the middle of the night. But when the roosters started to crow, he awoke and saw that he was not only free of the bonds of his chains, but also of the disease of madness with which he had struggled. He immediately turned his entire mind to praising God with psalms and hymns and he sang them with such great joy, even though he was alone, and so loudly that he awoke all those who were sleeping near his room. Then he arose and went to the door where his brothers were on guard. He asked them to let him out to satisfy the demands of nature. But they thought that this was a trick of the insane man and didn't dare to agree. Instead, they summoned their host, the one who had locked him up there, and asked him to speak with [their brother]. After he had spoken with him and knew by the reasonableness of his answers that he was now of sound mind, he opened the door and allowed him to go where he wished. When he returned, he met him and asked what had happened to the chains with which he had locked him up in that room. [Waltbert] answered that, "The chain with which you bound me is unbroken, and if you wish to know where it is, look for it and you will find it." After they had lit a candle, they found the chain lying in front of the bed on which they had made him lie down; it was joined together in the same way and secured with the same bonds as it had been when they bound him on that very bed with it and left him alone in that small room. Who should we believe did this except the one who created all things from nothing and who can do among the things he has created [amazing things] that can neither be understood by human reason nor explained by words? Who, in fact, can either logically surmise in his mind or describe in words how that priest was released from those chains? For I am absolutely certain that no one on his own could remove himself from bonds of that sort if he was bound by them like that priest was when he was locked in that small room by himself. Those [other brothers], who had left him there, returned later and found him cured and in full possession of his mind and memory. They went home happy and with him they praised God. I learned how this event happened not from the accounts of other people, but I knew of it on my own since, by God's will, I was still there [in Seligenstadt] at the time. Thus I [can] write of it with great confidence, since [as] it happened I knew of it, as they say, by visible faith. But since everything that I have decided to write down about the [miraculous] powers of the martyrs cannot be finished in this present book, let it end here, for those things that remain [to be told] would begin more suitably if they had their own introduction.

[Book Four]

[Preface]

In relating the signs and miracles that I declared I would record in this [fourth] book, those that occurred in the palace should be set down first for they came not only to the attention of many people, but also to the attention of the ruler himself, his chief men, and, indeed, all his courtiers. [It is necessary to record these miracles] not just for this reason, but also because there were no other relics than those of the blessed martyrs Marcellinus and Peter [kept] at that time in my chapel where these miracles happened. Thus, whatever cures or signs are known to have happened there should belong to and should be attributed individually and collectively to those [saints], whose relics were the only ones present. The most blessed martyrs also worked their many powers and miracles, as I shall demonstrate in the following [chapters], in the places of other saints. The [miracles] that happened in their churches could reasonably be viewed as joint ones brought about by those saints along with [Marcellinus and Peter], especially since [the saints] are believed to have equal merit before God. It is not unreasonable to think that the saints work together in performing miracles. But that this was not the case is proved and clearly demonstrated by this argument: that no miracles were made in those churches before the relics of the blessed martyrs were brought there. But for right now, as I promised, let me set out the miracles that occurred in the palace.

1. There was a certain young man, a Greek by the name of Drogo, who was one of the king's chamberlains. He was seized by a fever and [had] already suffered, either because of the negligence of his companions or the ignorance of his physicians, from a lengthy bout of ill health for many months. After Abbot Hilduin returned the relics of the blessed Marcellinus to me, as was described in the second book, [Drogo] was advised in his sleep to come to my chapel and to light a candle, purchased there for four denarii. He was to pray to Saint Marcellinus, whose head [that is, his skull] was present there, to help him. He was assured that if he did this, he would quickly be freed from the illness with which he had struggled for such a long time. He believed the one urging him and did what had been ordered as quickly as he could. He was immediately cured and after he had recovered the strength of his limbs, he walked home on his own feet.

2. In the same place there was also another young man by the name of Gerlach from the city of Rheims. He was one of those men who had been commanded to come from that city [to Aachen] in order to erect the buildings of the palace. Almost six months earlier in that same town, he was seized by such a powerful and immense tightening of his tendons that his feet were stuck to his rear end and his knees to his chin. His friends and relatives carried him in their arms to my chapel. They made him lie face down, since he could not lie down in any other position, and they prayed with great piety for the holy martyr to restore his health. He was brought there on a Sunday at the third hour of the day and he lay there until the ninth hour. The service of that hour had been solemnly completed by the clergy, when lo and behold such a powerful fragrance of the most alluring and unusual kind came from the chest containing the sacred relics of the blessed martyr that it entirely filled the small room of the chapel. Everyone who was present there immediately stood up in amazement at it and with puzzled looks asked each other if everyone had sensed the same thing. Suddenly they saw that [Gerlach], who was lying nearby, was being pulled, as though by [unseen] hands, and that his limbs, which had been contorted by the disease, were being stretched out. These people understood that they were in the presence of divine power and [so] they lifted up the man and placed him before the altar. After he had been placed there he begged and cried for divine assistance. With everyone looking on, [Gerlach] was so straightened out that though he had been transported into the chapel on strange hands, he left the chapel on his own [two] feet. Nevertheless, a trace of the affliction he suffered is still to be seen on his body, for afterwards he limped so [markedly] in his left leg and foot that he always needed a cane to help him walk. Let people say what they want to about why he was not completely cured. For my part, I can only speculate that some sign of external illness remained with him to help him strive for internal salvation.

3. There is an ancient city called Jülich [see Map 2] that is eight leagues from the town of Aachen. A certain girl from that region was also afflicted with a similar disease. Her mother and other relatives brought her to my chapel. Since a large crowd of people had, as it happened, gathered together there at that time to hear Mass, she could not be carried into [the chapel] and so they laid her down outside the east window of the chapel. They were waiting for the opportunity, once that crowd of people had dispersed, to carry her more easily into the chapel. But at almost the middle of the service, when the Gospel had been read out and the offering of the eucharist was over, they observed that she was in some trouble and had collapsed as if she were asleep.

Sweat covered her entire body. They were not wrong to conclude from these signs that divine power was present and [so] they raised her up from that spot and set her down, [still] apparently asleep, on a square stone that lay nearby. There, in the presence of everyone who had rushed to see this miracle, she recovered with the Lord's help and within the space of a single hour the complete use of all her limbs.

Among the other spectators in the chapel there were some Jews, one of whom was named David. After the fulfilment of this sign, he quickly ran to the window of the small room where I was and called me. He described for me the miracle he had seen and gave thanks to God, who through his martyrs had deigned to achieve such great miracles for the health and welfare of humans.

4. In the same town there was an old blind man, who, as he himself stated, had been suddenly stricken with blindness three years earlier. He used to go door to door begging for donations along with the other poor. [Once] when he was sleeping in his hut, he saw in his sleep a man standing by his side, who said that if he wanted to see [again] he should go to my chapel. There was a physician there who could restore sight to one who requested it. He refused and spurned the sight he was offered. "What would I do with vision now," he said, "since I have been so long without it? It is better for me not to have it than to have it. Everyone clearly listens to a [blind] beggar and they give what he needs, [whereas] it is not right for the sighted to beg. Moreover, being old and frail I cannot work." Then the [dream figure] who was speaking to him said, "Go at once, for whether you want to or not you will recover your sight." He obeyed that commanding [figure], proceeded to the chapel, and spent the night there. When nothing happened that night, he returned to his hut. The one who had appeared to him before in his sleep appeared again, and, just as he had ordered him before, he commanded him to proceed to the chapel. [The blind man] did as he was ordered, but in fact nothing happened this time [either]. But after being admonished a third time he came [to the chapel] and knelt down before the altar to pray. [Then] he received back his sight. I myself had often seen this man, when he was still blind, begging at my house along with the other poor and sick. Thus I needed no other proof of the return of his sight, since I believed that the evidence of my own knowledge [of the case] was sufficient.

5. While the positive accounts of these and many other workings of [God's] miraculous power were spreading throughout the towns and districts [near Aachen], a woman from the land of the Ripuarians, who had been blind for a

long time and both wanted to recover her sight and believed she could, asked
to be taken to that chapel [of mine]. After she had arrived there, she stayed for
three whole days and nights fasting and praying. But at the point when she
saw no sign in her body of the cure she had hoped for, she was taken back
home. A few days later, with the realistic hope of recovering her sight [still
strong], she asked to be taken back again to the sacred relics. This time she
was taken back by a single servant, for those who had led her there earlier
thought her [renewed] hope was futile and pointless and did not wish to go
[back] with her again. When she [had], with her companion and guide,
reached the cemetery of the palace of Aachen, which is located on the mountain that rises up on the eastern side of the town, she recovered the vision she
had long desired. It was as if divine grace had come out to meet her at that
point. Then, full of wonder and astonishment, she now ordered the servant
who had [until then] led her to follow: "Until now," she said, "I followed
where you led me, but now I don't need you to lead, because I see the way
we must go. With God's help, I [can now] see this town that contains the
sacred relics I set out to visit. You need only see to it and insure that you take
me directly to the chapel of the martyrs in the town itself." After she had said
this, she proceeded to the chapel, gave thanks, and informed me of the miracle performed on her [body]. [Thus], with her sight [restored] and full of joy,
she returned home.

6. Eschweiler is a royal estate four leagues away from the palace of Aachen
[see Map 2]. There a certain man was stuck [at home] and was in great difficulty because of a lingering problem with his bowels. Moreover, his family so
despaired of his condition that it seemed [to them] that he could only be
cured by cauterization [the application of a hot iron]. A physician was called
upon to perform this [treatment] and a day was decided upon for the harmful
searing. In the meantime, it was revealed in a dream to a certain woman living on the same estate that to be cured that man should not submit to a measure of this sort, which could hardly be endured because of the pain.
[Moreover], since [this treatment] was useless, it would not bring health and
well-being to the patient. But if he wished to be cured, he should go to the
palace at Aachen and seek out my chapel. He should arrange to be set down
in it and should not depart from there for three whole days. In this way he
would regain his health entirely. When he had heard this, he called together
his friends and family and begged them to carry out for him the directions of
that revelation. They soon led him on horseback to the chapel and, setting
him down in it as had been ordered, they departed, intending to return after
the three days were over. Once he had been left [alone] there, he prayed for

the three days and three nights to the Lord for the restoration of his health. And he was so completely cured that he maintained that no trace of that disease of his bowels that had gripped him for so long remained. When his family [and friends] returned to him, just as they had promised, they discovered that he was cured, just as they had hoped. That man returned home not on the back of a horse, as he had come, but using his own feet and to the great happiness and joy of those people.

7. There is also a royal estate in the district of the Meuse [river] that lies about eight leagues from Aachen. Its inhabitants call it Gangelt. A woman there had a daughter almost eight years old who was so beset by an awful case of paralysis that for a long time she had been almost unable to move any of her limbs as needed. When her mother heard accounts of the miracles, she began to hope in her kind heart that her daughter's health could be regained. At once she underook to lift up and carry her [daughter] in her own arms to the chapel. When she reached there at noon, exactly at lunchtime, she found none of the clerics present, for they had [all] departed a little while before in order to eat. Nevertheless, she entered and set her daughter down near her on the hard floor. But she lit a tiny candle that she had brought as an offering and placed it on the ground in front of [her daughter] and bent down with the deepest devotion to pray in the presence of the sacred ashes. Immediately after that the girl, without her mother being aware of it [since she was deep in prayer], recovered the health and strength of all her limbs through divine grace. She stood and picked up the candle lying beside her and stood behind her [mother] who was [still] bent over [in prayer]. After she had finished praying, she raised her head from the floor, but she saw neither the candle nor her daughter in the place where she had left her. She stood up and, turning around, saw her daughter standing behind her holding the candle. She praised God and was filled with joy. She saw that there was no one there to whom she could relate the miracle that had [just] occurred, for aside from the poor who were sleeping outside the chapel in order to beg, there was no one inside the walls of the chapel except she and her daughter when that miracle happened. And so, after fulfilling her vows by giving thanks [to God], she walked home with her daughter now cured and well.

I shall briefly explain how I learned of this miracle. Gerward, the librarian of the palace, to whom the care of the palace's books and buildings had already at that time been entrusted by the king, was coming from Nijmegen to the palace of Aachen. When he stayed for a night on the estate [of Gangelt], he asked his host if he had recently heard of any news from the palace. He said to him that "At present the courtiers are mostly talking about the signs and miracles happening in Einhard's house by means of the saints whose relics he is said to keep in the chapel of his house. All my neighbors are daily rushing [there] to venerate them and whoever is brought there ill is cured on the spot." He began to tell him about that woman's daughter and how she had been cured a few days earlier. Then Gerward said, "Go and bring that woman to me so that she herself may speak to me, because I am anxious to hear her [story]." The woman came and clearly revealed everything, just as it had occurred. When Gerward appeared before the king the next day, he related to him what he had learned about this miracle from the report of that woman. Now when I, following custom, went in and stood before the [king], he carefully raised the matter of what Gerward had told him about this miracle both to me and to the others standing near him. He marveled and also praised the mercy and power of God. And so it happened that I myself learned of this miracle that [had] occurred without my knowledge in my own house from a report of this kind [by the king himself].

8. It should be sufficient to have recorded in this present book these [accounts] of the miracles of the blessed martyrs that happened in the palace. Now it is time to take up those miracles that were accomplished in the places to which the relics of those martyrs came to be venerated because religious men had sought them and I granted [their requests]. In those places they are still cherished today with deep devotion.

George, a priest and the abbot of the monastery of St-Salvius the Martyr, which is located in the district of Famars in the town called Valenciennes on the bank of the Scheldt River [see Map 1], was the first person to receive the relics from me. He sent them to that monastery from the palace at Aachen in the hands of a certain deacon. When [that deacon], who had only one companion with him, had arrived in the district of Hesbaye at the royal town people call Visé [see Map 2], he dismounted in a meadow close to that town in order to rest the horses. All at once one of the inhabitants of the place, who was bent over with a hump and whose jaw was also extremely swollen (for, as he himself said, he had suffered for a long time from a painful toothache), angrily entered that meadow carrying an iron pitchfork on his shoulder. With irritation he asked why [those horses] were grazing in his meadow. The deacon, who was bearing the martyrs' relics, was at that moment preparing to hang the relics on top of a rod that he had set up in that place for that purpose. He said to that man, "It [would be] better for you to prostrate yourself before these relics of the saints, which I hold here in my hands, and to beg God to deign to release you, because of the virtues of these saints, from the pain you are suffering. For the swelling that is seen on your face is a sign that your mouth is in great pain." At that the man threw away the pitchfork he was holding in his hand and fell face down before the relics. And, as the deacon had persuaded him, he prayed to the Lord for his health and well-being. Not long afterwards, he stood up from his praying so cured that the swelling was gone from his face, the pain in his teeth had disappeared, and so had the hump on his back that had weighed him down. Then, he quickly ran into the town and asked all his relatives and neighbors living there to praise God and thank the Lord Christ. A great crowd of people poured into that meadow and a throng from the surrounding area gathered together to give thanks on behalf of that man who had been cured. Everyone invited the deacon to spend the night there. He was unable to deny their request, because they were actually prepared, if he did not agree, to keep him there against his will. Then they kept watch all night long and the whole area resonated with the praise of God. But the next day, when the deacon had begun to continue on his way, that entire crowd of people gathered together and with great devotion accompanied the departing man. They did not wish to stop or go back until the deacon was joined by others, who were aroused by the fame of this miracle, and had come out to meet him.

9. It was in this manner that the sacred relics of the martyrs, from the time of this miracle, were welcomed by the people of those areas and carried with the Lord's guidance to the church of St-Salvius where George had sent them. It should be said that I learned of this miracle from the account of George himself. But I also received a small book from him about other [miracles] that should now be reported. The arrangement and sequence of this book takes the following form:

10. In the fourteenth year of Emperor Louis's reign [828], with Christ's favor, the Lord deigned, because of the relics of his saints, to reveal miracles and wonders in the very palace of the king in order to strengthen the faith of his Christian people, just as he had at the birth of the church. Thus, I, George, a priest at the palace of Aachen sought and obtained from Abbot Einhard relics of the blessed martyrs of Christ, Marcellinus and Peter. He himself had recently received their bodies, which had been carried from Rome by his own men. And he made arrangements to send those relics, which were stored in a chest that he had appropriately adorned with gold and jewels, by means of his own deacon, a man named Theothard, to the church of St-Salvius the Martyr, which he himself then held as a benefice of the king.

When that deacon had come to a royal villa called Visé, a hunchbacked man approached him. He was in such distress and pain from a toothache that he had not been able to eat anything for the last fifteen days, only to take some water. At the urging of the deacon, he prostrated himself and prayed before the relics [the deacon] was bearing and with devotion and prayer he called on the Lord Christ to take pity upon him. Through the intercession of the saints Marcellinus and Peter all his physical problems disappeared and he arose from prayer a cured man. This miracle occurred on the thirteenth [day before the] Kalends of July [that is, 19 June]. (I [Einhard] wrote a fuller account of this [miracle] above [in 5.4.8], because I undertook to compose it from the [oral] report of George.)

[23 June] On the third day [after leaving Aachen] the deacon arrived with the relics in Valenciennes and he carried them with reverence and honor into the church of St-Salvius, as he had been ordered. A young man by the name of Dominic from a royal villa called Les Estinnes [near Hainault in Belgium] had been so plagued for an entire year by the disease the Greeks call 'spasms' that his right hand could almost not be held still, but moved in a constant circular motion as if it were turning a mill. Immediately upon entering [the church] he was so cured by the merits of the blessed martyrs before the whole congregation that afterwards he no longer suffered from the disability of that awful shaking.

[24 June] On the fourth day, which was the feast day of blessed John the Baptist, an old woman by the name of Gerrada, who said that she had been blind for a year, called upon the blessed martyrs while Mass was being celebrated. Through the merits of those saints she recovered the sight, which she had full of faith sought, while everyone there looked on.

[26 June] As well, on the feast day of Saint Salvius, which falls on the sixth [day before the] Kalends of July, a certain deaf and mute man was deemed worthy during Mass to receive back both his hearing and speech through the intercession of the martyrs.

On the same day an old woman named Rodeltrude from the district of Laon, who had for three years not seen any light, regained her sight during the celebration of the same Mass.

[27 June] On the fifth [day before the] Kalends of July, a boy around seven years old named Donitian, who had been blind since birth, recovered his sight during a divine service because of the merits of the blessed martyrs.

[28 June] On the eve of the feast day of the blessed apostles Peter and Paul [that is, 29 June], which is the third [day before the] Kalends of July, a little girl named Theotbalda, who was thought to be nine years old and who had been completely blind for three years, stood in the midst of a throng of people [in the church] during the Mass. With divine mercy and because of the intercessory powers of the martyrs she recovered the sight she had lost.

On the same day a man by the name of Dado from a village called Little Bridge [came to the church]. He had been so stooped over for six years that he could not stand up straight and, as a consequence, walked with his head bent down and placed short crutches under his armpits to support himself. At the same hour and in the same place he was cured and stood up straight because of the mercy of God and the merits of the blessed martyrs.

[4 July] On the fourth [day before the] Nones of July, a widow named Adalrada, who had been completely blind for four years, heard accounts of these [miraculous] powers and full of faith began to hope that she would recover her sight. She picked up her cane and hurried off all alone and without a guide for Valenciennes. When she started to draw close to the town, she thought she perceived a single ray of sunlight with her right eye. For that reason and with a pure heart, she prayed for divine clemency to allow her through the intercession of his saints to see the church of St-Salvius. She was immediately heard and obtained at once, through the Lord's mercy, what she had wanted.

On the same day, as well, during Mass a woman named Ruoitla from the district of Noyon [see Map 1], who had been blind for five years, regained through the Lord Christ's gift and the merits of his saints the sight she had lost.

[6 July] On the octave after the apostles' [feast], that is, on the day before the Nones of July, a man by the name of Gunthard from the same district, who was paralyzed, was led by his relatives to the church of St-Salvius. They said that he had suffered from this illness for one year and that the left side of his body was so disabled that he could not raise his hand to his mouth, wash himself, or put on his shoes. During the morning service, while the Mass was being celebrated, this man was cured through God's mercy and the merits of his saints.

In addition, another man, who was named Hildebon, came [to Valenciennes] from a monastery called St-Martin-aux-Jumeaux. He had been blind from infancy and during his entire life had never seen sunlight. On the same day, during the celebration of the Mass in the same church, he received his sight by means of those same saints and by the mercy and intervention of the Lord himself he was [now] found worthy to see clearly all those things he had never seen before.

[7 July] On the Nones of July, a little girl by the name of Reginlindis, who seemed to be no more than seven years old and who had been blind for three years, stood along with others in the church to hear a divine service. With the merits of the saints intervening [for her] and before the entire congregation she recovered her sight.

[12 July] On the fourth [day before the] Ides of July, during Mass, a blind woman named Alagia, who had lacked sight for nearly two years, regained her sight from Lord Jesus Christ after the prayers of the saints had intervened on her behalf.

On the same day an old blind man named Ermenward from the village of Gheule, who had been unable to see anything for fourteen years, entered the church during the evening service. He prayed to the blessed martyrs and immediately his blindness disappeared and he regained with the Lord's help the vision he had wanted for so long.

[26 July] On the seventh [day before the] Kalends of August, a girl, who was possessed by a foul spirit, was led into the church while the holy Mass was being celebrated. By means of Christ's power and the merits of the blessed martyrs, the demon was expelled and she was deemed worthy to regain the complete health of her mind and her body.

11. These are the miracles and wonders our Lord Jesus Christ deigned to bring about because of the merits of his holy martyrs Marcellinus and Peter in the town of Valenciennes for the health and well-being of the human race. The priest George undertook to send me [an account of] these that he had collected together in short book and I thought that they should be inserted into this work of mine. George is a Venetian who had traveled from his own land to our emperor [in 826]. In the palace of Aachen he skillfully construct- ed an instrument the Greeks call a water-organ.

The monks serving God at the monastery of St-Bavo, which is located next to the Scheldt River in the place called Ghent, where that stream joins with the Leie [see Map 1], presented me with another small book. At their request I [had] sent relics of those martyrs of Christ to their monastery. These [miracles] are found arranged in this way in their little book:

12. [3 July] In the 828th year after the incarnation of our Lord Jesus Christ, on the fifth day [before the] Nones of July, on a Friday, on the sixth Indic- tion, the relics of the holy martyrs of Christ, Marcellinus and Peter, arrived at the monastery of St-Bavo.

[5 July] Now on the third day [the compiler in Roman fashion includes the first day, 3 July, as one of the days counted], that is the very next Lord's day, which was the third [day before the] Nones of July, a blind girl named Hartlinda from a village called Roeselare [see Map 1] was led before the altar upon which the sacred relics of the martyrs had been placed. Now according to her father and mother, she had been without the use of her eyes for eight years. But before all the people gathered there she regained, with the Lord's mercy, her sight.

[12 July] Eight days later, that is, on the fourth [day before the] Ides of July, another blind girl, [this one] by the name of Helmrada was led [to St-Bavo] from a village called Mechelen [see Map 1]. Her parents said that eight days after she had been baptized she had suddenly become blind. [But] in the presence of the sacred ashes of the martyrs through the Lord's gift she suddenly recovered the sight she had lost so long ago.

[14 July] Next, three days later, which was the day before the Ides of July, a girl, all bent over, by the name of Blidrada, arrived there from the village of Bourecq, which the monastery of St-Vaast holds. After she had humbly called on the Lord Christ to restore her health while she [kneeled] before the relics of the saints, she stood up straight before everyone gathered there and in a flash was deemed worthy to recover the normal posture of her body.

[21 July] Then, on the twelfth [day before the] Kalends of August, a woman by the name of Eddela, a servant of St-Amand, from a village called Baasrode, who was said to have lacked sight for many years, regained her vision while praying there faithfully.

On the same day a servant of St-Bavo by the name of Eberald, from the village of Mullen, who had also been blind for many years, was granted the vision he had so long desired [and this happened] while everyone there watched.

On that day as well two widows, who had been blind for many years, regained their sight there. It is said that one of those [women] came from the village of Eessene and was called Blidwara, while the other came from the village of Wormhoudt and was called Ricberta.

[15 August] Then after twenty-five days [had passed], that is, on the feast day of the Assumption of Saint Mary, a woman by the name of Anganhilda, from the village of Ghoy, proceeded into the presence of the sacred relics of the martyrs, while the whole congregation looked on and was amazed at what [it saw]. For she was so bent over that she almost could not raise herself up to look at the sky. On the following day, that is, on the seventeenth [day before the] Kalends of September [16 August], while the Gospel was being read out in that church and the same people were looking on, she was restored to such a straight and perfect posture that it was as if she had never been bent over toward the ground through some problem with her body.

[22 September] Next, on the twenty-second day of September, that is, on the tenth [day before the] Kalends of October, a man by the name of Liodold from the district of Turnhout [see Map 1], from a village named Heppen, who because of the weakness of his left leg and foot supported himself on two crutches in order to walk, was so completely cured there while the congregation looked on that afterwards he no longer needed the help of his crutches to walk.

[25 September] In fact on the fourth day after the occurrence of this miracle, that is on the seventh [day before the] Kalends of October, a young man named Hunwald from the village of Chièvres, who was deaf and mute and also had a deformed left hand, came [there]. After he had proceeded before the sacred relics of the martyrs and had humbly prayed there, all the troubles with which he had been afflicted were driven off by the miraculous power of Christ. He was so completely cured that it was as if he had never been deaf or mute or had ever in any way suffered from a tightening of the tendons in his hand.

[26 September] The next day, that, is on the sixth [day before the] Kalends of October, a woman by the name of Engilgarda, who for many years had suffered from a serious case of paralysis, was cured in the same church before the whole congregation through the merits of the blessed martyrs. She was a servant from a village called Warcoing and belonged to the bishopric of Tournai.

[27 September] Indeed, on the next day, that is, the fifth [day before the] Kalends of October, another woman, this one called Ramburga, from the village of Bettegem, who was extremely weak because of a similar sort of problem [that is, paralysis] in the lower part of her body, regained in the presence of the saints' relics the complete strength of her limbs while everyone gathered there watched. By the will of God she was, in a moment's time, released from a disease that was said to have afflicted her for a decade.

There on the same day a blind man named Germar from the village of Scaltheim, which is located on seashore of Frisia near the mouth of the Scheldt River, prayed for God's mercy and called on the blessed martyrs because of the misfortune he was suffering. He was then deemed worthy to regain with great joy the vision long denied to him.

[30 September] Moreover, on the fourth day after the Lord willed this miracle to happen, that is on the second [day before the Kalends] of October, a female servant of St-Bavo by the name of Gundrada, from the village of Audeghem, who for nearly three years had not seen the sun, prostrated herself in prayer before the altar. Through the Lord Christ's gift and the merits of his saints, she regained the sight she had lost.

13. The monks of the monastery of St-Servais the Confessor, which is located on a bank of the Meuse River, in the town that is called Maastricht today [see Map 2], brought me a third small book. That place lies about eight leagues from the palace of Aachen and is very crowded with a host of residents and especially merchants. The text of this book, if I recall clearly, seemed to be arranged as follows:

14. [4 June] The arrival of the holy martyrs of Christ, Marcellinus and Peter, in the town of Maastricht occurred on the day before the Nones of June. Now on that day a vast crowd of people had gathered to receive them. They came out from the town to meet them, praising and blessing God for his vast and ineffable mercy in deigning to visit through such great patron [saints] a people who believed and depended upon him. With praise and spiritual rejoicing the crowd came to the church of St-Servais, where after much thanksgiving by all a Mass was celebrated. After everyone had returned to their homes and work, the bier on which the sacred ashes had been transported, was arranged on the right side of the altar in the choir. That whole day was spent in great rejoicing and happiness by the people who lived in that town.

When I had, following custom, entered that church to celebrate the evening service, [I saw] among others a boy by the name of Berngisus. His relatives had led him there a few days earlier from the district of Condrieu, for he had been blind since birth. In the presence of everyone, he suddenly fell onto the hard floor and lay there for quite a while as if overcome by sleep. Then, with the Lord Christ granting [a cure] because of the merits of his saints, he soon opened his eyes and saw light, which he had never seen before.

[8 June] On the fifth day [after their arrival], that is, on the sixth [day before the] Ides of June, a man having the surname Hildimar, who was deaf and mute, regained both his hearing and speech through the miraculous power of Christ in the presence of the sacred relics of the saints.

On the same day as well a [servant] girl from the household of St-Lambert [of Liège] by the name of Adallinda, who was not only deaf and mute, but also blind and curled up in such a wretched way, because of the tightened tendons throughout her body, that her knees touched her chest, was set down beside the martyrs' sacred relics by her relatives. In the presence of everyone who was there, she regained by divine grace and with remarkable speed her sight, hearing, and speech, and indeed all her limbs became straight and strong.

[9 June] The next day, that is, on the fifth [day before the] Ides of June, a royal servant by the name of Berohad from the village of Crecy, whose body on the right side was entirely debilitated and useless because of tightened tendons, came before the saints' relics. He immediately stood up straight and was at once restored to the health he so desired.

Similarly a girl with the name of Theothild from the town of Maastricht itself, whose right hand was curled up and deformed by a similar tightening [of her tendons] to such a extent that it was entirely useless, was also cured on the same day before the saints' relics.

When these events had been witnessed, the people gathered in the church began, because of their great joy and happiness, to raise their voices and loudly chant praises to the Lord in hymns and litanies. All at once a deaf boy entered [the church] and stood amazed, as if thunderstruck, in the midst of the crowd of people. Then, after he had come before the altar of the holy Savior, which was set in the middle of the church, blood suddenly began pouring from his nose and the faculty of hearing that he had been without for a long time was restored to him.

[10 June] Now the next day, that is, on the fourth [day before the] Ides of June, it seemed to me that the bier holding the sacred ashes of the martyrs should be raised up higher, so that it might be somewhat higher than the altar beside which it was placed and so that it might be more easily seen by the people approaching it. A little while earlier, while we were doing this and were, while in the midst of our work, singing litanies in praise of God, a [servant] girl from the household of St-Servais was carried into the church by her family. They set her down in front of the bier. This girl's feet had been deformed by a tightening [of the tendons] since birth and her hands had also been weakened by stretched tendons. On top of that she was mute. But she was so suddenly cured, that within an hour she could speak, walk, and use her hands fully for everything that needed doing.

[13 June] A woman from the town of Maastricht itself had a blind servant by the name of Adalgarda. She entered the church and entrusted her to the holy martyrs Marcellinus and Peter, so that through their holy intercession she might be worthy to regain her sight. And so she left her there. After [Adalgarda] had remained in the church at the conclusion of the evening service, she suddenly fell down on the hard floor as if she had been struck by someone. She rolled about there for a long time, but finally stood up to the great bewilderment and amazement of the people standing nearby, for she could [now] see perfectly. This [miracle] occurred on the Ides of June at vespers, when dusk was falling.

[14 June] A man by the name of Theotgar from the district of Geneva in the province of Burgundy [see Map 4] was afflicted with that disorder which physicians call a 'spasm' after the Greek word, but which in Latin can appropriately be called 'trembling' because of the persistent agitation of the limbs. He entered the church and stood in the middle of the crowd of people that had as usual gathered to listen to the Mass that Sunday. After the Gospel reading was over and the creed of the Christian faith was being chanted, that trembling man suddenly fell to the ground and while the divine service was being brought to a close he laid there almost completely still more like a dead man than a living one. An immense amount of blood flowed from his nose.

After the sacred service had ended, the cured man stood up to the great amazement of the watching congregation and no longer trembled. This miracle occurred on the eighteenth [day before the] Kalends of July, which was a Sunday, as was stated above.

[17 June] Moreover, on Wednesday, that is, on the fifteenth [day before the] Kalends of July, a boy by the name of Folchard from a monastery called Meldert, who was deformed by a wretched tightening [of the tendons] in his legs and feet, was cured in the presence of the whole congregation in the same place.

[21 June] On the eleventh [day before the] Kalends of July, a man came to the church and entered along with others. His right hand and arm were moving round and round in an amazing way as if he had to turn a mill; and he did this without ceasing. He said that this agitation had befallen him, because he had against the commandment ground wheat one Sunday, and now for an entire year he had paid this particular penalty. After he had approached the martyrs' sacred relics and had faithfully called on them, that grinding motion suddenly stopped. This man said that he had come from the monastery of the Irish called Fosse and that his name was Dothius.

[23 June] On the eve of [the feast day of] Saint John the Baptist, which is the ninth [day before the] Kalends of July, a man came to the church of St-Servais in Maastricht. He said that he was from the city of Tournai [see Map 1]. As he himself [later] declared, he had been deaf and mute since his childhood. His relatives had led him to Saint Sebastian [in Soissons] where he had begun both to hear and speak, but not with success, since his speech could hardly be understood. When others spoke to him, he too could not hide how little he heard. When he came for the morning service, he fell down before the sacred relics and went to sleep. A little later he awoke as if someone was shaking him and asked people standing closeby who had punched him in the mouth. When they all answered that no one had, he got up and was at that very moment cured. He [now] spoke and heard perfectly without any problem.

On the same day, while the Mass was being celebrated, a woman by the name of Madallinda brought two candles to light in the church. With her right hand she gave one of these [candles] to one of the sacristans to light, but kept the other in her left hand as though she intended to light it later with [the flame of] the other candle. But in an amazing fashion, as the sacristan lit the candle he was given, the other one, the one the woman still held in her hand, was lit by divine intervention while everyone looked on.

A monastery of nuns, called Eike, is located on the Meuse River. There a woman by the name of Saliga, who was consecrated to God, lay immobilized by a terrible case of paralysis; her entire body except for her right arm was affected. In a dream she saw one of her neighbors standing beside her. He reproached her with words like these: "What are you doing?" he said. When she answered that she was only resting in her own bed, he said, "Have you [not] heard of the saints who have come to St-Servais in Maastricht?" When she said that she had heard nothing about them, he said: "Get up and rush there as quickly and hastily [as you can], for there you will regain strength in all your limbs!" But when she awoke and did not bother to do this, the same [figure] warned her in similar terms the next night to proceed to Maastricht. But again, as she did before, she ignored the voice that had warned and commanded her and postponed the trip. But on the third night she saw him standing at her side, with an angry look, asking why she had spurned his warnings. Then he hit her in the side with a rod he seemed to be holding in his hand and he ordered her to set out at once for Maastricht. This time she didn't dare disobey the command of the third vision and [so] she summoned her relatives and friends who led her to Maastricht as she had been ordered. She was placed beside the martyrs' sacred ashes in the church of St-Servais. There she waited for the return of her promised health. [Finally] on the fifth day after coming there, and to the great amazement of all, she was deemed worthy to regain perfect health throughout her body.

15. Two very special miracles still remain [to be considered]. Not only do I believe that these should not be forgotten, but in fact I am sure that I can bring about the most appropriate end to the fourth book, which is now at hand, by recording them. These miracles might seem to belong to the blessed Marcellinus and Peter [working] together with other saints, since one of these [miracles] occurred on the arrival of the relics of Saints Protius and Hyacinth and near those relics themselves. The other [miracle] is known to have happened close to the relics of Saint Hermes and on his feast day. Nevertheless, it seems in point of fact that these miracles should be attributed to [Marcellinus and Peter], since they happened in the very church where their most sacred bodies rest. In fact, confirmation [of the nature] of these events rests with those of us who were present and who, with divine assistance, were permitted to see them. For this reason, let me, without introductory remark, take up these miracles that need to be related.

16. Pope Gregory [IV; see Fig. 2], who succeeded Eugenius [II] and Valentine in the office of the papacy, wished to expand the titular church of St-Mark the Evangelist, where he had been priest, and to erect a monastery within it. So he looked in the cemeteries and the churches established farther from

Rome to see if he might find bodies of the holy martyrs. After he found them, he undertook to transport them to the titular church he was erecting with magnificent workmanship. It was by accident, therefore, that it happened that it was at the very time when the tomb of the most blessed Hermes was about to be opened and his sacred body raised from there that one of my men, who had traveled to Rome that year to pray as penitents do, took his place with other pilgrims in the crowd gathered in the church of the martyr. After he had closely observed the proceedings, he conceived in his simple heart, but not unreasonably, the hope of obtaining relics of that martyr. He went to see the deacon Deusdona, whom I mentioned so frequently in the first book, and in the strongest possible terms begged him to acquire a portion of those relics no matter how small from the sacristans of that place and to present it to him so that he could bring it to me. [Deusdona] immediately consented to his pleas and promised that he would act without delay. He paid a sum of money to the sacristans and received relics not just of Saint Hermes, but also of the saints Protius and Hyacinth, whose bodies had been laid in the same church. In fact, he undertook to send me those relics through a member of his own household, whose surname was Sabbatinus, and also through my own man, the one who had talked him into doing this. But the portion of the body of the blessed Hermes that he had been able to obtain, he himself brought and conferred on me as a great gift. But when I learned of the arrival of the relics of the saints Protius and Hyacinth, we marched out in procession to greet them and we honorably received them, as was only appropriate, and carried them to the church with hymns and prayers. We set them down on the bier on which they had traveled beside the bodies of the blessed Marcellinus and Peter.

It was there the next day that a woman from a neighboring estate called Baldradesstadt, who was possessed by a demon, entered [the church] with other people. That evil spirit began to roar and threw her face down onto the hard ground. It made its evil manifest by revealing it openly to everyone there. When [the demon] was asked by the priest, who was exorcising that spirit, who he was, where he had come from, and when and why he had entered into her, he responded to each question. He claimed that he was not only a demon, but actually the worst of all living things. When the priest asked him the reason for this great evilness, he confessed that an evil will had done this to him. When he was also asked whether he had ever been in heaven, he admitted that he had been in heaven and that he had been expelled from there because of his pride. When his investigator asked whether he had ever seen the Lord Christ, he said that he had seen him in hell when, in order to save the human race, [Christ] had deigned to die and had descended there [into the infernal regions]. But when it came time to ask him if he knew the names of the martyrs whose relics had been carried into that church a day earlier, he said, "Their names are certainly well known to me, because when they were martyred I was there standing beside them. I have [ever since] been tormented by my great envy for their everlasting glory. Even here and now I am experiencing their persistent resistance, for they are punishing me with unbelievable torment and are compelling me to leave the vessel [of this body] in which I have hidden for a long time." The priest said to him, "When you have left [her], where will you go?" He said, "I shall travel along the worst road and shall seek out distant and deserted places." After this, once he had revealed to the priest, who had ordered him to speak, both when and how he had entered into [the girl], he turned to the woman and said: "Before I leave you, you unhappy woman, I intend to smash and break your bones. I shall leave you crippled as a remembrance of our meeting." When that woman, as though she were aware of her affliction, began in a humble and subdued voice to plead for help from the saints, that [demon] immediately began to roar and bellow in the foulest manner using her mouth [to do so] and he ordered her to shut up as she tried to speak. To those of us who were there it was quite remarkable to see that foul spirit speaking through the mouth of that little woman in such different voices, for at one moment she spoke so clearly with a man's voice and at the next with a woman's, that it seemed that there was not one, but two persons in her who were bitterly wrestling with each other and taking turns shouting abuse at the other. In fact, there were two persons there, resisting each other with their different wills; one was the demon who wanted to destroy the body he inhabited, the other was the woman who wanted to be free of the enemy holding her. The difference between their wills could clearly and easily be recognized, since their voices were dissimilar and the words they shouted at each other in turn were very different. Now when, as usual, the service of the divine mystery was finished, it was time for me to leave the church and to look after my body's needs, I ordered the woman to wait there with the guardians [of the relics] until I returned, for I was confident that by means of the power of Christ and his martyrs' merits the one who so treacherously inhabited her would quickly depart. And my hope was not in vain, for when I returned to the church after eating, I found that the demon had been expelled and that [the woman] was [now] safe and sound, in complete control of her mind, and rejoicing in the praise of God. Indeed, it is widely known that this miracle occurred upon the arrival of the relics of Christ's blessed martyrs, Protius and Hyacinth, in the way I have just recorded.

But the miracle attributed to Saint Hermes and how it happened will be described in the next narrative.

17. Cologne is a metropolitan city located in the territory of the Ripuarians on the Rhine River [see Map 2]. A certain woman from there had been for a long time afflicted to such an extent by a stretching of the tendons below her waist that, since her legs and feet would not work, she could not walk. Instead, she sat with her feet out in front and leaned on her hands, which rested on the ground, and so moved herself forward. After she heard of the miracles and wonders the Lord had worked through his holy martyrs Marcellinus and Peter in curing the sick and crippled, she was extremely anxious to travel to their church. And since she was not able to go there easily in any other way, she was transported on the boat of [some] merchants who were traveling there for the feast day of those saints [2 June]. She arrived there on the day of their martyrdom and remained there for quite some time in the hope of regaining her health. But when she saw that her cure had been delayed, she decided to proceed to Mainz. In truth her cure had [merely] been delayed, not denied, for it would happen not in some other place, but there [in the saints' church] and not at that time but later. It was then nearly the feast day of the martyr Saint Alban [22 June], whose church and famous monastery were in that city [of Mainz]. After she had arrived there and had prayed to the Lord beside the tomb of the martyr for the restoration of her health, she saw in her sleep that a young cleric was standing beside her holding new shoes in his hand. He ordered her to take them and put them on her feet, which she did. Then he ordered her to return to the place she had left with these shoes on her feet and to wait there for the arrival of the physician who would, without doubt, cure her. When she awoke, she trusted her vision and returned as quickly as she could to the curative church of the holy martyrs. For two months she remained in that place with other poor people and awaited the fulfilment of her vision.

In the meantime around the middle of August [830, see 1.16 above], the deacon Deusdona (about whom I spoke at great length in the first book of this work) came from Rome and brought me a great gift, a single joint of the blessed martyr Hermes's finger. I received it and placed [the joint] stored in a small reliquary in the upper part of the church above the western entranceway. But that woman, as I have said, had traveled [back] there, because she had been [so] advised by a heavenly vision. But when two months had passed and she still saw no indication of the help she had been promised, she suspected that she had been deceived by a false dream and [so] she began to think about returning home. She arranged with traders, who were themselves departing for home the next Sunday, which would be the fifth [day before the] Kalends of September [28 August] and also the anniversary day of Saint Hermes, to return to her land on their boat. Now as night fell [on the eve] of the day fixed for her departure, after the evening service, I as usual left the church to go to bed. As others as well were exiting, that woman wanted to enter and sat down at the door itself. There, with everyone watching, she was overcome by a stupor and fell silent for a time. Next, after some blood had poured from all around her toenails, she returned to normal and reached out her hand to the people standing near her. Once she had been lifted onto her feet, she began to walk to the tomb of the martyrs. When she had arrived there, she threw herself down in prayer before the altar and lay there a long time until the hymn that the rejoicing and happy crowd was devoutly singing in praise of God was over. When [the hymn] was finished, the woman stood up cured, but she no longer wanted to return to her homeland.

Thus, that miracle is appropriately attributed to the blessed Hermes, since it is known to have happened on the day of his martyrdom and beneath his relics [which were above the door]. But the most holy martyrs Marcellinus and Peter cannot have been entirely left out of this work, [since] the miracle was brought about in their church and that woman herself, who was cured, was always throughout her entire pilgrimage calling upon them to help her.

18. These then are some of the innumerable miracles of the saints that I either saw or learned of from the accounts of the faithful and that I decided to commit to letters and lasting memory. I have no doubt that the lovers of Christ and those who venerate his martyrs will be grateful to read [of these miraculous cures], since nothing seems impossible for them to achieve, if it suits the almighty God. But I recommend that unbelievers and those who disparage the glory of the saints not try to read them at all, for I am sure that they would be unappealing [to them] and they may be so outraged by the vulagarity of my language, that they may be unable to avoid blasphemy and spite, and so demonstrate that they hate God and their fellow human beings, whom they are commanded to love.

6. THE COLLECTED LETTERS

A collection of Einhard's later letters was apparently preserved at St-Bavo. The letters translated below are in the order in which they occur in the unique manuscript (Paris, B.N. lat.11379, fols. 3-14r, but reference numbers from Karl Hampe's edition are supplied in parentheses for those readers wishing to examine the Latin texts.

Source: translated from Einharti Epistolae, ed. K. Hampe, Monumenta Gemaniae Historica: Epistolae, vol. 5 (Hanover: Weidmann, 1898-99), pp. 105-142.

1 (Hampe 1). To Ansegisus, the abbot of Fontanelle (St-Wandrille). 823-825

To the venerable Ansegisus, a most beloved brother in Christ, [I wish] everlasting salvation in the Lord.

I am appealing to your Kindness not to receive [this letter] with annoyance, but rather with sympathy and friendship, since I am intervening with you on behalf of the interests of N., who was once my man, but is now Lord Lothar's man [that is, his vassal]. I ask you to allow him to hold the benefice that I gave him [presumably when Einhard was lay-abbot] under any financial terms that suit you until I am able, with the Lord's help, to supply some compensation to that man with another benefice [obtained] through the generosity of our lords [Louis the Pious and Lothar]. You will find that I am even more eager and committed to pursuing your causes and interests, if you deign to look after my request in this business.

I hope that you may always prosper in the Lord.

2 (Hampe 39). To Gozbert, the abbot of St-Gall. 816-836

Einhard, a sinner, [sends his greetings] to the venerable Abbot Gozbert, a devout servant of Christ.

I beg your Holiness to deign to consider the case of that man of yours named Bebo. I myself gave him a benefice from the monastery of St-Cloud, because he served me well. But after I commended him to Lord Lothar, I secured from the lord emperor [Louis the Pious an understanding] that he would make a confirmation of that same benefice on him for the rest of his life. For this reason, I ask and beg your Kindness not to allow any problem to arise for that man over this benefice until, with the Lord allowing it, I can talk to you. I am writing to you in this way, because I am [well] aware of the evil intentions and infinite greed of some people, who do not care about their neighbors' losses if they can satisfy their own greedy ambitions.

I hope that you may always prosper in the Lord.

3 (Hampe 4). To Amalarius, liturgist and priest of Metz. 828-29

Einhard, a sinner, [sends his greetings] to Amalarius, a most revered servant of Christ.

I do not know who came before the arrival of your servant, the one who brought your letter to me, and arranged for you to be ordered to come to the emperor on the day following Palm Sunday. But after I myself received your letter and asked the emperor [Louis] about the business you were interested in, he directed me to write you that you should have celebrated Easter Sunday at home. [He also said] that you should command the rest of your retinue to follow you so that when they catch up with you at the palace, after you have received your instructions and the purpose for your mission has been made clear, you might be able to set off on your journey without delay.

I hope that you may always prosper in the Lord.

4 (Hampe 43). To Otgar, the archbishop of Mainz. 826-840

Einhard, a sinner, [sends his greetings] to the holy lord and justly venerable Otgar, the most revered archbishop.

This brother named Werdric is from the congregation of St-Boniface [that is, Fulda] and is staying with me by permission of his abbot [Hrabanus Maurus], since he is a relative of mine. I have, therefore, now sent him to you, so that you may arrange to ordain him a deacon, once you have determined that it can be done canonically according to the reasons laid out in his abbot's letter. [Hrabanus] sent that [letter] to me recently, when I asked for and sought his advice about the matter. I have sent that letter with this same brother for you to read. From it, I think, you [should] immediately be able to tell whether that consecration can occur now or must be postponed until a later date.

I pray and hope that divine grace will always and everywhere protect your Holiness, most holy and revered father, since you serve [God] with devotion.

5 (Hampe 54). To Bishop James. Before 840

Einhard, a sinner, [sends his greetings] to the most revered bishop, James, venerable in Christ.

That cleric of yours by the name of Otmar delivered the letter of your Holiness in which you ask me to give permission for this same cleric, who was born and raised in this area, to stay with you. After weighing the strength of his case, I have decided to give my approval to your request, but on these terms. This cleric [Otmar] along with his brothers and mother shall have the right to remain with you, as you requested, but they shall pay their dues each year to St-Servais [of Maastricht], exactly as [those dues] were assigned to them by our brothers. Let the matter of the ordination of this same cleric lie within your power to do about it whatever seems best to you, since you know and are fully aware of his habits and way of life, and whether he is a suitable [candidate] to take up some holy order.

I hope your Holiness remembers me and that you may always prosper in Christ.

6 (Hampe 24). To Egilolf and Hunbert. Late 832

[Einhard wishes] eternal salvation in the Lord to Egilolf and Hunbert, most beloved brothers in Christ and his devoted servants.

I know that you are not unaware that Bishop Wolfgar [of Würzburg] of blessed memory [who died in 832] granted upon my request a benefice of three homesteads and twelve dependents from the resources of St-Kilian [a monastery in Würzburg], in the district of Durbargau, in a place called Mergentheim, to my man Gerbert. But since he could stay there only as long as [Wolfgar] lived, I beg your Kindness to permit that Gerbert to hold that benefice, as he now does, until a [new] bishop is ordained in that see and he [the new bishop] and I reach an agreement on what ought to happen about that benefice in the future.

I hope that you may always prosper in the Lord.

7 (Hampe 47). To Count Poppo. 828-840

Einhard [wishes] salvation in the Lord to a magnificent, honorable, and illustrious man, the gracious Count Poppo.

Two poor people have fled to the church of Christ's blessed martyrs, Marcellinus and Peter [in Seligenstadt], and have confessed that they are guilty. In your presence they were found guilty of robbery, which they committed when they stole wild animals in the lord's forest. They have already paid part of the fine, and should still pay the rest. But they claim that they do not have the means to pay [at present] because of their poverty. Therefore, I beg your

Kindness to consider sparing them, as far as it is possible, out of love for the martyrs of Christ, to whom they fled, so that they may not be completely ruined by a crime of this kind, but rather may realize that, in your eyes, it helped them that they fled to the tombs of the holy martyrs.

I hope that you may always prosper in the Lord.

8 (Hampe 44). To Otgar, the archbishop of Mainz. 826–840

To the holy lord and justly venerable Otgar, the most revered archbishop.

A priest by the name of Hruodrad came to see me and said that he was from your estate, [the town of] Mayen [see Map 2], and had received permission from your suffragan bishop and his brothers to proceed to Rome in the month of March. But, sometime later, after he had come to Mainz, he was not able to find people with whom he could continue that journey. For this reason, he turned to a certain countryman of mine by the name of Hildebert, whom he knew, and stayed with him until he could find people traveling to Rome. He says that he has now found these people and he asked me to request your permission for him to proceed on that journey. For he wishes, as he himself maintains, to complete that journey as quickly as he can and [then] return to his proper place. For this reason I beg your Holiness to consider granting him the permission he requested and that it not be held against him that he was delayed so long on the way. Many unavoidable problems were put in his way, which he could not solve.

I hope that your Holiness remembers my Feebleness and that you, most holy and revered father, always prosper in Christ.

9 (Hampe 6). To Geboin, the count of the palace. Prior to 830

Einhard [wishes] salvation in the Lord to his much loved brother Geboin, the glorious count of the palace.

I am appealing to your Kindness to consider hearing out a fellow countryman of mine, whose name is David. He wants to explain his problems to you, and if you see that his case is a reasonable one, [he hopes] you might give him the opportunity to protest to the lord emperor [Louis]. For he is a man [vassal] of Lord Lothar and, therefore, you should help him not just because of my request, but also out of love and respect for his superior [that is, Lothar].

I hope that I may be lucky enough to see you safe and sound sometime soon.

10 (Hampe 45). To Hetti, the archbishop of Trier. 828–840

Einhard, a sinner, [sends his greetings] to the holy and justly venerable Hetti, a most revered archbishop.

As [soon as] I learned from your Holiness's letter [what] you wished done, I undertook to do [it] at once, namely by sending you the relics that you wrote of wishing to acquire for the dedication of your new church. Indeed, I did that happily, because I have such great confidence in you and [I know] that whatever portion of the sacred ashes of the blessed martyrs comes to you will be shown the kind of honor we ought to have shown to their complete bodies, if laziness and neglect did not slow [us] from honoring them as they deserve.

I am, however, not able to tell you anything more certain about the matter you wished to learn from me, because almost no news normally comes to me from that place [the palace]. Nor am I very interested in those things, for I take little pleasure and gain no benefit from knowing about them.

I hope that your Holiness remembers my Feebleness and that you, most holy and revered father, always prosper in the Lord.

11 (Hampe 7). To Count Hruotbert. Prior to 830

[Einhard wishes] eternal salvation in the Lord to a magnificent, honorable, and illustrious man, Hruotbert, the glorious count.

I am appealing to your kindness to deign to write to me about what you want done now in the case of my man Alafrid. Should [that case] be completely dropped or ought he to hold out hope that he may be deemed worthy to attain his just due through your assistance? For I laid out the entire case for the lord emperor, including how you made inquiries among truthful people, along with the counts of his palace, Adalard and Geboin. [The emperor] told me that he was surprised that the case had not yet been concluded. Therefore, I beg your kindness to consider writing me now about what my man [Alafrid] should do about his case.

I hope you may always flourish in the Lord.

12 (Hampe 55). To the Priest Liuthard and Einhard's Deputy Erembert. Before 840

In the name of Christ. Abbot Einhard [wishes] salvation in the Lord to his faithful men, the priest Liuthard and his deputy Erembert.

Let it be known to you that I have ordered the priest Willibald, as I know him to be my man, to collect our revenues from our men both at St-Bavo and at the monastery of Blandin [at Ghent]. For this reason I am sending him to you, since I wish you to assist him in this business so that he might receive those revenues fully and in good silver. After he has received [those monies], I wish you to render assistance to him so that he can bring them to me.

I hope you may always prosper in the Lord.

13 (Hampe 8). To Count Poppo. Prior to 830

Einhard [wishes] eternal salvation in the Lord to a magnificent, honorable, and illustrious man, Poppo, the glorious count.

I was told that you had asked me to reassure you on three matters. It is difficult for me to do that on at least one of those [matters], that is, whether you can, without censure, marry a woman, whom you know better than me. As to the provisions you received in Aachen, I wish no other payment than your friendship. As to Jupille [near Liège], I am prepared to act according to what we agreed upon when we spoke together [about this business]. Thus, I cannot now provide you with more information in my letter.

I hope you may always prosper in the Lord.

14 (Hampe 52). To the Monk Gerward. Early 830s

Einhard [wishes] perpetual salvation in the Lord to the dearest monk Gerward.

It is not clear to me what I should think about you, whether, that is, you did not understand my letter or did not care about my peril. But I am led more easily to [the former] interpretation, for I would rather think that as a result of certain preoccupations my letter was not carefully read and understood by you than to believe that your Kindness had no concern for the danger threatening me.

For you encourage me, or rather advise me, to abandon my watch over the martyrs, with whom I was ordered to stay and to be constantly present, and to come to the palace, since I might run the risk of a future penalty if I delay for a week. But a delay cannot be avoided, not just in setting out for the palace, but also on the journey it is necessary to make to the palace, particularly in my case. I have rarely been able to travel from Aachen to the church of the martyrs [at Seligenstadt] in less than a week both because of the difficulty of the road and because of the feebleness of [my] body. But I now ask you and stubbornly beg you to reread again and understand the letter I sent you. You should not refuse to write back to me, as I had asked you to in my letter quite some time ago, about how that revelation [see 5.3.13] and the commands by which I was bound struck you. Messengers are not lacking, if you wish to send what you have written to my deputy Bonottus.

I hope that you may always prosper in the Lord, dearest and most beloved brother and lord.

15 (Hampe 37). Einhard's Wife, Emma, to Blidthrut. 828-836

Emma, a friend hoping the best for you, [wishes] eternal salvation in the Lord to her most beloved sister Blidthrut.

A certain servant of yours from Mosbach [see Map 3] by the name of Wenilo married a certain free woman, and now, fearing your anger and also that of his lord, Albuin, has fled to the church of the saints Marcellinus and Peter [at Seligenstadt]. On his behalf I ask that your Kindness consider interceding with [Albuin] in my stead, so that with [Albuin's] permission and yours he might retain that woman whom he married.

I hope that you may always be well.

16 (Hampe 46). To Count Hatto. 828-840

Einhard [wishes] eternal salvation in the Lord to my dearest friend Hatto, the glorious count.

A certain man of yours by the name of Hunno came to the church of the saints Marcellinus and Peter [at Seligenstadt] seeking forgiveness because he had married his own fellow dependent, your servant, without your permission. For this reason, I entreat your Kindness, so that he may be found worthy to receive your indulgence in this business, if his offense is found to be worth forgiving.

I hope that you may always prosper in the Lord.

17 (Hampe 42). To Abbot Hrabanus [Maurus]. 822-840

Einhard, a sinner, [sends his greetings] to that most revered servant of Christ, the venerable abbot, Hrabanus.

A certain man of yours by the name of Gundhart asked me to intercede on his behalf with your holiness, so that he might, without giving you offense and indeed with your approval, be given permission to avoid the military expedition that is being planned at the present time and might remain at home. He claims that he is forced to remain at home out of great need, since he has been threatened by revenge and does not dare to go on this expedition with his enemies and with those who are plotting against his life, particularly with that count whom he is ordered to accompany, for he says he is his bitterest [enemy]. Thus, he asks you not to issue an order that would place him in such great danger. He is anxious to look after the matter himself, in order to make peace with the collector of the heerban [the fine for not appearing when summoned], if he should come and compel him, without troubling you. I would not have asked you [for help] in this matter, if I had not learned for certain of this man's dire straits and the dangers [to him].

I hope that you may always be well.

18 (Hampe 48). To the Deputy, Marchrad. 828–840

Einhard [wishes] eternal salvation in the Lord to my dear friend Marchrad, the distinguished deputy.

Two servants of St-Martin [of Mainz], from the village of Hedabahc, by the names of Williram and Otbert, fled to the church of Marcellinus and Peter, Christ's blessed martyrs, [at Seligenstadt] because their brother had killed one of his companions. They asked to be allowed to pay the assigned wergeld on their brother's behalf, so that his life might be pardoned. Therefore, I ask your Kindness, as far as it is possible, to consider sparing him out of love for God and his saints, to whose church they have fled.

I hope that you always prosper in the Lord.

19 (Hampe 20). The Emperor Louis to Count G. 832

In the name of the Lord God and our Savior Jesus Christ, Louis, the emperor augustus by the design of divine providence, [sends greetings] to Count G.

Let it be known to you that we want you, once this letter of mine has reached you, to ready yourself at once and without delay to come to a village of ours called Heilbronn [see Map 3] on the fifteenth [day before the] Kalends of January [18 December], that is, six days before Christmas, to meet our *missus* [*dominicus*], H. Whatever he orders you and the other counts and vassals to do, on our authority, you should strive to do and accomplish as directed, inasmuch as we have firm confidence in your fealty.

Farewell.

20 (Hampe 21). The Emperor Louis to his Vassal H. November 832

In the name of the Lord God and our Savior Jesus Christ, Louis, the emperor augustus by the design of divine providence, [sends greetings] to our faithful man, H.

Let it be known to you that we want you to command one of your sons, our vassal, whom you know to be best suited for this [duty], to stand ready so that, when Count R. [Hruotbert] and our *missus* H. want to inform us of something through him, he can proceed at once and with all speed to Tours. With God's grace, either we ourselves or our beloved wife [Judith] will be found there. Be sure, then, that you are not negligent, if you wish to enjoy our favor.

I hope you may always prosper in the Lord.

21 (Hampe 22). The Emperor Louis to his Vassal T. Late 832

In the name of the Lord God and our Savior Jesus Christ, Louis, the emperor augustus by the design of divine providence, [sends greetings] to our faithful man, T.

Let it be known to you that we want you to stand ready, so that, whenever Count Hr[uotber]t and our *missus* H. wish to inform us of something through you, you will be able to proceed at once and with all speed with that message to Tours. With God's grace, either we ourselves or our beloved wife [Judith] will be found there. Be sure, then, that you are not negligent [in this duty], if you wish to enjoy our favor.

22 (Hampe 23). To the Imperial *Missus* A. Late 832

Einhard [wishes] perpetual salvation in the Lord to his beloved brother and friend, A., a *missus dominicus*.

I thought that you knew that our men, whom we have in that area, were on guard [duty] along the coast as arranged and ordered by the lord emperor not only at that time when he set out for [Tribur], but also when he continued on to Orléans. For this reason it does not seem fair to me that men, who were exactly where the emperor himself had ordered them [to be], should have to pay the heerban [the fine for not appearing when summoned]. Therefore, I call on your Kindness to grant us the time then until the lord emperor [himself] arrives. I shall remind him of his order and he will then issue a ruling, as it suits him.

I hope that you may always prosper in the Lord.

23 (Hampe 5). To his Deputy at Maastricht. Around 828

In the name of Christ, I, Abbot Einhard, send greetings to my deputy and faithful man.

Let it be known that I wish you to send some people to Aachen to fix up and restore my buildings. You should [also] arrange, as is customary, to deliver at the right time those things that we need to have there, that is, flour, grain prepared for brewing, wine, cheese, and other things. But you should arrange for the cattle, which need to be slaughtered, to be brought to Lanaeken [near Maastricht on the Meuse] and slaughtered there. I want you to arrange for one of these [oxen] to be given to Hruotlouge. I wish the entrails and offal [of the slaughtered cattle], which cannot be preserved for our needs, to be given to the people of the household at the same place. With the Lord's assistance, I wish to reach the palace around [the time of the] Mass of Saint Martin [on 11 November], if I am still alive. For this reason, I wish you to inform the subordinates of the church about all these matters and to command them on my authority to carry out these things at my expense, and so I have [now] ordered you to do.

Farewell.

24 (Hampe 56). To a Deputy. Before 840

In the name of Christ. Einhard, called the abbot, sends greetings in the Lord to N.

I am making it known to you that we require wax for our service and are not able to obtain this [material] in those places because the production of honey was small [over the last] two years in those areas. For this reason, I wish you to discuss and consider with N. in what way, if it is feasible, you might arrange to send one load [on a beast of burden] to me with those vassals of mine who are returning to me from those parts after the feast day of Saint Bavo [1 October].

Farewell and pray for us.

25 (Hampe 49). To an Archbishop. 828-840

Einhard, a sinner, [sends greetings] to the holy lord and justly venerable and most revered N.

A certain servant of St-Mary's by the name of N., who falls under the authority of your holiness, came to the church of Christ's blessed martyrs, Marcellinus and Peter [at Seligenstadt], seeking forgiveness for a crime, which he committed by slaying a companion over a dispute that broke out between them. Therefore, I beg your holiness to consider sparing him out of reverence for those same martyrs, to whose church he fled, so that after having submitted his body to the punishment of a whipping he be allowed to make restitution with a cash payment and [so] make right what he committed with an evil will.

I hope your holiness, most holy and revered father, always prospers in Christ.

26 (Hampe 27). To a Certain U. Late 833

Einhard [wishes] eternal salvation to U.

Frumold, the son of Count N., whose sister is the wife of N. [another individual], holds a moderately sized benefice in Burgundy in the district of Geneva, where his father was [once] count. He has been [incapacitated] more from illness than old age, for he is troubled by an ongoing and serious case of gout. He fears that he will lose that [benefice], unless your Kindness will help him, since due to the illness from which he suffers he cannot travel to the palace. For that reason, he begs you to consider asking the lord emperor [Lothar] to permit him, because of his pressing need, to hold [that] benefice which his grandfather [Charlemagne] granted him and his father [Louis the Pious had] allowed him to hold, until he has recovered his strength and [can] appear before him and commend himself in the usual fashion.

Farewell, most beloved of colleagues, your old and sick colleague so wishes.

27 (Hampe 28). To a Count. Late 833

Einhard [wishes] eternal salvation in the Lord to a magnificent, honorable, and illustrious man, N., the glorious count.

N. [Frumold], the lord's vassal and brother of Count N.'s wife, wanted to come to the lord emperor [Lothar], but was troubled by gout and old age and was not able [to travel] because of his illness. As soon as he can, he will come [to do] his duty. In the meantime, he requests that he be permitted to hold his benefice, the one in Burgundy in the district of Geneva that the lord Emperor Charles gave him, until he [can] appear before him and commend himself into his hands. It also seems right and useful to me that this be done just as he wished, because he is a good and prudent man and of good reputation among his neighbors. You would be doing the right thing, if you could consider helping him in this business.

I hope that you may always prosper in the Lord.

28 (Hampe 29). To a Certain Count. Late 833

Einhard [wishes] eternal salvation in the Lord to the magnificent, honorable, and illustrious N., a glorious count.

I ask your kindness to consider helping this young man, N., with our lord emperor [Lothar], so that he and his brother may not lose a benefice they [presently] possess. For they hold fifteen homesteads in the Tournai district and five homesteads on the other side of the Rhine [the former district was in Lothar's kingdom, the latter in Louis the German's]. He himself wishes to serve our lord emperor [Lothar] for the benefice that is in the Tournai district, and [hopes] that his brother may commend himself to N. [Louis the German] for that [benefice] that lies beyond the Rhine. But [he still wishes] them to hold jointly the entire benefice [that is, in the two kingdoms]. But [his brother] does not wish to agree to this arrangement, unless the lord emperor should order him. But unless it is done, they [will] lose their benefice lying beyond the Rhine. Thus, he begs your Goodness to consider asking the lord emperor to order his brother to do this. He himself stands ready to make whatever agreement pleases the lord emperor, because he wishes to hold his benefice jointly and continuously with his brother.

I hope that you may always prosper in the Lord.

29 (Hampe 31). To a Priest. Late 833?

Einhard, a sinner, [sends his greetings] to the holy and justly venerable lord, N., a priest of the supreme God.

I happily received your relative and faithful man Eburo, who came to me. I thought that he would stay here for a long time, but since he is in a rush to return to you, I did not wish to let him depart without a letter from me. If he returned empty-handed, you might think that he had not come here at all. But, with respect to those matters about which he believed he would bring some definite news to you, I can inform you of nothing definite [in writing] and cannot indicate [anything verbally] through him, since the changing nature of things that has recently occurred in this kingdom has shaken me to such an extent that I am almost entirely unsure what I should do except, in the words of Jehoshaphat, "to turn our eyes to the Lord" [2 Par.20:12], and, in Philo's words, "to ask for divine assistance, since human assistance fails." I commend Eburo, the bearer of this letter, even though he is a close relative of yours, to your favorable attention. For I trust in God that, although it cannot be achieved now, on another occasion I would, with the help of divine clemency, send him back to you happy and full of joy.

I hope that divine favor may always and everywhere keep your Holiness well and mindful of me.

30 (Hampe 57). To Vussin. Before 840

[Einhard wishes] salvation in the Lord to my dearest son Vussin.

I fear and worry a great deal, son, that now that you have left the fold [of the monastery] you may not pay [proper] attention to yourself or to me. An immature young man, unless checked by the restraints of discipline, does not easily take to the paths of justice. Therefore, my son, strive to follow an upright way of life, so as not to offend by any means that one whom I have always urged you to follow. Keep in mind your profession [of faith], to the extent that he has approved of it, and hold fast to the teachings of the one to whom you have devoted yourself completely. Having been instructed in these things and having become accustomed to how they work, you will lack none of the advantages of [this] vital science. [For,] just as I advised you in person, apply yourself to the business of learning. Leave nothing unexamined that you can learn of this noble science from the most clear and abundant ability of that great orator. Chiefly, however, remember to follow the upright way of life of that one, at which he excels, since grammar, rhetoric, and the study of the other liberal arts are useless and, indeed, harmful to the servants of God, unless by means of divine grace they are thought to contribute to the forma-tion of good habits, for "knowledge puffs up, but charity edifies." [1 Cor. 8.1] In fact, I would prefer to see you dead rather than puffed up and filled with vices. For the Savior ordered us to learn of his gentleness and humbleness of heart, not the miracles he performed. What more can I say? You have fre-quently heard me lecture you on these things and others of this sort. I hope that someday you will be attracted to those things through which, with God's help, the purity of one's heart and body is acquired.

I have sent you, therefore, [some] obscure words and names from the books of Vitruvius [on ancient architecture], which came to mind at present, so that you may look them up in that book. And I suspect that for the most part they can be demonstrated to you on the reliquary that Lord E. fashioned with ivory columns in the likeness of ancient artifacts. As to what Vitruvius calls *scenographia* [that is, drawing in perspective], check out what Virgil calls a stage in the third book of the *Georgics*, where he says:

[How] it is a delight [to lead solemn processions]
To the shrines, and to see the slain steers
Or how the stage changes when the front is shifted,
And how the depicted Britons [seem to] lift the purple curtain.
Farewell.

31 (Hampe 2). To Bernharius, the bishop of Worms. 825–826

Einhard [wishes] perpetual salvation in the Lord to the holy and justly venerable lord, Bishop N.

Although I was very disturbed to learn from your letter that you, dearest lord, have been so terribly ill, I still take some comfort from knowing that this suffering will help you, for it is part of the purgation of your soul. For I believe that [his] divine mercy has let you suffer from this disease for such a long time, so that it might receive you [already] purified when you depart from this body. About praying for you, I assure your Kindness that, to the extent that God will see fit to give me the strength and the opportunity, I shall exert myself through those [saints] whom I believe are inclined to listen, just as I recognize that you have faith in my Timidness. Even though one should never despair of recovering one's physical health, since God has the power to do whatever he wants with what he has created [see 5.3.11 and 20], it is still better for each of us to prepare for the [absolutely] certain [that is, death] than to neglect what is inevitable in the hope of a better outcome, which is uncertain.

I hope that you may always prosper in the Lord.

32 (Hampe 3). Bernharius, the bishop of Worms, responds to Einhard. 826

To my dearest Einhard [greetings from] Bernharius, now in [my] final moments, but still and as long as breath remains [in me], faithful to you and yours, as God can testify.

I commend my soul to your kind affection, my most beloved [friend], so that once it has departed from this sinful body you may think it appropriate to remember it when you and your own faithful men gather together, so that [my] sorry soul, once it has been assisted by the appeals of the holy prayers and pleas of your pious brothers, may deserve to obtain some place of [peaceful] rest.

[Now] that these matters have been reviewed, rather briefly because of the very great restrictions [placed on] the flesh or the spirit, I plead with you, my most beloved, that for the love of God and [your] friendship with me, however unworthy [I am], you might devote your great attention to the churches which were entrusted to my small talents. In this way, after my death, hungry wolves will not be able to invade that holy place and scatter that very vulnerable flock, but instead a [new] ruler will be be given to them, one who will know that he should love or, rather, fear God and mercifully help those placed under him.

Indeed, our most faithful brothers, who are also yours, at the monastery of N. [Weissenburg] have selected Folquicus to preside over them. Of them, he is the one [who has been] closest to me. He may, in fact, be young in age, but I believe him to be mature in his character and conduct. You know his family background well: he is the son of N., the brother of N., and the relative of many nobles. They sent him to Worms and, since I was still alive, they commended him in person, while N. deigned to visit me. With Count N. standing at his side, [Folquicus] with many tears made promises to me and my relatives. Lord N. [that is, not the count], who was moved by the request, also agreed that, if God brought it about, [the brothers] might select [Folquicus] in my place. Therefore, remember, my dearest [Einhard], that this [matter] is not to be put off, but try as hard as you can to bring it about [at once].

I am sending along a pallium which I ask you to arrange to give to the brothers at St-Servais [Einhard's monastery at Maastricht], so that they may make mention of me [in their prayers]. To your Kindness I have arranged to give my mule. Let Emma [Einhard's wife], a most beloved sister [to me], assist you in this business. I commend my soul to you.

My dire straits do not now permit me to say more, but once again I commend my soul to your prayers.

33 (Hampe 51). To a Count and Judge. 828–840

Einhard [wishes] salvation in the Lord to his dear brothers and friends in Christ, Count N. and Judge N., glorious *missi* of the lord emperor.

My men who have come to me from those regions frequently tell me of your good will and of your kindness towards me, inasmuch as you watch over my people and spare them whenever you can, both as to the heerban and to other business falling under your office. For this reason I thank you deeply, which is only fitting, and I ask God and his saints [Marcellinus and Peter] to consider rewarding you appropriately for your [good] deeds not only here in this present life, but also in [your] future life. I also promise you that you can count on my Smallness to be ready to do your will.

Farewell.

34 (Hampe 11). To the Emperor Lothar. 830

May my lord, the most pious emperor, live forever.

I am not easily able to express in words how much concern and anxiety my Tininess has for your Greatness. Indeed, I have always equally loved you and my most pious lord, your father [Louis], and I have always equally wished for the well-being of both of you, after he lifted you up, with the approval of all the people [nobles] of the kingdom, into sharing the [imperial] title [in 817]. And he ordered my Smallness to devote myself to your care and to impress upon you the need to regulate your conduct and actively pursue an upright and beneficial way [of life]. But, although you have found my efforts in this regard less beneficial to you than they should have been, [my] faithful commitment [to help you] still did not leave me and, in fact, remains [strong] even now. That commitment [will] not allow me to stay quiet, but rather forces me to remind you of your salvation and to explain briefly in what matters you should guard against your endangerment.

Your Greatness should be aware that it had come to the attention of my Smallness that certain men, who were pursuing their own interests, rather than yours, were inciting your gentle nature and were attempting to convince you to disregard your father's plans [for you] and to forsake the obedience owed to him, so that you might reject the role of ruling and overseeing [a kingdom] as assigned to you by your very pious father and [instead] come to him against his desire, wishes, and commands and remain with him [as his keeper] although that displeased him. Can anything more perverse or inappropriate be imagined?

Look at what sort of convincing [they did] and how full of evil it is. In the first place, it seems to my Tininess that [their persuasion] urges you to regard as worthless that commandment of God that insists upon honor being shown to parents and [it also urges you] to regard as empty the promise of a long [life] granted to those keeping that commandment. Next, [it urges you] once [filial] obedience has been rejected to replace it with disobedience and to rise arrogantly and treacherously against the one under whom you should have humbly submitted yourself. Then, through contempt and disobedience, with charity having been driven out [of your heart], discord, which never [previously] existed between [the two of] you and which should not be called [forth now], grows to such an extent that hatred [now] arises between those who should love each other. That should not happen and must be avoided at all costs. For I believe that it is not hidden to your Prudence how great an abomination it is in God's eyes for a son to be rebellious and disobedient toward his parents, since God commanded through Moses that such a man should be stoned to death by all the people, as you can read in Deuteronomy [21:20-21]. Thus, I thought that your Piety should be admonished so that through the prudence granted to you by God you may guard against your endangerment and not think that this divine opinion can be rejected by anyone, despite being written down in the Old Testament. For it is one of many [such] divine opinions that our elders and teachers, namely the holy fathers [of the church], both recently and in ancient times, both in Christian and

Jewish ages, believed must be followed. God knows that I love you and that, for this reason, I am admonishing you with all loyalty; nor ought you to consider the low station of the person doing the admonishing, but rather the healthy nature of the advice.

I hope [that you may always prosper in the Lord].

35 (Hampe 32). To an Abbot. Late 833?

[Einhard], a sinner, [sends greetings] to the holy and justly venerable N., a most revered abbot.

I have learned from the disclosure of my friends that N.—I do not know if I should call him an abbot or bishop, [but] you know who he is—is in the habit of listening to your healthy and extremely prudent advice in matters pertaining to his own interests. Therefore, it seemed [proper] for me to beg your Holiness to consider speaking to that man on behalf of his nephew Eburo, who is now staying with me, and to consider asking him not to deceive [Eburo] in the hope he had given him, but instead to decide to persist in the kindness promised to him, namely to consider helping [Eburo], who is stuck in a state of poverty, from his own resources. In this way, he may not, because of penury and a lack of necessities, be forced to give up that place, in which he himself [had] established him. That situation will certainly occur, unless [that lord] sees to it that it does not occur. That matter can, however, easily be looked after, if [that lord] sticks to those promises of his with which he [had] persuaded [Eburo] to submit to him.

I hope that your Holiness, mindful of my Smallness, always prospers in Christ the Lord.

36 (Hampe 58). To a Monk and Good Friend. Before 840

Einhard [wishes] eternal salvation in the Lord to his beloved brother and dearest friend N.

Count N. asked me, in the case of those pigs you placed in his care for fattening, to beg you to let him hold onto those pigs until they become larger and better, and that he himself might purchase them for a fair price for the lord's service. Since that man knows of our friendship, he thought that I could secure this request from you. For my part, I, being confident of your affection [toward me], do ask you not to refuse to fulfill his wish in this business.

I hope that you may always prosper in the Lord.

37 (Hampe 9). To his Deputy at Fritzlar. 828–830

Einhard, in the name of Christ, to his deputy, N.

I am very surprised that everything I asked you to do could have been left as it has been. For I have learned that you have sent none of the grain needed to make flour or malt, which you were supposed to have sent to Mulinheim [Seligenstadt]. [Indeed,] you have sent nothing but thirty pigs, and those were not very good sized ones, but small, and three modia [a dry measure close to a peck] of vegetables. Beyond that, [you have sent] nothing. And not only that, but also this [is at issue], since during that entire winter I saw neither you nor any messenger of yours who might have given me details [about where things stood]. But if I can derive no greater benefit [income] out of Fritzlar [see Map 3] than [the little] you have produced for me from that place, then why should I [bother to] hold that benefice? Now, therefore, if you care at all about my opinion, I request that you strive to correct your negligence and that you reassure me at once about what I can look forward [to receiving] from you.

38 (Hampe 59). To a Monk. Before 840

Einhard [wishes] salvation in the Lord to his beloved brother N.

I wish you, on my authority, to order Egmunel to make for me sixty square slabs measuring two feet on each side and four inches thick, and two hundred others, also square, but smaller, measuring ten inches on each side and three inches thick. I have sent you [instructions] through this man concerning the seed [perhaps, the herb sorrel] that I want you to have planted in a large space, for it normally grows into a large plant.

Farewell.

39 (Hampe 12). The Emperor Louis to the People of Merida in Spain. 830

In the name of the Lord God and our Savior, Jesus Christ, N. [that is, Louis the Pious], emperor and augustus by the design of divine providence, [sends his] greetings in the Lord to all the leading men and to the entire population of Merida.

We have heard of your troubles and of the various difficulties you are enduring because of the savagery of King Abd ar-Rahman [II, the emir of Cordova], who has oppressed you constantly and violently with his greedy desire for your possessions, which he has attempted to steal from you. We know that his father Abul Aas [Al-Hakam, the emir of Cordova until 822] did the same, forcing you through the imposition of unfair charges to pay taxes to him though you were not indebted to him. In this way [Abul Aas] made enemies out of his friends and rebellious and disobedient [subjects] out of obedient ones, for he was attempting to take away your freedom and to oppress and humble you with unfair taxes and tribute. But we have heard that you always courageously fought back as courageous men against the damage done to you by evil kings and that you have bravely resisted their cruelty and greed. We have [also] learned from the accounts of many people that you are doing this [even] now.

Therefore, it pleased us to send this letter to you to console you and urge you to persevere in that very defense of your freedom, which you have [already] begun, against an extremely cruel king, and to refuse to submit to his fury and raging madness, as you have so far done. And since that very king is our absolute enemy and opponent as much as he is yours, we should resist his raging madness with shared resolve.

For we want, with the almighty God's help, to send our army next summer to our [Spanish] march, where it might set up camp and remain ready and waiting for you to send word that it should advance [into Spain]. If it seems appropriate to you, we shall, in order to assist you, [first] send this army against our common enemies living in our march, so that if Abd ar-Rahman or his army wants to proceed against you, they will be stopped by our army and no one [from the march] will be able to proceed against you in order to help [Abd ar-Rahman] and his army.

For we reassure you that if you wish to abandon him and to come over to us, we shall grant you your ancient rights to the fullest extent without any reduction and we shall permit you to be free of tax or tribute and shall command you to follow no other law than the one under which you wish to live. Nor do we desire to treat and regard you except honorably as friends and allies in the defense of our kingdom.

We hope that you always prosper in the Lord.

40 (Hampe 13). To the Empress Judith. 830

May our most pious lady deign to understand that after leaving Aachen I, your servant, became so ill that it took me almost ten days to reach Valenciennes from Maastricht [a distance of 110 miles or 176 kms.]. At that point I was overcome by so much pain in my kidneys and spleen, that I was not able, in fact, to ride one mile a day.

Thus, I implore your Piety to allow me, with your permission, to go by

13. An image of Empress Judith from Hrabanus Maurus's *Exposition on the Book of Judith*. The manuscript may come from Rheims in the second quarter of the ninth century. Now in Geneva, Bibliothèque Publique et Universitaire, lat. 22, fol. 3v.

boat to St-[Bavo] and to rest there until almighty God shall deign to grant me the strength to make the journey. For as soon as I am able to ride [again], I shall come as quickly as I can to you or to the lord emperor [Louis]. But at the present time I humbly beg your Piety to deign to apologize for me to my most merciful lord [Louis], when you see him, since I did not appear before you. God knows that I have not written anything untrue to you about my illness. Indeed, I not only have this [health] problem, but others even more serious, from which I suffer, but I can only speak about them with a close friend [see 6.41].

But you should [also] know this, that you could not now obtain any greater reward before God, than if you see to it that I am allowed to hurry, when I am well [enough], to the service of the holy martyrs of Christ. In fact, I can get there by boat in fifteen days from St-[Bavo].

41 (Hampe 14). To a Friend (Gerward?). April 830

If illness did not prevent me, I would not be sending this letter, but would instead come myself and [also] be present along with you while those [events] are occuring around you. But now that I find myself in dire straits, I beg your Kindness to agree to intercede on my behalf with our most pious lord and emperor.

For when queen [Judith] was departing from Aachen and I was unable to accompany her at the same time, she commanded me to join her in Compiègne later. [While I was attempting] to comply with her order, I [had] come with great difficulty to Valenciennes after ten days. From there, since I was no longer able to ride, I traveled by boat to St-[Bavo]. A great loosening of my bowels [diarrhea] and a [sharp] pain in my kidneys came on one after the other so [regularly] that there was not a single day after leaving Aachen that I did not suffer with one or the other [ailment]. Likewise I was troubled by other [afflictions] which derived from that illness that laid me low last year, namely, a continual numbness of my right thigh and an almost intolerable pain in my spleen. Beset by these [multiple] afflictions my life is dismal and almost entirely without joy, primarily because I fear that I shall die not where I would want [to die] and because I am engaged in other business than in the service of the holy martyrs of Christ.

For that reason, I call upon and entreat you through Marcellinus and Peter, Christ's blessed martyrs, to agree to intercede for my Smallness with the most pious emperor, lest he be inclined to be angry with me because I did not meet him like those who were able. I would by all means have come if I had been able [to do so], and I shall come as soon as I am able [to]. Whether present or absent, I shall remain faithful to him. I request your Kindness, therefore, to deign to fill me in by letter as soon as you can both about what has transpired and what should take place there [at the palace].

I hope that you may always prosper in the Lord.

[P.S.] Everything that is now happening in this kingdom was foretold two years ago in the revelations [brought about] by Christ's martyrs. [See 5.3.6 and 5.3.13]

42 (Hampe 15). To the Emperor Louis. April 830

A small servant [sends greetings] to a great lord.

[I trust] that [you], my most pious lord, remember that you gave me permission, when my lady [Empress Judith] saw you, to proceed myself at that time to the work of serving the blessed martyrs of Christ [at Seligenstadt]. I wished to do that, but my lady ordered me [instead] to follow her to Compiègne. I complied with her orders and set out after her, as soon as my horses were ready, for Compiègne. But I was soon seized by pain in both my spleen and kidneys and was so sick that it took me almost ten days to travel from Maastricht to Valenciennes. At that point, since I did not believe that I could ride any longer, I located a boat and went by water to St-[Bavo]. Now that I am there and placed in dire straits and pain, I ask and pray that your Piety will deign to grant me permission to proceed to the place [Seligenstadt] where the sacred bodies of your pious patrons rest. In fact, I can reach that place by boat in fifteen days from St-[Bavo]. You could obtain a great reward for yourself before God, if you permit me to proceed to the service of his saints, [that is], if I am able to get there while still alive. I believe that those holy martyrs should intercede for you with God if you wish to place my service to them ahead of my service to you. For I can achieve nothing greater for you in any other part of your kingdom than there, if you will help me in this.

43 (Hampe 16). To a Bishop. May 830

Einhard, a sinner, [sends greetings] to the holy and justly venerated lord, N., the most revered bishop.

I have not stopped giving as many thanks as I can to the almighty God and to our Lord Jesus Christ, since I learned that my most glorious lord and augustus Lothar, protected now and always by God, had arrived safe and sound from Italy and that you, my dearest [friend], had come with him. I hope and pray that that great man will soon allow me to come there, where I might have the privilege and pleasure of being in your presence. In the meantime I still commend my Smallness to your Kindness and through you to his Piety [Lothar], and I beg you not to deign to suspect anything [bad] about my Tininess because of the evil talk of any person [at court]. I call upon God and the holy martyrs Marcellinus and Peter to bear witness that I am unable in words to reveal the love and devotion that I know I feel towards you. Thus, I confidently seek that, when I visit, I should deserve to find your regard for me such as, I do not doubt, I deserve from you.

I hope that your holiness always prospers in Christ and remains mindful of my frailty.

44 (Hampe 17). To a Certain E. The middle of 830

Einhard [wishes] perpetual salvation to the holy lord and justly venerable bishop.

Although there are a great many things that I would still like to learn, there are two things about which I have greater curiosity right now. First, where and when will that general assembly [which finally met at Nijmegen in October 830] be held and, second, must Lord Lothar return to Italy or stay with his father? [I hope] your Kindness does not object to filling me in about these two matters, for I need information about them more than about the other things happening around you. For what I should do depends on that news, if divine piety will deign to allow me to have the strength to do something of value.

I hope very soon, dearest of my friends, to see you in good and prosperous form.

45 (Hampe 18). To Count G. 830

Einhard [wishes] perpetual salvation in the Lord to his beloved brother G[eboin], the glorious count and magnate.

I have always felt your kind affection toward me, but never more than now, when you obtained permission for me to proceed to the service of the saints Marcellinus and Peter [at Seligenstadt], who because of this will intercede [for you] with God. And thus I thank your kindness as much as I can, and stubbornly implore that, in keeping with your good nature, you always deign to speak on my behalf both with the lord and emperor [Louis] and with his sons, particularly with the young lord and augustus Lothar, in whose piety I, although unworthy, have great confidence.

Besides that, I ask you to consider rewarding and helping the painter N., your devoted subordinate, and [also] to consider interceding on his behalf with the lord and emperor [Louis], that is, if you should find an appropriate opportunity [to do so], so that he may not lose his benefice, the one gained by serving his lords so well, because of someone's envy. I do not need to tell you who those [envious] people are that he fears in this business, since both you and I know who they are. I ask only that you consider helping him to the extent that you are able.

I hope you may always prosper in the Lord.

46 (Hampe 36). To an Abbot. Autumn 834

Einhard, a sinner, [sends his greetings] with the highest veneration to a most revered abbot [Folco].

Just as I have not forgotten my request, I suspect that you have not forgotten your promise, although a great variety of difficulties later appeared that were able not only to force our talk aside for a time, but even to cast it into the state of the permanently forgotten. I refer to that conversation which we had when we were both in attendance at the palace [and spoke] of the roof of the church of Marcellinus and Peter, the blessed martyrs of Christ [at Seligenstadt], which I am now attempting to construct, but with great difficulty. We agreed [you will remember] to purchase lead for the price of fifty pounds. But although that work on the church has not yet reached the stage [of building the roof], the need for that covering compels me to remind you [now]. On account of the uncertain end of mortal life it always seems necessary to hurry, so that the good work which we have begun with God's help might be brought to completion. Thus, I beg your kindness to consider reassuring me in a letter about the purchase of that lead, so that I might learn if anything has yet been done and, if nothing has, in what way that business will be done and, with God's help, brought to completion. Therefore, I [would] implore your Kindness not to refuse to reassure me in a letter about this matter.

I hope you may always prosper in the Lord and remember me.

47 (Hampe 35). To a Certain F. Autumn 834

Einhard [wishes] perpetual salvation to F.

I request that you write me nothing about the state of things at the palace, because none of the things happening there is pleasant to hear. About you and my friends—if I still have any other than you—I am very keen to learn where you are and what you are doing. Thus, I undertook to send this letter to your Kindness to remind you in the strongest possible terms to write to

me about what is happening to you, that is, what sort of health you are enjoying, and where and when we might, if still alive, see each other. For I have
often wanted both to see and speak to you, but never more eagerly than right
now, because the need was never greater for me to confer and discuss with a
friend about the life I should live. I can speak more openly with you than
with anyone else, for I place greater trust in the loyalty of no other.

I have sent a letter to Abbot [Folco of Fontanelle or St-Wandrille] with
this servant. I [would] ask that, if he is able to continue on, you arrange for
him to be led to that [abbot] by some of your men. But, if perhaps his horses
are tired, as often happens, and he cannot go farther, I beg that you take the
letter I am sending to Folco and you send it on to him by means of someone
else. You should beg him to answer me and to give [whatever] answer he
might wish to make back to you. You should [then] arrange for that answer to
reach me as soon as you have found a suitable messenger.

I hope that you, the dearest of my friends, always prosper in Christ and
remember me.

48 (Hampe 30). To a Bishop. Late 833?

Einhard, a sinner, [sends his greetings] to the holy and justly venerable lord,
the most revered N.

That priest of yours by the name of N. has frequently asked me to intercede with you on his behalf, so that you might consider treating him with
mercy. He says that he was stuck in great poverty, but it is worse now, since
that small benefice he held in Bavaria was taken away from him and was
granted to another. Now he does not know what he should do or how he
should serve his lord, unless by means of your intercession the Lord Lothar
considers giving him some help in maintaining his present life.

I hope that you remember me and that you may always prosper in the
Lord and that you will consider commending my Smallness to that most
pious emperor [Lothar].

49 (Hampe 19). To a Noble Friend. 830?

Einhard [wishes] eternal salvation in the Lord to his beloved brother and
most faithful friend, N., the glorious magnate.

Since I know that your faith [in me] has been so often demonstrated, I
cannot at all doubt that I should turn to the assistance of your charity in all
the emergencies [that face] me and my friends. Thus, I have sent you along
with this letter my countrymen and dependents, Aristeus and Theothous. I

beg you to consider receiving them in your usual generous way and to consider assisting them with the lord and augustus Lothar and his most pious father [Louis] in their pressing needs, which they will describe to you. In this way, those men will [come to] possess the same great confidence in you that I have.

I hope that you may always be well, my best and dearest friend.

50 (Hampe 50). To a Count. 828–840

Einhard [wishes] eternal salvation in the Lord to a magnificent, honorable, and illustrious man, N., the glorious [count].

Since I rely a great deal upon your friendship, ... I do not hesitate to ask about the [property] rights of the blessed martyrs of Christ, Marcellinus and Peter, which are [held] in your monastery [and] likewise about certain dependents ... which my current deputy, N., attempted to obtain before you and which he hopes he can acquire with your help. Therefore, I beg your Kindness to consider helping him not only in this case, but also in some other business, so that through this you may be thought worthy to have those martyrs of Christ as your patrons and intercessors with God.

51 (Hampe 33). To Louis the German. Early 834?

My lord, your most pious father, ordered N. from the monastery N. to help and work with me to construct the church of Marcellinus and Peter, the blessed martyrs of Christ, your patrons [at Seligenstadt]. But those men, it seems to me, will do none of that work, unless they receive an order from your Clemency directing them once again to help us in this work as directed by the lord, your father [Louis the Pious]. And therefore, in order to fill you in about the reason for this work, I have undertaken to send this letter of entreaty from my Smallness to your Greatness, in which I ask and humbly seek that, for the love and honor of Christ's martyrs and your patrons, you deign to pay [particular] attention to the construction of their church, so that with your assistance this [construction] might be achieved. [I also ask] that, on our behalf, you give the bishops mentioned your sacred order in the form of a letter [carrying] your most glorious authority, which they would surely not dare to defy. In this way, your reward before God should grow and the blessed martyrs should intercede for you, so that your kingdom may always be blessed, strengthened, and remain safe and defended against the intrigues and the attacks of malignant spirits and malicious men.

I hope and pray that my lord king may prosper and live forever.

52 (Hampe 34). To King Louis [the German]. 833-834

I wish to beseech your Piety on behalf of a certain friend and dependent of mine, namely your faithful man N., so that you may consider receiving him and, once he has commended himself into your hands, consider granting him some support from the benefices which are known to be free and available here in our district. For he is noble, trustworthy, and has learned to serve your interests in whatever business is asked of him. For he served your grandfather [Charles] and your father [Louis] faithfully and with vigor, and is prepared to do the same for you if God chooses to grant him life and health. Until now he has been extremely sick, and thus he cannot appear before your Piety, [but] he will come as soon as he can. For this reason, I beg your Piety to permit me to know what I may promise him in the name of your goodness, so that he may live with positive hope until he can appear before you.

53 (Hampe 25). To King Louis [the German]. After 30 June 833

[I ask] my lord and most glorious king not to be displeased with me because I came neither [to your court] nor afterwards into your presence. I did not do this to offend you or because of laziness, but because I was sick and had a fever, as I still do. I was scarcely able to present myself before your brother, Lord Lothar, and then to return, once he had given [me] permission, to the holy martyrs [at Seligenstadt], when that [meeting] was brought to a close by the two of you.

And I [went home] only because I did not know that a division of the kingdom had been made between you, though it had. In fact, a rumor spread that the very part of the eastern regions of the Franks in which I live and hold a small benefice, ought to belong to Lothar's kingdom. Since I am worried, I beg your Clemency to allow me to hold and enjoy that benefice, until [such time as] I shall receive Lord Lothar's permission to come to you and commend myself into your hands—if I am able to secure that [permission] in any way. For I propose to come to you as one [fully] loyal and devoted to your service, if God will deign to grant me life and health.

54 (Hampe 26). To a Priest and to a Deputy. Before October 833

In the name of Christ, Abbot Einhard [sends] greetings in the Lord to N., a priest, and N., a deputy, our loyal men.

Let it be known to you that I wish you to arrange for customary gifts to be prepared, such as a man is accustomed to make on behalf of his lord, [in this instance] on behalf of both Lord Lothar and his wife [Ermengard]. And when [Lothar] has returned from Orville to Compiègne, I wish those [gifts] to be presented then and there. Then I want you to inform me how those [gifts] were received by him or by her.

Farewell.

55 (Hampe 60). To a Vassal. Before 840

In the name of Christ, Abbot Einhard [sends his] greetings to his faithful man.

You know that, to the extent that I was able, I undertook to fulfill your wish, in that I worked to return your daughter to you. Therefore, I ask you, for the honor and love of Saint N. and me, to agree with me in this: that, if I should arrange for this man's freedom, you would allow him to marry your daughter. It seems better to me that she be joined to that man again, [once] he is made free, than that she should be scorned by everyone.

Farewell.

56 (Hampe 61). To R. Before 840

Einhard [wishes] eternal salvation in the Lord to his dearest son R.

The man, whom you sent to me, came on the tenth [day before the] Kalends of September [23 August], and since you wrote that you had no reservations about his loyalty, I did not hesitate to trust him with anything about these matters I wished passed along to you. In fact, I think that it is better to trust a loyal man than a written document, since if a document or piece of parchment falls [out of the hands] of its bearer, every secret it holds is revealed, but a loyal messenger, [even if] tortured, does not betray the message entrusted to him. Therefore, everything that I wished to say to you, had you been present, I have told your loyal man, whom I found devoted and faithful to you in all things, particularly since he did not hide or put off [telling me] anything you directed him to tell me.

I hope that you may prosper.

57 (Hampe 38). Emma to N. Before 836

Emma, your loyal [friend wishes] perpetual salvation in the Lord to her venerable and beloved lord and son, N.

After your faithful *missus* N. came to us and brought back your letter for me, I happily undertook to do whatever I was able to see needed doing from it. It belongs to you to weigh and judge whether those things that you have decided between you to do are seen to be not only beneficial, but also honorable for both parties and that there is no legal blame attached to those who did this for the benefit of many.... I perceive that [this matter] can only be done, if it is done at the right time, because as you know very well from Solomon [Eccles. 3:1], only those things achieve success and are proper that happen at the right time.

I hope, dearest son, you always prosper in Christ.

58 (Hampe 62). To a Vassal. Before 840

In the name of Christ, Einhard, a humble abbot, [wishes] eternal salvation in the Lord to his faithful and beloved man.

I do not doubt that you recall how you commended yourself and yours to me. Since you decided to do this of your own will, it is also my wish in turn and by all means to supply you and yours, whenever the opportunity arises, with fitting support to the extent that I know how and possess the ability. Thus, let it be known to your Kindness that my vassal and your daughter desire with the Lord [God's] approval and your permission to take each other in marriage. For that reason, I decided to send to you [some] men to inform you that it seems appropriate to [his] mother, brother, and all [his] relatives for this [marriage] to happen, if it suits you. In addition, I myself not only wish this [marriage] to be approved, but I even wish to supply [him] deservedly and honorably, as quickly as it can be arranged, both with benefices and other things, if you give me the authority to do so. In addition, that same vassal will provide a dowry and supply abundant gifts. To conclude this business [all] that remains is either for you not to defer coming yourself at the present time in order to bring this matter to a close or to allow me to finish it. For I know that I can, with God's favor, do it at the present time, but I do not know what another day might bring. So it was written: "Let neither your hand nor your foot be still, but do at once whatever you do." [see Eccles. 9:10] With these things having been so surveyed, I ask you to make sure to inform me about this business either by means of this messenger or through a letter from you ...

Be well ... [in] Christ.

59 (Hampe 63). To a Bishop. Before 840

Einhard, a sinner, [sends his greetings] to the holy and justly venerable lord, N., a priest of the most high God.

That vassal of yours named Agantheo, who is my relative, was in my service for a considerable length of time, but because he now wants to spend his days under your authority, it pleased my Smallness that he had elected to be in a place so familiar [to me], and so I decided to give him this letter of recommendation. In this way, by means of my intervention, since I have declared him to be my relative, he may have an easier introduction to your Holiness and may reside with you. Therefore, I beg you to deign to receive him and maintain him in service to you. I suspect that you will find him to be a useful servant.

I hope that you may always prosper in the Lord.

60 (Hampe 64). To a Bishop. Before 840

Einhard, a sinner, [sends his greetings] to his Lord N.

Necessity compels me, since there are too few priests at the altar [here], to implore your holiness to consider ordaining our cleric, named N., to the rank of deacon. He is suitable for this [office] not only in age, but also in learning. And thus I have sent that man to appear before your Kindness, in order that we may deserve to receive him back again, consecrated by you in that same rank.

I hope you always prosper in the Christ.

61 (Hampe 40). To the Emperor Louis the Pious. After June 837

The almost unanimous opinion of the ancients was that the strange and unexpected appearance of stars [that is, comets] signified that unfortunate and sad things rather than happy and beneficial ones were about to fall upon human beings. Only the holy Gospel [Matt. 2:2] supplies an example of the appearance of a new star that was benefical, for the wise men of Chaldea are reported to have seen [such] and, since they concluded from its brilliance that the eternal king had just been born, they bore gifts in veneration that were suitable for such a great one.

But everyone who said that they saw the star that appeared recently [on 11 April 837] reported that it was frightening and that its appearance was not at all pleasing, [for] its fiery blaze was menacing. I suspect that this [comet] supplies [us] with fitting signs of our just deserts and announces an approaching disaster that we deserve. For what does it matter whether humans are forewarned of [God's] impending anger by a human, by an angel, or by a star announcing [it]? Only this is necessary: to understand that the appearance of the star was not without meaning, but warned humans that by being penitent and calling upon the mercy of God they may work toward avoiding future danger. Thus, in Jonah's prophecy [Jon.3:2], the destruction of the city [of Nineveh], which he had foretold, was postponed by divine mercy when humans were transformed by the remedies of penance. And God treated those [penitent] people as he had promised the prophet Jeremiah he would when he ordered him to go down to the potter's house and to hear his words while the potter worked there [Jer.18:1-10]. I am also confident that he wishes to treat us [the same], if like them we don't neglect to do sincere penance.

I wish that the disaster the fleet of the Northmen is said to have brought recently [July 837] upon parts of this kingdom could have made complete payment for the appearance of that horrible star. But I fear that the punishment that awaits [us] will be [even] heavier, for such [a heavier penalty] was signified by that dire omen. Still those people experienced a serious and bitter enough penalty to themselves and all their property, when that great onslaught [of Northmen] fell so violently upon them from the sea.

May [you] my most pious lord and emperor prosper and be happy in all things.

62 (Hampe 65). To an Unnamed Person. Before 840

Einhard [wishes] perpetual salvation in the Lord to his beloved and venerable brother in Christ, N.

... of my man N. are prepared ... your pigs. For so I was told, and because the same man N. has served me with devotion and loyalty for a long time now, thus I ask your Kindness, in so far as it is possible, to consider sparing him in the matter of that compensation, which he owes you by law; so that I may hold him to his necessary service to me. You may in justice always find me even readier and more anxious to carry out your wishes.

I hope that you may always prosper.

63 (Hampe 41). To a Count. 839?

Einhard [wishes] eternal salvation in the Lord to a magnificent, honorable, and illustrious man, N., the glorious count.

By means of Dagolf, the [royal] hunter, the lord emperor ordered Count N. to arrange for all those counts who are in Austrasia, that is, Hatto, Poppo, and Gebehard, and their other allies, to assemble in one place in order to discuss among themselves what ought to be done if an insurrection should arise in Bavaria [where Louis the German had retreated in 839]. It also seemed good to them that both you and Atto should be present at that same assembly.

Thus, they ask you to consider that and to let them know [by letter] where it would be best for you to speak with them. It seems to N. that this would be good.

64 (Hampe 53). To the Monks of Seligenstadt. 834–840

In the name of the most high God, [Einhard], a sinner, [wishes] everlasting salvation in the Lord to his dear brothers living in the monastery of the blessed martyrs of Christ, Marcellinus and Peter.

Let it be known to your fraternity that with the Lord's help I am safe and sound, and that I am anxious to read and learn the same thing about you. In addition, I advise the brothers to undertake to remember me carefully, as you promised, in the presence of the holy martyrs, our patron [saints], whom you are known to serve daily. In this way the pious Lord may allow me to find you safe through their intercession. I beg you, therefore, with a father's concern, my dearest ones, to remain mindful of your promise [to me] and that you are [daily] commending yourselves to the Lord and his saints, ... and that you are always anxiously on guard so that the ancient enemy [Satan] may not be able to deceive and seduce you with any trickery. Pereptually intent upon divine praises and ... and obedience with attendance at the churches of God, and in turns assisting you ..., carrying burdens, that you may be able here with some ease successfully to gain the eternal kingdom with the help of Christ and his holy martyrs [Marcellinus and Peter]....With these there are ..., according to the Apostle, I say, with all honor and diligence ... priests of Christ by your example [setting] a model of salvation for the younger [monks] ..., the days that are about to come, with kindness in turn ... and happy to continue to the celebrations of Easter, by divine grace ... strive to maintain your..., just as I established it for you; and occupy yourselves demonstrating complete obedience and diligence to your vow, as long as your honor stays strong into the future, and the advancement of your souls with God's help should progress greatly from day to day.

May your holy fraternity be well and prosper ... my beloved brothers.

[P.S.] Let this letter of mine be devoutly read out in the presence of all the brothers, and let it be obeyed.

65 (Hampe 66). Blessings for a Monarch. Before 840

This royal acclamation is found in the collection of Einhard's letters, but cannot with absolute certainty be attributed to him. Moreover, it falls at the end of Einhard's letters and is followed by several pieces not by him. The acclamation may refer to Louis the Pious's full return to imperial power on 2 February 835, the feast of the Purification of the Blessed Virgin, at Thionville.

A minuscule person presumes to offer prayers of benediction to the piety of a brilliant lord. For, in fact, such great psalms [are sometimes sung] alongside other little speeches after the Purification of the Virgin Mary [2 February]. May the immortal king grant you good health in this present life and allow you to rejoice with his saints in the glory of heaven for eternity!

> The right hand [of God], which governs life throughout
> the ages with divine piety,
> Lifted up the key-bearer [Peter], so that he not drown
> in the sea [Matt. 14:30-31].

The last five letters in the collection (66-70; Hampe 67-71) were neither written by nor sent to Einhard and so have been omitted here.

APPENDIX:

A. (Hampe 10). To Emperor Louis. 830-832

On folio 20 of Paris, B.N. lat. 11379, a separate leaf written by a different hand contains the following letter by Einhard and a partial copy of letter 34 (Hampe 11).

Although I most certainly believe that my most pious lord [Louis] is always mindful of his patron saints, the blessed martyrs of Christ, Marcellinus and Peter, who by God's secret judgment abandoned Rome and came to Francia for the advancement and protection of your kingdom, and for some reason I am unaware of they deigned to stay with me, a sinner, I still feel that it is absolutely necessary to remind you frequently of matters that pertain to their honor, so that I do not, by some chance, bring danger and damage to my soul if I am less devoted to their memory than I should be. Although those famous [saints] are most merciful and even spared their own tormentor, I am afraid to offend their king, our Lord Jesus Christ, for whose love they died without hesitation. [I would not want] him to find me slow in paying suitable honor in their veneration.

Therefore, most pious lord, I humbly urge and ask your excellency to deign to recall that [contractual] exchange of the place [Seligenstadt] where the revered bodies of the martyrs [now] rest, which was made with Bishop Otgar [of Mainz], and to make that place their [permanent] property. In order to free up [that land] you transferred [a piece of] your own property to St-Martin [of Mainz].

Similarly I take the liberty of reminding your Mercy of the requests I made when I was ill and terrified that my death was close. It was then that I suggested to you that you should deign to grant some of your benefices to those same most gentle [saints], your patrons, for the upkeep of those who will serve God there in the presence of the most sacred bodies of those holy martyrs. You [also] led me to hope by your very kind promises at that time, that I would not be misled in my desires. Not only for that reason, but also in this business, you should direct your mercy towards those whom I trained for your service and assist them through those very benefices. I am fully confident that, if you deign to fulfill my wish in this matter, you should in this way satisfy God and his saints.

Similarly I ask you to deign to reflect upon and consider what rewards [will] await you in heaven and the praise of you that will spread in this world, if during your time [here] you increase, decorate, and venerate the resting place of the holy martyrs with both buildings and other necessities. This building campaign will, of course, be credited to your name. Indeed, your memory and the memory of the martyrs will forever be joined together and celebrated by all peoples.

Lastly, I ask and stubbornly call upon your great Gentleness to deign to look upon me, a wretched sinner who is now old and infirm, with mercy and pious affection. [I ask as well for you] to release and free me from [my] worldly concerns and to permit me to remain in peace and quiet at the tombs of the blessed martyrs of Christ, your patron [saints], and [to stay there] attached to those same saints in the service of God and our Lord Jesus Christ under your protection. In this way, that inevitable and final day, which usually happens to one at the age I have now reached, may find me not preoccupied with superficial and trivial concerns, but rather devoted to prayer and reading, and engaged in thinking and meditating on the divine law [the Bible].

B. The Church of Sens Petitions Einhard,
7 December 828–6 June 829

The following letter survives outside the collection of Einhard's letters. An almost identical letter was sent to the empress, Judith, and a longer version to the archchaplain, Hilduin.

Source: translated from *Frotharii episcopi Tullensis epistolae*, ed. K. Hampe, Monumenta Gemaniae Historica: Epistolae, vol. 5 (Hanover: Weidmann, 1898–99), p. 286.

The most humble devotion of the Church of Sens [is sent] to the most holy Lord Einhard, glorious and outstanding in his nobility.

We have with humility assumed, my lord, that the reasons for our petition have reached your Clemency, so that we may quickly be worthy to receive through your piety consolation in these matters. We believe that it is known to you, that it was [once] granted to us, the most unworthy, by the lord emperor [Louis the Pious], that we could possess the right to elect [our archbishop] from among our number. But when we had elected that man, whom you know, he was not entirely acceptable to the serene lord emperor. It was again granted to us to find another from among our number, if we could, who would be suitable for that office. But when he had been found, as we believe, to be suitable for service to God and the lord emperor, we do not know for what reason but he was not received with complete sympathy by the *missi dominici*. For this reason we beg your Kindness to deign to assist us in this matter, so that we ourselves might present that man, about whom we are speaking, to the emperor. And as he orders, it should be examined and proved that [that man] will be of benefit to us and whether or not he is suited to the service of God.

We hope that you are always guarded by divine protection and that someday you will be rewarded with the crown of immortality, most pious and venerable lord.

To the most holy and pious lord Einhard, justly venerable, the lowly and abject congregation of the city of Sens [bids farewell].

7. THE CORRESPONDENCE WITH LUPUS OF FERRIÈRES, INCLUDING 'ON THE ADORATION OF THE CROSS'

Source: translated from Servati Lupi Epistulae, ed. P.K. Marshall (Leipzig: Teubner, 1984), pp. 1–15; and Einharti Quaestio de adoranda cruce, ed. Karl Hampe, in Monumenta Germaniae Historica: Epistolae 5 (Berlin: Weidmann, 1898–99), pp. 146–148.

1. Lupus's First Letter to Einhard, 830

Lupus's two trips to Fulda were in 830 and 835-836. He tells us in the following letter – the first in his collection of letters – that Archbishop Aldric [of Sens, 829-35] sent him to Fulda, but Aldric had been the abbot of Ferrières between 821-29, so it is possible that the abbot sent Lupus at the end of his abbacy, but took up his new office while Lupus was at Fulda.

Lupus [sends his] greetings to the dearest man, Einhard.

I have delayed for a long time, O most desirable of men, over whether or not I should be so bold as to write to your Excellency. Although there were many reasons, what mostly stopped me from writing was the prospect of offending you while trying to win your friendship. [I was worried that], with an overly hasty and unwarranted directness, I, who had not yet made your acquaintance, would start off [by assuming] that we were already friends. Thus, [although I was] entirely unsure what to do, the easy and unassuming nature of your spirit, which doubtless matches [your] philosophy, allowed me to hope that I might [still] obtain my great goal. Nevertheless, I should [at least] appear to supply you with some reason [for writing now]. But I [shall] pass over the opinions about friendship found in pagan literature, since you have devoted your special attention to them, lest I justly receive [back from you] that saying of Horace so often repeated by learned people: "Don't carry wood into a forest." But our God not only does not support the abandonment of friends, he demands the opposite, that our enemies should be loved. Thus, I ask, that you patiently and kindly bear with me while I rehearse my deeper thoughts, so that you may know that I am not attempting this falsely or from a young man's lack of seriousness.

Almost from early boyhhood I had a love of letters and did not spurn [learning] as an idle or pointless occupation as it is described by many today. If instructors had continued to be available and if the study of the ancients had not almost disappeared after long-standing neglect, then perhaps with God's help I might have been able to satisfy my eagerness [to learn]. Within your memory, indeed, learning began to be revived by that very famous emperor Charles, to whom writing ought to bear witness until it has secured an everlasting memory for him. In fact, [learning] lifted up its head a little and proved very well that that superb saying of Cicero was true: "Honor cultivates the arts [of learning] and, for the sake of glory, all are enflamed to study."

Today those who aspire to learn something are a burden. The unlearned, who commonly look upon the learned as though they are superior, should they detect any flaw in them, attribute that not to human failing, but to the nature of their education. Thus, [many] have withdrawn from this splendid work, some because they do not win fitting recompense for their wisdom and others because they are afraid that their fame will not be worthy [of all their work and learning].

It seems to me that wisdom should be sought for its own sake. I was sent out to pursue it by the holy Archbishop Aldric [of Sens, 829-35], obtained a teacher of grammar, and received the lessons of that discipline from him. But to pass from grammar to rhetoric and, then, in regular order, to the other liberal arts, is a commonplace [occurrence] at this time [of life]. Then, after I had begun to spend a little time with the books of the ancients, the works produced in our own age displeased me, because they [had] drifted so far from the seriousness of Cicero and the other [ancients], which even outstanding Christians had imitated. [It was then that] your book [*The Life of Charlemagne*], in which you describe in an outstanding way the most outstanding deeds of the famed emperor, came into my hands. Let me say this without being suspected of trying to flatter you. I was overjoyed to find in it an elegance of thought and a rarity of conjunctions, which I had seen in the [ancient] authors, and also sentences not too long and complicated or too short. I wanted, therefore, some opportunity to speak to you in person, not just because of your reputation, which I had earlier known to be worthy of a wise man, but then especially because of my impression of the accomplished eloquence of your book. Just as your integrity and wisdom have made you well known to my Smallness, so may my love for you and for the discipline of learning recommend me to your Highness. Nor shall I stop hoping for this, so long as I know that you are alive and well.

I am now more encouraged to hope that this [meeting] may come to pass, since I have now moved from Gaul into this region beyond the Rhine and find myself living closer to you. For I was sent by the bishop I mentioned [that is, Aldric of Sens] to the venerable Hrabanus [abbot of Fulda, 822-842], so that I might be instructed by him in the basics of Holy Scipture. Then, when I had learned that his messenger was about to travel from here to you, I first thought of sending along certain obscure words that you might explain. But it seemed [upon reflection] better for me to send you this letter. If it is welcomed by you, I shall give thanks that I experienced this much desired reward.

Since I have once and for all passed beyond the limits of what is appropriate, I also ask this, that you might lend me, while I am here [at Fulda], certain of your books, but it is much less [difficult] to beg for books than for friendship. These books are: the *De rhetorica* of Cicero, which is a book I already possess, but [my copy] is corrupt in many places. I compared my copy against a copy I found here [at Fulda], which I thought would be better, but found even more corrupt. Likewise, [I would like to borrow] the three books by the same author on rhetoric in the form of a disputation and dialogue concerning the orator [*De oratore*], which I believe you have, since in the list of your volumes after the mention of the *Ad Herennium* and several other books, I found the *De rhetorica* of Cicero noted. Likewise [I would like to borrow] the *Commentary on the Books of Cicero* and, in particular, the *Attic Nights* of A[ulus] Gellius. There are many other books on that list, which, if God grants me some influence with you, I desire most avidly to consult. When those books [just mentioned] have been returned, I would have copies of [still] others made for me while I am here.

I beg you to relieve my embarassment by doing what I ask. [Since] I am [still] examining the sour roots of learning and you have already been filled with its sweetest fruits, inspire me with your overflowing eloquence. If I am worthy of these things, I shall remember the grace of such great favors for as long as I live. What compensation will flow to you in payment for these favors is not for me to say.

My mind suggests to me thousands of other things I should write about, but I ought not to delay your [busy] mind any further with my petty problems, since I know that you are either preoccupied with issues of the world or intent upon exploring the inner and hidden workings of philosophy.

2. Lupus writes to Einhard in early 836 after Emma's Death

Lupus [sends his greetings] to his most beloved teacher, Einhard.

I was shocked by the dreadful news of the death of your venerable wife. Now more than ever I wish I was with you to lighten the load of your sadness with my compassion or to console [you] with constant talk of impressions [on the subject of death] formed from [reading] the Bible. But until God renders this possible, I recommend that you reflect on the human condition, which we have incurred because of sin [that is, the First Sin], and that you endure with moderation and wisdom what has transpired. For you who have, with your vigorous mind, always risen above the seductions of good fortune, should not give in now to this bad fortune. Thus, after you have called on God, you should then demonstrate that strength of endurance, to which you would doubtless direct your own dear [friends] under similar circumstances.

I hope that you are well.

3. Einhard's Response to Lupus. Early 836

Einhard [sends his] greetings to his Lupus.

The overwhelming pain that I received from the death of she who was once my most devoted wife and most recently my dearest sister and companion has banished and driven out of me all enthusiasm and concern for my own affairs or those of my friends. Nor does [this pain] seem likely to end, since [my] memory so stubbornly dwells on the nature of her death that it cannot be completely torn away from it. On top of that, what constantly adds to that pain and makes an already sore wound worse is, without doubt, that my prayers were unable to accomplish anything and the hope I had placed in the merits and intervention of the martyrs [Marcellinus and Peter] entirely misled [me in] my expectations. Thus, in my case, the words of those consoling me, which normally relieve the sadness of others, instead cause the wound in my heart to become raw and open once again, since these people tell me to endure calmly misfortunes they are not experiencing themselves and they advise me to be happy over a situation in which they cannot show [me] any reason for joy or happiness. For what human being full of reason and sound mind would not weep over his fate and count himself unhappy and the most pitiful [of all humans], when, overcome by toubles, he learns that the one he had believed would support his prayers [that is, Christ or the saints] had turned against him and was unmoved?

Do these [troubles] not seem to you [to have been] of the kind that could provoke sighs and tears in [such] a small and puny man, that could force him to moaning and wailing, and even cast him into an abyss of despair? And they would certainly have cast [me down there to stay] if I had not, propped up by the power of divine mercy, turned at once to discover what greater and better men had proclaimed ought to be believed and followed in matters and misfortunes of this sort. Outstanding doctors [of the church] were within reach [in my library] and they were not to be spurned, but rather to be listened to and followed in every way: namely, the glorious martyr Cyprian and those brilliant interpreters of Sacred Scipture Augustine and Jerome. Inspired by their opinions and wholesome arguments, I tried to lift up a heart pulled down by heavy sadness, and I purposely began to ponder how I ought to feel about the death of that dearest partner of mine, whose mortal life rather than her [true] life I saw come to an end.

I even attempted to see if I could bring about by myself through reason what the long passage of time normally achieves, namely, that the wound with which the sudden blow of an unexpected death struck my mind should begin to form a scab and to heal with the medicine of my own mind's conso-lation. But the immensity of the wound makes treatment difficult. Although extremely beneficial things are advised by those doctors [of the church] act-ing as the most skilled and gentle physicians in order to alleviate a heavy pain, the wound which continues to bleed is still not prepared to heal.

You may well be astonished by this and say that the pain arising from an event of this sort ought not to last so long, as if it is [ever] in the power of the one suffering to say when it should end, since he neither knew in advance nor had the capacity to know when the suffering would begin. It, neverthe-less, seems that the size and length of one's pain and sorrow can only be mea-sured in terms of the [individual] losses suffered. Since I am acutely aware of my loss every day in every action, in every affair, in every matter of the house and household, and in all the necessary assignments and arrangements per-taining to [my] divine and human duties, how can that wound which has lev-eled so many and such great misfortunes upon me not reopen and grow sore again, rather than heal over and become solid [skin], when it is so often touched upon?

For I suppose (and I doubt that the supposition deceives me) that this pain and anxiety, which came upon me because of the death of my dearest partner, will be with me forever until that point in time, which God granted me for the purpose of living this wretched earthly life, is brought to its appointed end. Nevertheless, this experience has so far been good for me rather than harmful, since it slows and holds back, as if with bit and reins, my spirit, which was rushing after pleasure and success, and reminds me of death's approach. The ease and forgetfulness of old age had seduced me into hoping and longing for a long life. I see [now] that I do not have much longer to live, but how much longer that may be is utterly unknown to me. But I most assuredly know that a newborn child can die soon and that an old man can-not live long. And so I believe it would be far more useful and blessed for me to pass the brief and uncertain period of time [left to me] in mourning rather than joy. For if, according to Scripture, those will be blessed and happy who lamented and mourned in this life, then those on the contrary who do not fear to end their days in constant and undending joy will end up unhappy and wretched.

I give thanks and am grateful for your kindness, especially since you deigned to console me with your letter. For you could give no greater or surer sign of your affection for me than to hold out a comforting hand to one who had laid down sick and to urge me to rise up. For you were not able to neglect one who was laid low in his mind and weighed down by grief.

Farewell, dearest and most beloved son.

4. Einhard, 'On the Adoration of the Cross'

When I was attempting, despite the very great disturbance to my spirit [at present], to satisfy your curiosity, my dearest Lupus, and to solve the problem you put to me about the adoration of the cross, a question far greater and more encompassing arose from that inquiry, which I had thought would be easy [to answer]. I refer to the adoration of God and about how one should call upon and beseech him, since if he is asked otherwise than he should be or for something other than what one ought [to ask for], it is not surprising that our prayer is not heard or that what we desired to secure is not obtained. For James says: "You ask and receive not, because you ask wrongly." [James 4:3] The Apostle [Paul in his letter] to the Romans said: "we know not what we should pray for as we ought." [Rom.8:26] Thus it seems to me that there is a pressing need for us to examine and understand what it means, according to the words of James, to ask wrongly and, according to the teaching of Paul, not to know what is to be prayed for as we ought, because it can happen that one who does not know for what or how he ought to ask asks wrongly, and thus may not receive what he asks for. For he seems to ask wrongly and not to know how to ask who does not pray to God, to whom he prays, in the way [God] taught [him] to pray.

In the complete run of the Gospels no mention is ever made that our Lord Jesus Christ had taught or commanded prayer to himself, but rather, since he speaks most often of prayer that should be made to God, he advises [us] to pray to the Father, to ask the Father, to entreat the Father, and to beg him [for help] in all [our times of] need. For himself and likewise for others, he decrees, as if he could provide nothing through himself, that the Father should be prayed to. But our faith holds this most firmly, that just as the divinity and substance of the Father and Son is one, so is their power one and the same, and that the prayer, which the one [God] gave and taught, both should hear together, since both together wanted it to be given and taught.

But it seems as if it is not permitted for [Christ] to be prayed to otherwise than the Father is called upon when we pray or that something other might be asked for from him, except what the Son revealed as fit to be asked for in the prayer which he taught [Matt. 6:5-13]. And through this [we understand] that he who asks otherwise [than he should] or for something other [than he should] asks wrongly, according to the statement of blessed James, and thus does not deserve to receive what he asks for. The Apostle Paul also seems to indicate the same when he says: "we know not what we should pray for as we ought." When we entreat God, seeking to gain something other than that which is laid out in the Lord's Prayer, then the attainment of that request remains in doubt because we are praying not for what he commanded, but for what pleases us.

Thus, we read that it was set down in a certain article of a Council of Carthage [held in 397]: "that in prayers no one should name the Father for the Son or the Son for the Father, and that prayer, when one is standing at the altar, should always be directed to the Father." Those who came together at the same council, agreed upon this and deemed it, as it were, to be most fitting that the church should hold and preserve in its public ceremonies that universal form of prayer that the Lord and our Savior transmitted and taught, [and that] he himself even showed to be worthy of preserving and holding by always praying to and calling upon the Father. I do not recall having read anything about other things concerning private and secret prayers and requests and about what was set down and decreed [about them] in synodal ordinances except what I found added to the previous article, where it is said: "that whosoever shall copy out prayers for himself from some other source should not use them, unless he has first discussed them with more learned brothers."

At this point a question about our Lord Christ suggests itself to human curiosity, one that should not only be studied, but should even be expertly investigated and elucidated. If only God the Father should be called upon and beseeched in the public prayers that occur at the altar, where and in what prayers should the Lord Christ, that is, the Son, be entreated?

Likewise what ought to be believed concerning the apostles, the martyrs, and others, whose spirits, we have no doubt, are with God? Where, when, and how should they be called upon or should they be called upon at all? For I recall that there have been some who have said that the requests of the saints, who have now departed from this world, are particularly beneficial to those still alive and breathing and that the requests of the living can assist those same saints, if they wish to pray on their behalf.

You should not expect me to explain in detail how these matters appear to my Smallness. Nor should you take the things I have set out here to be this [investigation], since I [only] laid them out as matters that need explaining.

You should [also] know that, while I searched out relevant authorities in order to solve the question you put to me, this knotty problem forced itself upon me, which if it were not divine [or Christian] in its origins, I would have called Herculean. Indeed, concerning this knotty problem, let these words suffice for the present.

I wish now to answer, according to my ability, the small question about the veneration of the cross your Kindness put to me. It does seem to me that the cross should be adored; why it seems so, I shall try to explain. I suspect that that will be easier for me to do if I am able to explain the difference and distinction, as I see it, between prayer and adoration.

To pray, in my opinion, is to beseech in mind or voice, or at the same time in mind and voice without a gesture of the body, the unseen God; or it is to beseech something else in which the hope of help can be placed or in which it is appropriate for it to be placed.

But to adore is to exhibit veneration to a visible thing placed before one and [actually] present either by bowing one's head or by bending or prostrating one's whole body or by extending one's arms and spreading one's hands or in any way whatsoever that constitutes a gesture of the body. For we venerate many things to which we cannot and ought not pray. In Sacred Scripture this veneration is normally called adoration. So, when it says, "I will adore at your temple" [Ps. 137:2], it is as if [Scripture] says, 'I bow my head or I kneel before your temple'. This adoration signifies only veneration, as [indicated] above.

Similarly, in the book of Kings [3 Kings 1:16, 28, 31], the prophet Nathan and [Bethsabee] the mother of Solomon are said to have adored King David. One should not believe that they had called upon [him as] God, but that they venerated [him as] a man worthy of honor. Likewise, in the fourth book of the same account [4 Kings 2:15], when the sons of the prophets are said to have adored the reverent Elisha while they were prone on the ground at the spot where Elijah was seized, it is appropriate to understand that they did this for the sake of veneration. The Old Testament abounds in so many other examples [of this sort] that it would seem to be excessive rather than necessary to gather them all together. In those examples it seems clear enough that adoration is most often set down in place of veneration. But we see that veneration is frequently and appropriately shown not only to living and sentient beings, as for example to angels and humans, but also to insensible objects and things lacking all life, as for example to churches, the tombs of saints, or relics.

But to pray, that is, to beseech or call upon, does not belong to anything, except to that which lives and can help the one who prays to and beseeches him. For this reason I wonder why, in the Gospel of John [4:20-24], when a conversation concerning the subject of adoration arose between God and the Samaritan woman, it was recorded that they spoke not concerning prayer, which [belongs] to God, but concerning adoration, which is shown to a variety of things for the sake of veneration. For the adoration, which according to the word of the Lord [John 4:23], true adorers will make in spirit and truth to God, ought not to be made with a gesture of the body, which belongs to veneration. But, perhaps this instance, and there are many such places in divine Scripture, occurs there, because 'adoration' was improperly set down for 'prayer'. Nevertheless the one who wrote this account wished prayer in the Lord's [own] words, with which God is called upon, and not veneration, with which other things ought to be honored, to be understood. Or, if this seems more suitable, we should understand that just as prayer applies to God, so does adoration, because God is everywhere. And he, who is everywhere, is certainly always present.

Therefore, when for the sake of adoration you prostrate yourself on the ground, you will at the same time be praying in your mind to God and adoring with an action of your body him, who is everywhere, as if he were in front of you and present. So it happens that even God may be adored, as if for the sake of veneration, just as the other things which we said belong to adoration.

Nevertheless, you should know that the Greeks draw this distinction between prayer and adoration: they call prayer *proseuchis* and adoration *proschineusis*. A distinction of this sort is made because the former refers to the function of the mind, the latter to the body. When in Matthew [6:5-7], the Lord instructed the disciples about how they should pray, this word written in Greek is *proseuchis*, which pertains to the mind. But at that place where Herod speaks to the magi and says, "that I may come and adore him" [Matt. 2:8], *proschineusis* is found, which refers solely to adoration and to bodily function.

Since this distinction, which can be freely adapted to anything, is clear, I think it is now evident that adoration of the holy cross should not be spurned, but rather, as Saint Jerome recalled about Saint Paula coming to Jerusalem: "that one, prostrated before the cross, adored as if she saw the Lord still suspended there." And we believe that we too ought to do this, namely to prostrate ourselves before the cross and, with our inner eye open, to adore him, who is suspended on the cross. And so the cross, which is without doubt holy, will obtain the honor appropriate to it, and God, in whom, by whom, and through whom, as Saint Augustine says, all things that are holy are holy, because he himself made them holy, [will be] venerably adored.

5. Lupus's Letter of Consolation. April 836

I have carefully read and was very touched by that letter from your Dignity in which you complained deeply about the disaster that recently befell you. I was extremely sad that your mind was worn down by mourning and worry over such a long time. Although the comforting words of your friends, who are far superior to me, have attempted to lift such a great sorrow, nevertheless it is quite apparent from your letter that they have utterly failed. They were unsuccessful because they did not fully identify with your plight, to the point that some of them even urged you to be happy over the death of your dear wife, but that [advice] does not, in my opinion, have anything to do with consolation. It is not so much from the shallowness of my age or [any] confidence in my talents, which I know to be slight, that I am not afraid once again to insist upon these things, of whatever use they might be, in order to console you, but rather because of my great love for you. Indeed, I know that I too have suffered personally and alongside you from the death of that most noble woman, and your letter, I realize, has forced that pain to the surface again and savagely provoked it. Thus, I should not despair that the Lord has saved for me some [form of] solace, which has not yet been supplied by others, with which I might move you. A cure is often sought from lower sources when those made of the most expensive and skillfully prepared [medicines] were tried for a time and failed.

In the letter you sent back to me you divided the reasons for your pain, which seems justified to you, into two parts. The first of these, which is the most serious, is that your prayers and the hope that you had fixed on the intercession of the holy martyrs failed you as though they were useless. The other, which lies close to the first, is that you have been forced by the press of daily business to reckon how great a loss was imposed upon you by that dreadful death. Now the weight of both your domestic and religious affairs, which the sure companionship of that memorable woman once made lighter, has fallen entirely upon your shoulders, and it is overwhelming. In fact, both of these [causes of your pain] are valid and might easily oppress anyone with their weight, but not the wise man who has learned to bear adversity with an even temper.

In fact, I shall not try to undermine or remove completely the first [reason] that I set out, for I see that that would be absolutely impossible even for perfect orators, if they existed, and [it is] even more impossible for me. But I shall try to lighten and render it weak with the help of reason. You are, of course, disturbed and troubled because those profitless prayers misled you and the hope placed in the martyrs, rather, I mean, in God, was illusory. It is as if you were absolutely certain that you were asking so forcefully [in order] to bring about the salvation of you and your wife. But if you had explored the matter fully, [you would have realized] that the cause of your bitter and understandable grief seemed immense so long as divine judgment was reproving you not as a son, but raging against you as though you were resisting it. Nevertheless, even so, it is not necessary to plunge into a deep pit of despair, for the angered divinity was appeased with constant prayers and patient persuasion. Now, however, since God wants all people to be saved and no one should request something in the name of that one who is known as the Savior unless he seeks something of benefit to his own salvation and since you asked in good faith in the name of the Savior, who does not believe that [while] your prayer for temporal [gain] went unheard, your prayer for eternal salvation was clearly heard? For my part I certainly and most firmly believe that he has looked after the best interests of you and your wife, even in the matter of her premature death.

How, you ask? Surely it is because spouses, who are transformed from two bodies into one, although they might have lived together in perfect peace, are not released together [at the same time] by death. Rather the normal course of things is such that one will necessarily outlive the other. Your prudence already knows this, since the divine judgment against humans was: "you are dust and to dust you shall return." [Gen. 5:19] This [fate] can be put off for a time, but it cannot be avoided forever. Faithful spouses should hope that, since one of them will remain behind, the one who outlives the other is the one who is better able to bear disaster and is the one more suited to tend to [burial] arrangements in the Christian way. For the difference in strength [between parties] should not be understood as one of sex, but rather of spirit. If not, I do not see how Christian spouses could be bound to each other in sincere love. Since a firm reason persuades one of this, therefore, it is apparent that God has likely bestowed a great boon not only upon that venerable woman, but also upon you. For what [God] himself freely imposed upon you, although by a secret, but nevertheless just judgment, you would have chosen of your own accord.

Certainly that woman learned much from being in your company, so that she far exceeded not only those of her own sex, but even average men in her excellent prudence, seriousness, and honesty, which things bring great worth to human life. Although in a woman's body, she advanced in spirit to equal that of a man. But she would never have completely attained the pinnacle of your wisdom; never would she have equaled in her attainments your great strength and perseverance, which everyone specially admires in you; and never, had she lived, could she have achieved as much for your everlasting salvation as you have for hers and for your own salvation.

Thus, while we are stuck in this fragile body, we cannot be entirely removed from disturbance, but must be afflicted from time to time by illness. I would hope that that capacity which philosophers believe only belongs to the wise man comes to you, that is, to soften gradually by the wisdom of your mind events that at first glance seem adverse, for the unlearned mass of humans is [normally] overcome by adverse events. It would be even better to submit your will to God's. Then, because Holy Scripture illuminates the darkest shadows of this life, as [when it says]: "your word is a lamp to my feet and a light to my paths" [Ps. 118:105], we must examine deeply how God himself shapes this life. Everyday in the Lord's Prayer we say, "Thy will be done" [Matt. 6:10], namely not our will, which, often being ignorant of the things good for it, is accustomed to fail, but your will, that is to say God's own, foreknows the future. Also our Savior, with the passion close at hand, when he had said, "father, if possible, let this chalice pass from me" [Matt. 26:39], made strong with his divine power the weakness of humans, which he had taken on, or rather the frailty of its [bodily] parts, for which he had descended with these words of prayer: "nevertheless not as I wish, but as you do." That is, the master does not know how to deceive or to be deceived, because God has taught us by his example to try to drive away with prayers those adversities when they crowd in upon us, so that we may with profit welcome the execution of his will even at those points where it runs counter to our wishes.

Think of Paul, I beg you, whose eminence was so great that when he was caught up in the third heaven he heard the secret words of the Holy Trinity that no human is allowed to speak. Three times he had prayed that the Lord would take away the angel of Satan who was harassing him, yet he did not receive what he wanted, but what was good for him. Recall [also] that David wounded himself in order to secure life for his son, and that though he was a very great prophet, he in fact received no divine response, though he was overwhelmed by great grief. "For whatever was written for our instruction was written so that through patience and the consolation of Scriptures we may have hope." [Rom. 15:4] Therefore, ponder how David learned of the uselessness of his own prayers and, having humbly submitted himself to the justice of God, took up and gained his consolation through reason. You are not one who has this firm strength. Take as your response the saying of the Apostle [Paul]: "My grace is sufficient for you; for strength is made perfect in weakness." [2 Cor.: 12:9] In fact, he himself put aside the pain caused by the rejection of his prayer, if any [resentment] occurred to him, since he had been admonished in his vision to do just that. The fields of Sacred Scripture overflow with precepts and examples of this sort. But since as the great poet [Virgil] says, "we do not sing to the deaf," and the restrictions of a letter confine me, I [shall] pass on and leave these things for you to ponder.

It should have been enough [for me] to have touched upon these things that alone can, so it seems to me, with the help of God soothe and cure this swollen wound. Another idea also occurs to me as I think of these many things: that this judgment of God can be seen as an absolutely certain sign of [his] mercy rather than of [his] anger. "For, since he flailed every son whom he received" [Heb. 12:6], perhaps he [would] not allow your commitment [to him] to be diminished by your love for your wife, and so it might be supposed that he had called you back to love of him alone. If it was the case that you indulged more than you should have in an immoderate love of her body, [God] has punished you with the removal of her body. Through a prophet, God says: "punishment does not occur twice" [Nah. 1:9] (which is so interpreted in the Septuagint, "God does not judge the same case twice."). He has deemed it right to correct you here (for no one is free from sin), since you have as a human being exceeded [proper bounds], so that he may not have to decide something even more serious against you later. You should, therefore, embrace the tremendous mercy of God who has judged you worthy of his correction and, rather than fearing his anger, accept the blows of his discipline. Solomon says: "My son, do not withdraw from the discipline of the Lord and do not grow weary of his correction, since you are censured by him. For the Lord corrects the one he loves, just as a father acts against a son whom he much loves." [Prov. 3:11-12; Heb. 12:5] Thus, the anger of God rages against those after death, whom he did not punish for their sins in this life and whom he allowed to pursue their own wishes. About such things, we read in the Psalm [72:5]: "They are free of life's burdens and are not afflicted like other men." Likewise in Job: "They live out their days in wealth and in a moment go down to the nether world." [Job 21:13]

Moreover, something occurs to me: God wished you to experience in these circumstances just how unfortunate is the person who is cut off forever from that very one [God] in whom there is everlasting and true pleasure, since even the momentary separation from one human being, albeit a faithful and dear one, has so deeply affected you. Since all these things seem to be true, abandon, I beg you, as much as you can, this grief about which we speak, and say with Job: "The Lord gave and the Lord has taken away; it was done according to the Lord's pleasure; blessed be the name of the Lord." [Job 1:21] With the Apostle, spread praises in the name of God: "Blessed be the God and Father of our Lord Jesus Christ, the Father of mercy and the God of all consolation; who consoles us in all our troubles." [2 Cor. 1:3-4]

The other part of this business [the treatment of the second complaint] remains, which must be briefly touched upon, but I should not, in attempting to be a source of comfort to you, say too much and, perhaps, wear you out.

You have asserted that the wound of your sorrow begins again or, rather, continues, since your work is each day doubled and this reminds you of the good thing you have lost, especially since it seems that it cannot be brought to an end. I myself admit that this is very true and strongly approve of and judge to be fully catholic that statement, which you placed among others, that human beings cannot freely put an end to sorrows which they did not see coming and which they could not escape when they threatened. For, "it is certainly not in the power of humans to select their paths, but the steps of humans are directed by God." [Prov. 20:24] The freedom of the human will completely depends upon the assistance of God's grace.

But clearly what has been done cannot be undone, nor can sadness ever bring back the past. There is not in humans the capacity to seek help from themselves. Thus, when we are overwhelmed by troubles of any kind, in the face of which we feel ourselves to be even weaker, it is necessary for us to fly all that much more quickly to the aid of divine mercy as if to the safest harbor of all. That truth is elegantly stated: "It is necessary for divine assistance to appear when human assistance falls short." Nor should a long struggle wear us out, if only we try [to overcome it]. For he who calls [us] to himself in this way, "Come to me, all you who labor" [Matt. 11:28], helps those who try, enlightens those who seek him out, and surely crowns those who remain with him.

You said that the memory of this sorrow will be with you for as long as you live. I suspect that the great depth of your love was a product of long experience. But let me urge you, to the degree that I dare, not to give into a stubborn state of mind, for in fact immoderate [grief] will produce nothing of benefit to her, for whose sake that grief emerged, and it will harm you a great deal, if it is not displaced.

Why not, instead, entrust yourself entirely to the care and healing of God, for whom this is an easy matter, whereas for human nature it is very difficult? For who [ever] placed his hope in God and was deceived? I beg you to empty your whole heart to God in prayer. He who advised humans to pray when [he said] "ask and you shall receive" [John 16:24], wishes to answer you. Ask, so that he may inspire you with the urge to pray and so that he may grant you the fulfilment of your request. Say what that most distinguished and persuasive author Augustine said: "Give what you [that is, God] order and order what you wish." By his own grace, in fact, God precedes and follows us, so that we are able to wish and achieve something good. We learned this clearly in the Psalms where it is written: "My God, his mercy shall go before me" [Ps. 58:10] and, likewise, "Your mercy will follow me all the days of my life." [Ps. 22:6] Follow the Holy Spirit who advises [us] through David: "Cast your burden upon the Lord and he will sustain you" [Ps. 54:23], and say faithfully to God, "You are my shelter from the troubles that surround me." [Ps. 31:7] And, now rejoicing with the Apostle in the praise of God, you will be able to say again: "I am able to do all things through him [Christ] who comforts me." [Phil. 4:13] "The sorrow of this world produces death" [2 Cor. 7:10)], for there is no doubt that it inflicts not just a spiritual death, as you certainly know, but a physical one [as well].

We should, therefore, be unhappy over the hardships [caused] by the vices with which we are oppressed and we should attempt to separate ourselves from their false appeal with as much hostility as we can manage. Let us bear with moderation our existence in this world, for life cannot be lived without strife. In spite of that, let us rejoice in our faith while we await God's favor. For that is promised in the Gospels: "Blessed are they who mourn, for they will be comforted." [Matt. 5:5] This is rightly understood [to refer] not to those who mourn the loss of loved ones or worldly advantages, but to those who, having first cut themselves off from the deadly allure of sin, lament until, because of their worth, they receive consolation by the grace of the Holy Spirit. Or [it may refer] to those who are, to their own good advantage, afflicted by their own sins and those of the people close to them and [also] by their delay in attaining that blessed life to which we aspire in all our prayers. Consequently, while you are seeking perpetual repose for your late wife, who I believe did not incur death but stepped beyond death, ask our lord God to grant you patience, perseverance, and success in achieving good deeds. Then he will soon flood your heart with consolation and you will hear the Apostle's admonition: "Rejoice in the Lord always. I shall say it again: rejoice!" [Phil. 4:4]

Since you deigned to reveal your troubles to me, I shall attempt to pray even more devoutly for her and for you. I believe that God, not through any merit of mine, should be pleased by your humility, since without any regard for your greatness you were not afraid to share such serious business with someone of my smallness. I have demonstrated as best I could by human reasoning and divine authorities that you must patiently accept that your prayer was not answered and [have suggested] how that wound of sorrow, which has seemed so incurable, can be softened. It will be [an example] of your prudence and ususal dignity if you piously reread [this letter], which was written with the pious intention not of instructing [you], but of reminding [you of these divine teachings]. If anything useful can be found in it, [please] consider it as your own for friendship's sake.

I consider that little book 'On the Adoration of the Cross' [see 7.4], that you dedicated to me to be extremely useful and I greatly appreciated it, as I should. I am also hoping that you will humor me and unravel all those problems I sent you and not refuse to explain those I left behind this year. Your work on these would certainly profit not only me, but many others. Indeed, for this [book] that you sent to me, much to my surprise, and for other things, with which I am now, just as before, taught by you, I have and maintain the greatest gratitude. I, your anxious [friend], am waiting [to hear] how God plans to animate your Piety.

I have decided to depart from here [Fulda] in the middle of May, if I am still well. At which time, if God allows, I shall visit you as you will remember I told you [I would] and spend a few days with you. [At that time] I shall return your books to you and shall learn what I require and shall enjoy a pleasant time, however brief, talking to you. [Then], I shall be [truly] taught by that most welcome example of your dignity and integrity. A useless report deceived you into thinking that I was about to depart now [for Ferrières]. Even if that was the case, and I absolutely wish it not to be, I would still rush to see you [before departing from eastern Francia]. My love for you is so great, that I would never return home without seeing you and [seeking] the protection of the holy martyrs [Marcellinus and Peter at Seligenstadt].

I hope that you, my most beloved lord and father, remain strong in your faith, enjoy continued success, and think well of me in all things.

6. Lupus Postpones his Visit. May 836

Lupus [sends his] greetings to his steadfast father Einhard.

It is not easy to speak of how grateful I am that you are thinking of me, particularly since your Preeminence's loftiness has lowered itself so that I might enjoy the reward of spontaneous greetings [from you] in return. But I had hoped to be encouraged by your letter and to learn the degree to which the passions raised by your loss have cooled, and if you were convinced by anything my Smallness [wrote]. Just as I promised, I am specially entreating the Lord every day on behalf of the eternal repose of that dearly beloved woman, and I have not stopped asking with careful constancy for what I believe will be beneficial to you in [your] present and future life. Whether I am doing any good is for you to determine. Nevertheless, I shall never hesitate to rest the fruits of my entreaties in the mercy of God and to await their sure maturation, however slow that might seem to our impatient natures. Nevertheless, [those fruits] will mature on account of the great weight of divine justice. I beg you, moreover, to read book 21, chapter 27, of Saint Augustine's *City of God* and to see if that man, who was filled with divine inspiration, did not feel the same about such disasters as what I wrote [you].

Indeed, I had not read that [chapter] before, but when I ran across it after [I wrote] that letter, I was amazed that my thoughts were so similar [to his] in basic understanding, that they seemed to have taken their very tone from his.

I have been forced to put off for a short time my return home and, as a consequence, my visit to you. For the venerable Marcward [the abbot of Prüm], through whom my return home was being arranged, was sent as [the emperor's] representative to Italy; but first he summoned me to have an extremely cordial meeting [with him]. I was [still] determined to visit your holiness, leaving here on the day I had [already] indicated to you. But the illustrious Abbot Hrabanus returned a little later from the palace, but was not sure of his [arrival] time here, since he had been given an [imperial] assignment. For this reason, he advised me to put off my return until the Nones of June [5 June 836], since he would surely be [at Fulda] on the feast day of Saint Boniface [that is, the same day], that is, unless the authority of an imperial command – and, even then, only one of the most serious kind – should override [his commitment to return]. Thus, when Marcward, after his departure, sent [a messenger] to ask when I wanted to return [home], I requested that he see to it that the horses chosen for this mission were brought here on the day before the Nones of June [4 June], so that, with Christ's help, I might be able to begin my journey to you on the eighth [day before the] Ides of the same month [6 June]. That man [Marcward] will surely arrange this, if he is still alive and well. I do not dare to specify the exact day on which I shall arrive, but I [can] confirm that with God's help I shall arrive sometime during the week that begins on the Nones of June [5 June]. O that I might be lucky enough to find your mind freed of all aggravation and worry, so that you will not only be able to join with me, in the name of customary dignity, in whatever friends share, but that even your sharpest understanding will be brought to bear on matters upon which my opinion and those of others are deficient. In order to avoid the charge of flattery, I do not want to say any more about the degree to which I respect your intelligence, how much I submit to it, and how much I believe, in short, I have been helped or [soon] will be assisted by it. [Only] God, whose grace supplied [your intelligence], knows that.

In the meantime, please consider, with that fatherly devotion with which you always regard me, those [problems] I sent [to you] so that having seen them in advance you may explain them more easily to me [when I arrive]. In the first book, chapter four, of the *Arithmetic*, Boethius says: "quod autem dictum est: secundum duorum generum contrarias passiones, huiusmodi est." From that point until "spatio est maxima parvissima quantitate," is less clear than I would wish. In the same book, in the thirty-first chapter, in addition to "partes multiplices superpartientis," which he himself explained, he denies that it is "difficult for the interested" to locate the other things according to the "method" demonstrated. I shall understand that [method] if can learn from you what he meant by: "vocabunturque hi secundum proprias partes duplex superbipartiens." The following bits will [then] not be too difficult for me [to understand]. The same outstanding author, in the second book, second chapter, of the same work, says: "ut ait Nichomachus inmusitaton (or 'enmusitaton teorema proficiens' as I have found elsewhere) teorema proficiens." I am not sure I understand what these Greek words mean. In the same book, in the twenty-fifth chapter, at the place where he wrote: "omnis quoque cibus qui ex tetragonorum superficie improfunditatem corporis crevit," until "angulos uero VIII, quorum singulus sub tribus eiusmodi continetur, quales priores fuere tetragoni, unde cibus ipse productus est," which I quote directly, I do not follow the [actual] shape of this complex thing and I need you to help me grasp its meaning. I also desire, with the grace of God and your instruction, to begin studying the calculus of Victorius.

Also, in the matter of words such as *aratrum*, *salubris*, and similar words, which seem to possess a long penult not only by position, but also by nature, great confusion exists. I admit that I have pondered for a long time whether or not they ought to follow nature, [that is,] whether a long penult should be pronounced, as it is; or whether according to the statement of Donatus: "if a penult is long by position, it shall be accented (as Catullus treats it); nevertheless if it is long by position, it shall not have been composed of a mute and a liquid, for that would change the [place of the] accent (as is the case with *faretra*)"; [or finally], whether when syllables produced together [are long] by nature and by such a position, the common syllable should determine in advance the nature and the accent should be transferred onto the antepenult. It seems to me that both of these interpretations could be argued either way, for I have not yet been able to discover any sure resolution [of the matter] among the experts. It falls to your wisdom, therefore, to clear up this uncertainty and to support one of these [interpretations] with the strongest proofs. In fact, to compound the problem of not finding any expert's certain rule [on the matter], it also happens that in scanning a word like *aratrum* I always find the penult long. But, if a syllable stays common in those that are naturally long, it is obvious that in the nominative, accusative, and vocative plurals *aratra* can be used in dactylic [verse].

There are many other questions fit to be asked [here], which I have noted and which, if you and God will allow, I shall ask more appropriately in person. And, [knowing] of the devotion that you have always freely shown to me, I beg that when I have arrived you will deign to dip into the hidden recesses of your memory and, for the sake of charity and friendship, quickly bring forth those things that you know I require and that I cannot learn from any-one else. In sowing the seeds of your knowledge in me, you may transmit to many others the very fruits of your knowledge.

In addition [to these things], the royal scribe Bertcaud is said to possess a scheme of ancient letters, at least of those that are particularly large and that are thought by some to be called 'uncials' [or capitals; see Fig. 14]. Therefore, if you are in possession of this, I beg you to send it to me through this painter, when he returns, but in a codex carefully protected by a seal.

I would have sent the Aulus Gellius [text], if the abbot [Hrabanus Maurus] had not held onto it and was not still seeking to have it copied for himself. Nevertheless, he said that he will write to you [to explain] that he had removed that book from me by force. But if God allows me to, I shall myself return to you that book and all the others, which I am enjoying because of your generosity.

At the very least, do not refuse now to explain those obscure words, chiefly Greek, that are found in laws, and the other word from Servius, also in Greek, that I sent you at the start.

Best wishes, dearest teacher and kindest father, may you always flourish and have every success.

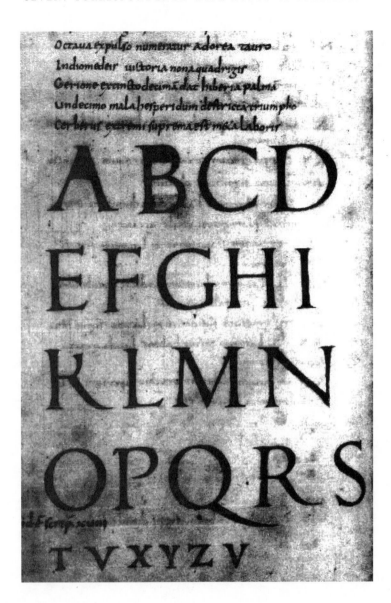

14. This copy of square capital letters is found at the end of a manuscript of Victorius of Aquitaine's calculus, which Bernhard Bischoff connected to Lupus of Ferrières. Perhaps, then, this is Lupus's copy of the book he asked Einhard about in 7.6 If so, this could be a copy of Bertcaud's sample letters. Berne, Burgerbibliothek, Cod. 250, fol. 11v.

INDEX

Entries are listed by part and document number and, in some cases, by book and section numbers. Thus, 2.5 is a reference to the *Life of Charlemagne*, chapter 5, while 5.3.17 refers to the *Translation and Miracles*, book 3, chapter 17. If the topic appears several times within a work, no book or chapter number may be given.

weapons 2.9, 2.23, 2.32

weather 5.1.12, 5.1.14, 5.3.19

weights and measures, false 5.3.14

Weissenburg, monastery of 6.32

Welatabi 2.12, 2.15

Wenilo, servant of Blidthrut from Mosbach 6.15

Werdric of Fulda, relative of Einhard 6.4

wergeld 6.18, 6.25

Wicbertus and Hildeberga, donors of
Blandin 3.8.5

widows 5.3.14, 5.4.10, 5.4.12

Wiesbaden 5.3.19

Wiggo, demon 5.3.14

Willibald, priest, dues collector for Einhard 6.12

Willibert, resident of Seligenstadt 5.3.3

Williram, servant of St-Martin, Mainz
6.18

Wilzi 2.12

wine 2.24, 5.3.11

wolf 1.6-7

Wolfar, archbishop of Rheims 2.33

Wolfgar, bishop of Würzburg 6.6

Wormhoudt, village of 5.4.12

Worms 6.32

writing 2.25, 5.3.13, 5.4.10, 6.56, 7.1, 7.6

Würzburg,
St-Killian, monastery of 6.6

Zacharias, pope 2.3